WASTED

WASTED

Mark Johnson

sphere

SPHERE

First published in Great Britain in 2007 by Sphere

Copyright © The Wise Project Ltd 2007

The moral right of the author has been asserted.

A CIP catalogue record for this book
is available from the British Library.

ISBN 978-1-84744-024-2

Typeset in Bembo by M Rules
Printed and bound in Great Britain by
Clays Ltd, St Ives plc

Sphere
An imprint of
Little, Brown Book Group
Brettenham House
Lancaster Place
London WC2E 7EN

A Member of the Hachette Livre Group of Companies

www.littlebrown.co.uk

This book is dedicated to the lost

If people can change, the world can change

Prologue

I'm off. I'm out of this place. I hate it, with its battered wardrobes, its smell of cleaning fluid, its collection of armchairs worn thin by squirming arses. It was easier to live on the streets than this. Everything was simple there. No rules, no therapists, no memories, no one, nothing. Just drugs. That was all I wanted and all I cared about. The pain of daily life was gone, replaced by the pain of having to find my next hit.

I switch on my lamp. The light is painful because my pupils still can't respond properly. I find an empty carrier bag. Sighing, I open it.

Where am I going? And how?

I don't have much to take, nothing more than a few clothes others have left behind when, like me, they've run away. I put them into the bag slowly. Then I reach under the bed for my art box. My joints creak as I bend down and pain shoots up my legs. Everything hurts when you come off heroin. My bones are bleached of their marrow. My cells are bereaved.

I open the art box and check that my Collection of Found Objects is complete. The paintbrushes. The spoon handle. The sewing needles. The notebook. The badges. All found in bins, other people's throwaways, and until recently my only possessions.

My heart races. I'm scared. I don't want to go. It's been such a long journey to rehab. But I don't want to stay.

'What's up?' asks a voice. My room-mate, Colin. It's so late I thought he must be asleep.

'I'm in bits,' I say. 'I've been here for over two weeks and I can't stand it any longer with nothing in my body.'

He sits up in bed and yawns. 'Pain still bad?'

'It's doing my fucking head in.'

He knows what I mean. He's a full-on crack-heroin addict too, a small, dark-skinned gypsy of about forty. He understands that, for years now, I've been taking drugs to stop myself from feeling anything at all. I haven't had real emotions for a long, long time. Now, as the chemicals recede, I'm becoming a human being again. All those emotions the drugs helped me avoid are happening at once. Terror, guilt, shame, hopelessness, helplessness, loneliness, sadness, a sense of loss, jealousy, anger . . . everything I should have felt in my wasted years I feel now. After being ignored for so long, these emotions have the power of a great locomotive and they're running right over me. They're crushing me, turning me into pulp.

Colin watches me. He's been in and out of rehab for years and he can talk the talk, although that hasn't stopped him relapsing regularly.

'I mean,' I say, 'all the fucking rules they have here. I can't keep to them. What is it they want from me?'

'It's not what they want. It's what you want.'

'I just want to be clean. I want a new life.'

'Well . . . there is a way.'

'Huh?'

'It's like this. All the stuff that's in the back of your mind, it'll have to come out. You've got to get honest. All the things that have been holding you down, all your secrets, you've got to tell, mate.'

I think for a minute while the tiny hairs stand up on the back of my neck. This keeps happening and it doesn't mean someone's walking across my grave. It means that another nerve ending is coming back now that my receptors are no longer blocked by drugs.

'You mean,' I say, 'I've got to tell about what it was really like out there? On the streets?'

Colin guffaws.

'I don't mean ego stuff about how hard you were. I don't mean feeling sorry for yourself stuff. I mean that you've got to tell your secrets. Real secrets. All the small embarrassing things you've never told anyone, the sneaky things, the spiteful things, the grassing-up-your-mates keep-it-to-yourself kind of things.'

My secrets. He must be kidding. There are a lot of things I'm not going to tell anyone. Ever.

He says: 'Talking about your weaknesses gives you back your power.'

I cross the room and open the window and smell the night. I breathe deeply, inhaling the salty air, inhaling the sea.

I hear Colin's voice, insistent, behind me.

'You've got to tell.'

I turn round and he's still looking at me.

'There's a lot of stuff that's keeping you sick. Your secrets poison your soul. It's called the Secret Side of Self. Think about it, mate, before you pack your bag.'

I lie awake all night, my body alive with pain, every nerve raw, my legs propellers that have to keep whirring, spinning, moving. I want to go but I've got nowhere to go. I don't want to do this but I've got nothing else to do. I don't want to take drugs but I can't live without them.

In the morning, I'm still here.

When I go into group therapy, I'm shit-scared. I cower in my chair and everyone can tell I'm going to talk for the first time. There's an air of anticipation. Or maybe it's curiosity.

'Ah,' says Alan, looking pleased. 'Is there a Significant Event you'd like to tell us about, Mark?'

'Yeah,' I say. I open my mouth and wait for myself to speak. For a minute nothing comes out. And then I start.

Chapter 1

I hate Sundays. It's the day Dad goes to the pub and Mum goes to church. And, if Dad isn't around to stop her, Mum takes us too. Today, he's not here. I can tell from the special silence, and the way Mum's so tight-lipped in the kitchen, that Dad didn't come home last night.

Mum gets ready for the meeting and so does our big sister Kelly, who always does what she's told and then tells us to do it too. Shane and I keep looking hopefully up Reynolds Street for Dad because we want him to come back, even if he's drunk, to save us from church. I look up and down the street between the double row of red ter- raced houses but there's no sign of Dad, no sign of anyone, just that special Sunday morning silence.

We dress slowly for the meeting. Dad still hasn't arrived so we set off, Shane and me trailing behind Mum and Kelly. We go down Reynolds Street. We pass apple trees. In the summer their branches were thick with leaves and their bark was scaly and I loved the way the tree was wrapped round me like a green blanket when I scrumped the apples. Now the branches are bare and dripping.

Mum takes my hand and drags me into the Kingdom Hall. It's a big room with a platform at the front. It smells of soap and no cig- arettes. We sit down on green chairs and some old elder stands on the platform and talks and talks for at least an hour. I am glad when there is singing, but the music has no rhythm and little tune. Then there's more talking. I can't sit still. I whisper to Shane, I squirm. I practise tying my shoelaces. Shane tells me I'm doing it wrong. I hit him. People turn round to glare and now Mum's angry. She'd like to shout but she can't because this is church so she takes hold of my wrist and marches me off to the toilets at the side of the room. The fur at the cuff of her purple coat tickles my face. Then she pulls me inside the cubicle and smacks me.

'No, no, Mum, please no!' I wail.

'Shhhhh,' she hisses, walloping my backside with her hand. Hair flies from her face in frizzy curls. When she hits me, I can smell her perfume, feel it scratching my throat. The plumpness round her cheeks suddenly isn't there any more: her face is hard with anger.

'Muuuuuuu—' But Mum slams one hand over my mouth and continues to hit me with the other. Bang, smack, wallop. I manage to make protesting noises through her fingers.

When she opens the door the room is silent. Every head is bent in prayer. Some people aren't praying, though. I know because they turn to stare at me. I am crying but, on a glare from Mum, I cry silently.

'We were trying to pray,' Kelly tells me as we file out afterwards. 'But all anyone could hear was you begging Mum not to smack you.'

We are glad to leave. The meeting hall is Mum's world, not ours. Even when we try to please Mum and the great God Jehovah by going to meetings and assemblies, we know we don't fit in there. We are not one of them. We are not saved. We are less than they are because they are promised eternal life and we are not and they know it.

Dad always laughs when Mum tells us about Jehovah. Not only does he refuse to let us go to meetings, he threatens to drive a lorry through the church doors.

Mum's voice is full of warning. She says: 'Jehovah's watching you. He sees everything that you do and He judges you.'

Dad bursts out laughing again, which makes us very happy because he doesn't often laugh. Nan and all our aunties and uncles who live in Reynolds Street probably laugh about Jehovah too, and they're not scared of Him either. They tell Mum to shut up when she starts talking about Him.

We are nervous as we approach the house. What will we find? Will Dad be there, sitting on the settee with an affable, drunken, Sunday smile? Will Mum start shrieking at him? We wait, tense, as Mum unlocks the front door. We enter quietly and, like a team of detectives, without discussing it, we search the house rapidly and silently. No Dad. Mum looks fierce. She goes into the kitchen and starts clattering things.

Nan arrives for Sunday lunch with her two youngest boys, George and Phil. They're uncles but they aren't much older than us so they're more like cousins. We hear Nan talking with Mum while they do womanly things with the roast. They keep their voices low. I don't listen. I don't want to. But I recognise that special tone of anger that is just for talking about Dad. They don't sound like the people around here because they come from Newcastle-upon-Tyne and their accents are more like singing. Here in Kidderminster, people don't sing when they talk, they sort of whine. Since all my relatives on both sides are from Newcastle, I spoke with a Geordie accent until I started at primary school last year. Now I sound like a Brummie.

I overhear them saying that Dad has probably slept the night at Her house. Her name is She. Maybe they're talking about the woman Shane and I glimpsed with Dad in the car last week. He accelerated when he saw us but we had time to notice that the woman was skinny like a coat hanger. She had long black hair and She was smiling. We told Mum about it and she's been angry ever since.

Nan is small and tough with a Woodbine at the corner of her mouth. I don't know if she ever smokes it or if she just glues it there in the mornings. I love Nan very much. She is strong. She is the head of our family. And right now, the head of the family is angry with Dad.

Mum has laid his place at the table. Kelly keeps glancing at the front door. Shane offers to run down to the Station Arms and see if Dad's there but Mum tells him not to. Her anger has set hard now.

Grimly, Nan carves the roast. Mum serves the vegetables in silence. Food is laid on Dad's plate. While we eat, we wait. The air smells of anticipation. The meat tastes of anger. When Dad's dinner is cold Mum silently takes it to the oven to warm.

As soon as dinner is over I go outside. I want to be somewhere else. I soon hook up with a couple of other kids and we end up at a girl's house down the road. Everything is in order here. I like that. The living room's tidy, her mum's in the kitchen, her dad's in the garden and there is calm. Our house is tidy, too, but it always feels as though there's going to be an explosion any minute and all the records and saucepans and chairs and clothes will be scattered over Reynolds Street and probably the whole of the West Midlands. But in this girl's house I like the Sunday afternoon calm.

Then, her big sister runs in, breathless.

'You're not to go out,' she says. 'There's a big fight in the street and you're not to see it.'

A fight. In the street.

'Where?' I ask. She doesn't answer and I don't need her to. I already know where the fight is.

'There's blood,' she says. 'Lots of it.'

And I am immediately out of the door, rushing towards the big fight I'm not supposed to see. From the end of the street I can hear shouting. A circle of people are huddled in their coats outside our house.

Neighbours and uncles and aunties and my big brother and sister are melting silently out of houses all down the street. As we approach the onlookers, Auntie Tanya ushers Kelly and Shane and me straight inside. I have time to glimpse my mum's bleeding face. She's yelling at Dad, circling him. He's standing there, much bigger than her and he doesn't move. He wears cowboy boots and blue jeans and a blue cowboy shirt and he has a cowboy moustache and his hair is dark and thick and wavy. Dad stands tall and strong like a real cowboy. Except that today there are stains all over his shirt. Blood and gravy. And round his feet is potato and roast beef. Fragments of plate scrunch as Mum circles him and this is a sound more awful than shouting.

Inside, nothing is different. The house is clean and tidy as usual.

A visitor could really think we're normal if they hadn't noticed the blood and dinner in the street. We go straight up to Mum and Dad's room and stand at the window holding each other close and watching everyone below. I am glad Kelly's arm is tight round me.

Down there, our mum's face is twisted into funny shapes and she is crying and bleeding at the same time. Her body is round. She's the opposite of that coat hanger woman in the car.

Dad is looking dangerous, fists at the ready, growling like thunder. And from here we can see that there is a third person in the fight. My nan. Her small, tough, skinny body is lying in the street. There's blood on her. But she's getting up now and shrieking at my dad. She's going to hit him. Dad gets his fists ready. A couple of neighbours leap over and hold her back.

Then the next-door neighbour talks to Dad and eventually leads him away. Dad is swaying a bit. They get in the neighbour's car and drive off. Probably they've gone to a pub.

In the night I wake up. The sky, through the overhead window, is black. I feel alone. I can hardly hear Shane breathing. I want to get up. I want to walk out of this house. I want to walk and walk and walk until I find another house where I can live with another family. I try to sit up but I can't. There are ropes wrapped round me. They are so tight I can barely breathe. I tell myself these are only imaginary ropes. I try to pull them off. But they are too tight.

I struggle and fight until, with Superman's strength, I drag my body up. I am sweating when the cold night air hits me.

I creep across the room and, very quietly, downstairs to the landing. The bedroom doors are open but no one moves, no one breathes. Maybe they all have ropes.

Cautiously, I go down the next flight of stairs to the cold, still dining room. I see something out of the window. I stop and look into the black garden. On the wall, just sitting on it, is a figure. I stare. The figure stares back at me. It is small and white and I know who it is. Jack Frost. He is shaped strangely, like a penguin, and he is pale and smooth. Probably he is made of ice crystals. There's a slender moon and he glitters in its small light. He's very beautiful. The dog, asleep out in her kennel, hasn't noticed him. Jack sits on the wall looking at me and I stand in the dining room looking back. Jack knows I'm Mark Johnson and I know he's Jack Frost. It makes me feel better that he's there, shining and still, on our garden wall.

I turn and the ropes pull me back up the stairs. I get into bed and the ropes feel looser now and not so heavy. My feet are as icy as Jack's and my whole body is hard with cold but now that I know Jack's out there I go quickly back to sleep.

The next day, Dad is quiet. He is humble. This makes us feel very uncomfortable. We are quick to forgive him for punching Mum and Nan. He's our dad and we love him and, anyway, Mum threw his dinner at him so what did she expect? But we tread round him carefully.

A few days later he goes away. Dad's always going off somewhere. The way he comes and goes makes him sort of magical. He is a very important person. Without men like my dad to fit all the pieces of steel together, there would be no power stations. That's why the whole family moved to the West Midlands in the first place, because Dad and Nan and Mum and all the uncles and aunties were helping to build a big power station so that people can turn on their lights. Now Dad works all over Britain and sometimes in Europe making power stations. He works in rain and snow. He works in summer until he is burnt brown and in winter only his moustache keeps his face warm. He is very handsome. He doesn't look old-fashioned and flabby like other people's dads. With his cowboy clothes and his collar-length hair he is 1976, he is now. He is big and strong and solid as a rock. He is my hero and I love him.

Chapter 2

Dad stays away for long periods and then he comes back for a few weeks. This is the rhythm of our lives. I always know when he's due because Mum has the house unnaturally clean. It smells of polish. Everything is in its place. There's a special waiting atmosphere. I'm waiting extra hard this time because I'm going to be in trouble with Dad. Mum has found some badges and stickers from the joke shop up in my bedroom and she thinks I've stolen them.

'I never!'

'Where'd you get them, then?'

'I bought them!'

'And where'd you get the money?'

'Tony. I was with Tony and he give them to me!'

'With the prices still on?'

'Yeah!'

I am outraged at these accusations. She never believes me. And she's going to tell Dad as soon as he gets back.

The day Dad's due I don't go straight home after school with my big brother. I skulk around in the street. Gradually kids appear from their houses and soon there's a whole gang of us. Our gangs are always forming and re-forming. People fight or they change or they grow up and join another gang. I'm out on the street all the time so I drift from group to group without really belonging in any of them.

I have friends who turn into enemies when I fight them. I have enemies who I decide to like or who beat me in a fight. We're like trains, always hooking and unhooking, except no one else can see it. No adult can see the patterns our groups make as they change size and shape.

Today someone's got an old bread tray, dug up from waste ground. We go down Station Hill to the pedestrian underpass by the big roundabout. The steps are made of shiny ceramic and they get slippery in the rain. We take it in turns to push each other down them on the tray. It's like bobsledding only there's no snow and it's bumpier. When we've finished we throw the tray in the canal. I'm looking for shopping trolleys to throw in too when everyone starts drifting off home because it's nearly dark. I don't want to go home. I never do.

I find some other, older kids back in Reynolds Street and hang around a bit with them and finally they go inside their houses too. I'm alone with all the tiny front gardens and gates and closed doors. I look down the street. Lights are on, a few curtains are drawn, people are sitting by their gas fires, watching TV, brushing their dogs, having their tea. I turn into 89 Reynolds Street. I push open the gate. The feel of its cold metal on my fingers is familiar. Its clang is a voice I hear every day. I walk very, very slowly to the front door. I kick some stones around. Finally, reluctantly, I bang the brass knocker.

Mum answers. She's had her hair done. I know because her long curls are so tight. And she's wearing a new sweater with her jeans.

'Where've you been?' she asks me.

'Over Tony's.'

'Just look at the state of you.'

My mum's hair, the way she's talking, the deep, deep silence behind her, can only mean one thing. He's home.

I step inside the house and it's so clean that it feels sterilised, even the air feels sterilised. It's not a living room, it's an operating theatre and I'm about to be dissected. Fashionable brown walls, brown settee, brown carpet, brown shelves, featuring rows and rows of my dad's cowboy books, and there, on the reclining chair but not actually reclining, is Dad.

He scares me more than anything else on earth. He is dressed in his usual cowboy uniform: blue jeans, blue shirt, boots. I'd like to slip right past him up the stairs without him noticing but he's already facing me. I look for a smile under his big cowboy moustache. There isn't one.

I say: 'All right, Dad?' I make for the stairs.

'Stay here. I want to talk to you.'

Where are Kelly and Shane? Why aren't they watching TV as usual with the gas fire glowing bright orange? They must have scented trouble and scarpered to their rooms. When Dad's furious his anger can fall on anyone. Well, anyone except Kelly.

My mum flutters around us. She can't really have a feather duster in her hand and a frilly apron wrapped round her but that's how it feels. As though Julie Andrews has breezed in to give us a song. And Dad's playing the Master of the House. This is what they do when Dad first gets back.

'Just because I'm away, doesn't mean I don't know what's frigging going on here. I do. I know what happens when I'm not around.' His voice is controlled, too controlled. He has the strongest Newcastle accent of all of us. Some people down here can't understand it. But I understand it. I hear the threat in his voice. It's because he puts up steel scaffolding. When he comes home there are big steel rods in his voice.

'I ain't done nuffin,' I tell him.

Dad says: 'You have. You've been at it again. Thieving. And you've only frigging gone and thieved from your auntie Tanya.'

It's not the joke shop. It's a completely different crime.

'I never!'

This makes Dad angrier. 'Everyone knows it was you.'

'I never! It must have been someone else, there were loads of people round at Auntie Tanya's!'

Dad interrupts me and I stop at once and his voice drops to a low monotone as though he's talking to himself. But he's not, he's talking to me.

'How did I get a frigging kid like this? That's what I want to know. I don't deserve it. I should chop his fingers off because that's what they do, yes, that's what they do in some of those hot countries, I should chop off his whole frigging hand. I am sick to frigging death of it . . .'

He doesn't shout. He gets scarier and scarier as his voice gets quieter. I try to say I didn't do it but my protests are swamped by his anger. Suddenly he's jumping up and dragging me to his bedroom. I feel the stairs bumping against my ankles. He throws me across the bed and my body bounces. He goes to the wardrobe, pulls out a pair of jeans and extracts the cowboy belt from the waist. I brace myself as the belt lands on my lower back. Pain shoots all over my body, running out in rivers from my spine. The pain feels red. My whole body feels red. He hits me again and this time it hurts but it doesn't hurt, because now a part of me is somewhere else, high on the ceiling or up maybe in some huge, green tree, watching him hit me. I'm detached and I'm not red, I'm cool, I'm cold, I'm like Jack Frost.

Down on the bed a kid is crying and a big blue man is standing over him.

'And you can just stop bubblin'!' the man spits. 'You sound like a frigging little poof.'

The kid doesn't stop crying.

'Get up the frigging stairs now, frigging poof,' hisses the big blue man and he goes out of the room.

Sniffing, I go to the attic room I share with my big brother. He's heard it all and he doesn't say anything but he understands. When Dad gives us a hiding our bodies hurt for a while but inside something hurts for a lot longer. The knowledge that he doesn't love us.

It's Friday night and that's men's night, according to Dad. Saturday night is family night but Friday night is for men. Dad will go to the Station Arms at the end of Reynolds Street. All the men in the street will be there. They walk up in a group which gets bigger and bigger as they come out of their houses.

I hear the front door slam and for a while there's a new kind of silence, the silence of relief. When I wake I don't know what time it is but I know that Dad isn't home yet or I'd have heard him. The moon's light, but not its shape, is visible through the frosted glass of the skylight. I can see, dimly, the footballers Shane hangs on the walls, kicking balls at each other.

Unless Dad's gone on a binge, he'll be back at closing time. My body tenses. Someone has wrapped the ropes round me again. I can't move at all, they're so tight. I can't breathe. I struggle and gasp for air. I just want to get the ropes off and run away down the street so I don't have to lie here any more. I hope Jack Frost's waiting for me on the garden wall.

Then the door slams. My muscles go hard and my body becomes cold metal as I wait. I don't breathe. My big brother doesn't say a word but I know that, over in his bed, he's listening too.

There's Dad's voice. Maybe it's one of those nights when he's come home happy and joking and laughing. But the noise level rises rapidly. Soon my mother is shrieking at him. She's talking about Her again. Then it's the usual stuff about Jehovah and the devil and the end of the world. I wish she'd stop. If she doesn't stop, he'll hit her. She doesn't stop. Her high-pitched voice goes on and on until I can't hear her words, just her music. When he replies angrily, their voices merge into one strange chord. Opera singers do that. Mum and Dad are singing an opera of fury.

I hear my brother get up.

'Where are you going?' I hiss, but I already know. We're power-less and it's worse if you lie in bed. I follow him down the stairs. We hover in the hallway. All the lights are on and Mum and Dad are standing there, Mum shrieking. There's a pause. It could be over. But no, he starts to punch her. His hands are the enormous, swollen hands of someone who works hard at power stations in rain and snow. Across the fingers of the left is tattooed LOVE. Lots of people have that tattoo, and they have HATE on the other hand, but Dad doesn't. He says it's because he doesn't hate anyone, so he has a cru-cifix on his right hand instead.

He doesn't use the hand that says LOVE to punch my mother, he holds her still with it and punches her with his other hand. She screams. I want to run away but I can't move. I clutch the doorframe. I feel sick.

Suddenly Shane is rushing into the room. He stands between

them, planting himself right in front of my mother, staring Dad out, daring him to hit her more. How can he be so brave? He's only two years older than me and not even at middle school yet. I glance at Dad's face and then I have to look away because it's so horrible. His eyes have become ice eyes. His anger's turned to ice and not nice Jack Frost ice either. I am really scared for Shane when I see that face. Shane tries to stare back at Dad, flinching a bit as though Dad's dazzling him. Then Dad holds my brother round the throat with the LOVE hand and hits him full on in the face with the fist that doesn't say HATE and I hear the smack of old knuckles on young flesh.

My mum screams and flings her arms round my brother and Dad storms out, pushing me roughly aside. I still can't look at his face.

Mum sobs. Shane sobs. Mum strokes him and I try to stroke him too but there isn't room for me so I sit crying by myself. I look around. The lounge is the same as always, neat and tidy, with its brown chairs and settee and its mirror, its cottagey prints, the shelves of Dad's cowboy books and his country 'n' western records. Nothing's out of place. But the air in here is different now. The world is different.

The next day is Saturday. When I pass my parents' bedroom I hear Dad snoring. In the kitchen, our big sister Kelly is applying a packet of frozen peas to the marks on Shane's face. He's been hit before, of course. Dad used to hit him for wetting the bed when he was younger. But this was a different kind of hit.

I look at Mum, leaning over the sink with her peeler in her hand and her Afro hair falling over her shoulders. She has a round, comfortable body that ought to be huggable and right now I need a hug. I sneak over to her and try to wrap my arms round her.

'Get off.' She pushes me away. But I hold her tighter and try to tell her that I love her. After yesterday, I need to say it. And, even though I've never heard anyone else in our family talk about love, not ever, I want Mum to say it to me.

'I love you, Mum.'

'Love!' squawks Mum. 'You need to think about how you can be a good boy and make Jehovah love you.'

'I am a good boy, I do love Jehovah.'

Actually I'm terrified of Jehovah. He's a bit like Mum and Dad rolled into one, knowing everything I've done wrong and very angry with me.

'I'm glad to hear that, Mark. I'm pleased to know you love Jehovah and I hope you'll try to be a good boy for Him, because He's watching you. All the time. And don't you forget it.'

'No, Mum.'

'If you came to meetings with me more often, you could live in Paradise forever, with Jehovah and all the animals.'

I wander off. Whatever you try to say to Mum, you always end up with Jehovah in Paradise.

Around opening time, Dad emerges from the bedroom and I see him and Mum talking in the kitchen as though nothing's happened.

'All right, sonna?' he says nicely when he sees my brother. Shane nods and reddens.

'Yeah, Dad.'

I know how he feels. Guilty because when Dad hits you then you know you've done something bad and it must be your fault. Miserable because you love Dad and he doesn't want your love. And sort of embarrassed for Dad although you're not sure why.

Soon, we hear the front door slam and the gate clang and we know he's gone to the pub. When he comes back he's quiet. He announces that, since Saturday night is family night, we'll all be going to the Cricketers' Arms this evening. It's spring and if we wear our coats it'll just about be warm enough for adults to sit outside and kids to play on the lawn. He tells us this and then he falls asleep on the settee.

When it's time to wake Dad up for tea, I am brave. He was in a good mood when he came back from the pub and he's my dad and I love him. I didn't have much success with Mum this morning but now I climb up beside Dad on the settee. Slowly. Carefully. And very, very quietly. He doesn't move. So far so good.

I start to put my arms round him. Because I love him. Without doubt or questions or conditions, I just love him and if I put my arms round him gradually, he won't even notice. Slowly. Slowly . . .

He opens one eye. I stop. My heart is thumping hard. Can he feel it banging away inside me? He closes his eye again and, after a long pause, slowly, slowly, watching him always, I wrap my arms round his neck. It is like sitting on a volcano. He doesn't move. He doesn't do anything. His eyes remain shut.

'Wake up, Dad. Tea-time,' I whisper, snuggling up to his big, warm body. It would be really nice here if it wasn't so scary.

We lie still for a minute and I continue to watch his stubbly face. His eyes open and gradually they focus on me. Then, in one quick, strong movement, he pushes me away and onto the floor.

'Geddoff,' he says.

I try to hug his leg and he shakes it until I am thrown off. He stands up. I move towards him again and his leg kicks out at me. He misses, but I'm crying anyway. He doesn't love me. He can't bear me close to him.

Dad sees my tears with disgust.

'Little poof,' he says, as he goes into the dining room. 'Little bubbling poof.'

I hate Saturday tea. It's always Campbell's Cream of Mushroom Soup and a pasty and our mum says there's only one way to eat it and that is with the pasty floating upside down in the soup. It looks horrible. I don't want it but under Dad's glaring eye I eventually swallow it all down. Then Mum's bustling about, finding her new sweater, and in the bathroom the top comes off a green bottle and the whole house is filled by the smell of sweet chemicals. Dad's Brut 33. Stinking, we head for the garden of the Cricketers' Arms.

We kids are supposed to be playing bowls but I stop and watch Dad. Is this the same man as last night's maniac? He's tall and handsome, you can tell from the way the women look at him when they sip their drinks. Even Auntie Tanya, who agrees with Nan that Dad's a monster and Mum should leave him, even Auntie Tanya nods a lot and bursts out laughing when he tells a funny story. Then he cracks a few jokes and keeps up a conversation with Uncle Steve that makes everyone laugh some more. He even comes over to the kids and messes around with the bowls for a bit and makes us laugh too and I love him and I'm proud of him. He's the cleverest, the biggest, the strongest, the hardest, the best. Because tonight he's that other dad, the dad who's had a few pints and feels playful. No drink and he's sullen and withdrawn and angry with us. Somewhere between two drinks and five he ripens like fruit and we've learned to enjoy him in those good minutes. After five or six drinks we know he's on his way to a binge. Our house will soon be full of fighting and fury and Shane or me or Mum will get beaten up: it could be any of us for any reason or no reason. The only certainty is that it won't happen to Kelly. I really hate her for that. I hate her anyway because she's my big sister and she's always good. I couldn't describe her or say what she's like or what she wears because I don't ever look at her. I pretend she's not there.

When Dad's got us so scared and miserable that we're all stuck inside our own little worlds of fear, when we barely speak to each other and we're creeping round the house hoping he won't notice us and will pick on someone else, then suddenly he goes away again. When he comes back, everything's perfect. Mum is Julie Andrews and Dad is Jehovah. He knows what we've done wrong while he's been away and he punishes us for it. Then, within days, order has collapsed and we're living in terror because he might pick on any of us and punish us for anything or nothing.

When Dad goes, we are relieved. It's much easier to love him when he's not there. Mum's sisters drop by more often with their children, the house is full of chatter. Uncle Mike even comes round to say he is organising a treat for us. He is going to take us to the West Midlands Safari Park.

There are six of us in Uncle Mike's Mini: Mum, Kelly, Shane, me, Uncle Mike and Nan. A Mini has only four seats so, as an extra-special treat, Uncle Mike lets me sit on his lap while he drives and I am allowed to steer the car part of the way.

Mum is wearing her leopard-print coat. When she waves her arms we shout that there's a leopard in the car. The leopard and Nan shriek when I take the corners too wide. Uncle Mike says to them: 'Don't worry, everything's under control,' even though it probably isn't. But here I am, six years old, surrounded by my family, knowing that Dad is far away, and I feel safe.

Driving is exciting but so is the park. We spot zebras and monkeys and then, as we go through the part where there are lions, the car splutters to a halt. Our faces peer out of the windows. The lions stare back at us.

'She's broken down,' says Mike. 'Probably overloaded.'

We look at the lions and then we look at each other.

'Well, get out and push then, Lorraine,' says Uncle Mike to my mother.

'I'm not doing that!' shrieks Mum. I am glad. It would be asking for trouble in her leopard-print coat. We make sure all the windows are wound up. The glass is soon covered by a layer of steam in which I can write my name. It is hot and airless in here. Through the fuzzy windscreen I can see a red glow. That means the sun is starting to go down. Someone points out that we have a choice: we could be mauled by lions or we could stay here all night and suffocate.

Uncle Mike laughs. Nan starts laughing, too. Finally Mum begins to giggle and that's our signal. Within moments, we three kids are hysterical with laughter too. When the staff of the West Midlands Safari Park arrive in their truck to rescue us from the wild animals, they find a Mini packed full of laughing hyenas. They stare as more and more of us emerge, giggling hysterically, into the fresh air.

The sun is setting. Someone has thrown a bottle of red ink across the sky. I notice the beauty of the shadow animals on the horizon as they walk lazily across the blood-coloured sky. I think that the West Midlands Safari Park right now is the most beautiful place on earth.

Chapter 3

Mum is going to have a baby. She's rounder than ever and the reason is that there's a baby inside her tummy.

The baby will be born in September but it won't have a birthday every year because we don't have them. That's because our mum is a Jehovah's Witness and she believes in Jehovah not birthdays. Even Jesus doesn't have a birthday if you're a Jehovah's Witness. My mum only celebrates Christmas because Dad tells her she has to. And all the time you can see she doesn't really want to.

Right now my best friend is called Angus. I don't know how long he'll stay my friend because I always end up fighting and changing friends but right now it's Angus and he likes to draw too so we draw together. Our teacher, Mr Jacobs, gives us enormous rolls of paper and gradually we fill them with a story in paint and felt pen. It is a story of many people and battles in strange places and the people and the battles change all the time like gangs of kids. The story unrolls with the paper and it never ends. I lag behind the other kids in everything but art and this is what I like best. I have painted, in bright reds, an elephant so spectacular that Mr Jacobs has given it pride of place on the classroom wall.

Maybe I like to draw battles because I am a fighter myself. I am not an angry sort of fighter. I don't make horrible faces like Mum does when she hits us. I can grin while I'm fighting someone. But I know how to land my punches in the playground and I use my fists to make sure people respect me. Some of the teachers don't like this and one break time after a fight I am sent back into the classroom to Mr Jacobs. But the classroom is empty.

The place is different with no one else here. My feet, as they walk across the room, sound different. The air feels different. There's my elephant pinned to the wall, here are the arithmetic exercise books open on the desks and, on Mr Jacobs' chair, sits not Mr Jacobs but his jacket.

I stroll up to Mr Jacobs' jacket and look over my shoulder. Nobody comes in. Nobody's outside the door.

Without thinking, my heart throbbing and my hands trembling, I delve into the pockets and find Mr Jacobs' wallet. A quick glance at the door. No one. I open the wallet. There is a thick paper line inside: a wad of notes. My heart thumping so loudly now that I'm scared I won't hear approaching footsteps, I pick out just one note, a blue one, and shove it in my pocket. Then, so fast I barely see my own hands, I close the wallet and slip it back into Mr Jacobs' jacket. No one saw me. Except the elephant. And Jehovah.

I am excited for the rest of the day. Will Mr Jacobs get out his wallet and count his money and know that a blue note is missing? Will the whole class be questioned and will anyone think of looking in my pocket?

But the day passes and nothing happens. Mr Jacobs does not open his wallet or he opens it without missing a note. On the way home I look at it and see that it is £5. Five pounds! I hide it in under my pillow because I don't want anyone else finding it and stealing it from me: our house is full of kids every day after school, mostly kids from the children's home where Mum's a cook. They follow her back after her shift and hang around for a bit of family life. They seem to like it here. Which is strange, as I often pretend I live at the children's home.

The next day I go to school almost sick with fear. By now, Mr Jacobs must certainly have discovered the theft. But he hasn't. This makes me happy and excited. I stole from Auntie Tanya and the joke shop and there were lots of other thefts no one even knows about but this is the best so far. All week I wait but the missing money is never mentioned. The fiver is mine! Five pounds is a fortune. What can I spend it on? Finally I decide to buy some sweets. Then I buy some brakes for a bike. I don't have a bike but one day I might have one. The most exciting thing of all is that, when the opportunity next arises, I can steal from him again. And all the time, a small voice inside me is asking me to stop doing this wrong thing. And all the time, I know I can't.

Mum is going to have her baby soon. She's always yelling at us now. Shane and I are a trial to her, she tells us so every day and she tells her friends from church too because one of them decides to help her.

Maureen has a thin face like a witch and it's her fault my mum's a Jehovah's Witness because she knocked on the door when I was a baby and persuaded Mum to join. It happened when my dad was in jail for a year for hurting someone. If he'd been there, he certainly would have put a stop to it.

When Dad isn't there to protect us from the Jehovah's Witnesses, Mum's friends come round a lot. Maureen doesn't like us. She looks down on us.

We have Maureen and her holiday in Scotland to thank for Mum's new best friend. She gets back waving a souvenir. It is a wooden spoon but it is no ordinary spoon. It is a deep mahogany colour and it is immense, as big as an oar. On it are carved the words: THE WORLD'S GREATEST STIRER! and one glance tells us what Maureen intends Mum to use it for. Mum hangs it in the dining room where she can grab it when necessary. We don't have to be very naughty to feel the cold, wooden hand of THE WORLD'S GREATEST STIRER! on our bottoms.

I try not to cry when Mum hits me with her spoon but when she wallops Shane and I hear his sobs, well then I want to sob too. Something about Shane makes me feel sad. When I look at his big ears and big head and big teeth and scrawny neck, when I see the way he looks sort of scruffy and unloved and a bit unhappy, then I love him and he makes my heart ache. If I get that aching, tearful feeling, I'm nice to him for a while. Then after a bit he's my big brother again and I'll fight him to death.

When Mum hits us she screams and her face gets pulled into terrible shapes and she's so angry that she can't stop hitting us. Once she couldn't find THE WORLD'S GREATEST STIRER! and she grabbed the broom and hit us so hard that the handle broke on Shane's head. When she's like this Shane and I know a terrible secret that hurts more than the spoon and more than the broom. We know our Mum's crazy.

I start stealing from her. Mr Jacobs has never noticed all the missing £5 notes so I begin taking small amounts out of Mum's handbag. When she doesn't accuse me, I take larger amounts. Then one day she catches me red-handed. She yells at me and THE WORLD'S GREATEST STIRER! comes down from the dining-room wall. Plus, she's going to tell Dad. I lie in bed worrying about what he will do to me when he finds I've been stealing again. I wish I could stop myself. But I can't. It's just something I have to do. And the ropes are here again, I'm lashed to the bed, struggling to move, struggling for breath, struggling to get away from the house, the family, myself.

Dad arrives. Almost immediately there is so much excitement that everyone forgets I'm in trouble because Mum has disappeared into hospital. Soon afterwards, Dad gets a phone call. He announces that we have a little sister.

Dad doesn't visit Mum in the hospital but in the evening he says he's going to see a friend. Since he's in charge of us, we have to go too. The friend is a woman. Shane and I instantly recognise the Coat Hanger. It's Her. Close-up, we see that her hair is raven-black.

'It's dyed,' says Kelly. She knows about that sort of stuff. 'And her face is brown because she smears false tan on.'

The Coat Hanger's face certainly is a strange colour. When I peer at her closely I see that Kelly's right: her face is covered by a layer of goo so thick she probably has to scratch it off. Gold jewellery hangs all over her body like decorations on a Christmas tree. Kelly tells us that the woman works behind a bar somewhere.

We make ourselves comfortable in the Coat Hanger's living room and, while she and Dad are busy in some other part of the house, we fall asleep. In the morning, Dad takes us home.

Later, he goes to the hospital to pick up Mum and the new baby girl. She is to be called Bethany and the sight of her, so small, her fingers tiny and her eyes big, makes me love her.

When I think no one is looking, I snatch the baby and take her into my arms. But everyone *is* looking – Mum, a midwife and all the family including Nan – and many pairs of arms reach out at once. They want to save the baby from me because they know I'm a bad boy. But I hold Bethany carefully. I look down at her little wrinkled face and I smile. She looks back up at me with wide eyes. She can't understand any of the things people say about me. She just trusts me. I do love her.

Chapter 4

I'm sitting in the front room and three bars of the fire are glowing and I'm talking to a lady. She's not old like Mum but she's a grown-up. She's a psychiatrist. The school has sent her. She's asking me why I'm always trying to hit the other kids.

I try to answer her questions helpfully but I'm not really here. I'm up in the branches of some high tree watching us. There's a lady leaning forward with an orange file on her lap and there's a kid slumped in a chair as if he can't get far enough away from her and that kid is me, except it isn't. Because she keeps talking about violence and I don't know what violence is. All that hitting in the playground is what I do, but that's some other person; it's not how I really am inside.

I see her a few times and then she makes a suggestion to Mum and Dad. It is such a fantastic suggestion that my eyes nearly pop out. She thinks boxing would be a good outlet for my aggression. I'm to have boxing lessons. So now I'll really be able to sharpen up my fighting skills and beat the shit out of the other kids, thanks to the psychiatrist.

But secretly, Shane and I agree something about the lady. We think it shouldn't be me talking to her. It should be Mum.

I am sent to visit a couple who live on our street. Mum cleans for them and for some reason she tells me to go over there on Sunday morning. I ask why but she just says they're expecting me. They're both teachers and Mrs Allbut teaches at my school. She's friends with Mr Jacobs. I'm in a new class now so my visits to the inside of Mr Jacobs' wallet have ended. He never did catch me. Sometimes, when I remember how I used to steal from him, I miss the excitement.

There's a gang of kids forming in the empty schoolyard as I pass and I don't want to waste my Sunday morning with a pair of teachers so I decide I'll stand on the doorstep and ask what they want me for. But when Brian Allbut answers my knock he gives me such a warm welcome that I walk straight in. He's an adult but he's not old and his face has strong lines as though someone carved it.

From the outside their house looks just like ours: the same red brick, the same windows, the same door, but from the minute I walk in everything's different. The rooms are light and bright and welcoming with books and nice pictures round the walls. The records look interesting, not like Mum's Johnny Mathis and Dad's country 'n' western. They ask if I'd like to do some painting and they lead me into the kitchen. I can smell flowers. The radio's on but it's not playing music; it's playing a conversation.

'*The Archers*,' says Jill Allbut. She smiles at me. 'It's nearly over anyway.'

She switches it off and I see that they've got painting stuff all laid out on the table. They show me how you can paint paper and fold it into different shapes and this is very interesting and I become totally absorbed.

They are very nice. When we stop for a snack they ask me questions and listen to the answers and then he says something and then she says something and then I say something and the talk flows easily. It's like passing a ball around. In our house, in the playground, there are grunts and people say only one word or don't say anything at all or at least not what they mean and you get told to shut up a lot and no one listens to what the last person said unless they're planning to disagree and the only real talk is an argument. I try to imagine what it's like to live in a world of conversation like the Allbuts, a world where you even hear conversations on the radio.

When it's time to go home for my Sunday dinner, I am surprised. It seems to me that I only came in five minutes ago. The

Allbuts admire my work and say they've enjoyed having me. They ask me to go back. I say I'd like to. I feel different as I walk back up Reynolds Street. A big gang of kids is playing in the deserted school-yard and a few people are on the roof, which is a great game and guaranteed to bring a police car out, but I walk right by them. Suddenly today I'm a good kid instead of that bad boy who hits people and steals a lot. And I like it.

Mum opens the front door to me. She doesn't look at me or smile and she turns at once to go back to the kitchen. I follow her through the house and everyone ignores me except for Bethany. She's a tod-dler now and I've learned to hate her, we all have, because everyone's always making a fuss of her, even Dad, and Mum never lets her go. Bethany gets all the hugs and kisses I think I should get. But today, when everyone else treats me as though I'm invisible, I'm glad that Bethany rushes up to me and looks pleased I'm here. I have a chat with her, like at the Allbuts'. It's one-sided but she seems to enjoy it. Then I stay in the kitchen while Kelly and Mum get dinner out of the oven.

'Don't just stand there, get the oven door closed,' Kelly snaps at me.

'Move!' says Mum.

They start to argue about how they'll carve the roast.

Compared to the bright, friendly warmth of the kitchen where I've spent the morning, this is a loveless place. I don't smell the Sunday lunch: all I can smell is the house's sour atmosphere.

A few weeks later I'm hanging around in the empty schoolyard on a Sunday afternoon when some skinheads stroll in with a few bottles of Strongbow. They're four or five years older. In fact, they're Kelly's age and she's at school with them so I sort of know them.

'Little fucker,' they say, a friendly enough greeting, and when they open the cider they pass me the bottle. I take it, pretending I've done this often. But I haven't. And from the first swallow I am amazed.

The Strongbow is sweet and bitter at the same time like apple and lemonade. It slips through my body until I can feel its fuzziness down as far as my fingers and toes and right up into my head. I drink some more. It is warm in my belly. I drink some more. Someone passes me a cigarette. I smoke it and spit a bit. I drink some more. The schoolyard's looking blurred and the building's leaning enough to topple. That's interesting. I am relaxed. I laugh. I'm not scared of anything. I'm big, I'm with a bunch of skinheads.

We are all drunk but I'm drunkest of all. The others watch me and they laugh at me and then we go, spitting, swearing, smoking, hitting out at any little kids in our way.

'Fuck off,' we shout at old ladies we pass. Then we laugh and spit some more.

I don't know where we're going. I don't care. The pavement is not at right-angles to the houses and it's not parallel with the road either and above us the sky is turning round like a kaleidoscope. We stagger. We clutch one another to stop ourselves from falling.

We arrive at the house of one of the lads and start to play on his drum kit. We play wild, crazy music and we laugh at ourselves. Then I stop thumping and lie down on the carpet. There's a big sister leaning over me and behind her is the ceiling and I know something's wrong. I'm going to be sick. She leads me to the bathroom and takes care of me.

When I get home I'm different. I have entered a new phase of my life. Even though I'm only eight years old I'm already grown-up because I've been drunk with the big skinheads. This evening there is a thumping inside my head, as though we're still playing the drums. But I don't mind. I feel relaxed, contented. I've arrived. And I don't wake up in the night to the tight ropes and my running-away feeling.

I go back often to the Allbuts' and with them I'm a kid again. It's generally on Sundays because I hate our house on Sundays. I arrive from hell with the shrieking and shouting ringing in my ears and the Allbuts come to the door and smile and even say things like: 'Good to see you!' 'You're a breath of fresh air.' If they know that I'm a refugee from a war zone, they don't let on.

I walk into the calm of their kitchen and I'm in a different world where I can be a different Mark. Jill fixes me a snack and Brian reaches up to a shelf and gets down an aeroplane kit. First we have to fit it together, then, best of all, we have to paint it. They start me off on their kitchen table and I paint my plane in really bright colours – reds and blues with startling circles at the end of the wings. I paint every little bit of it although that means painting my fingers too. When I come back a few days later the plane is dry and we put on our coats and fly it in the garden. It soars. It soars across the lawn, over the flowerbeds through the late afternoon twilight. Even though it's winter, you can see that their garden's neat and full of shrubs and the earth's been dug over tidily. The plane lands gently in a hedge.

I take the plane home and try flying it there. Of course, it isn't the same at our house. Mum and Dad's idea of gardening is to dig an enormous hole and throw all the rubbish in and then fill it back up. There's no lawn or shrubs and there are never any flowers. The plane crashes into the shed and gets tangled up in the pile of rusting bedsprings and handlebars.

When the Allbuts ask about the plane, I tell them how sad our garden makes me. They produce a Bees catalogue and say I can choose something to brighten it up. I might still have time to plant daffodils so I select some bulbs and a spectacular plant called a Red Hot Poker. The bulbs arrive almost at once and the Red Hot Poker will arrive in the spring as a tiny plug. I'll dig a hole for it and when it grows our garden will be transformed.

I plant the bulbs and wait.

When I am at the Allbuts' it's easy to be good. It never even occurs to me to steal from them. But no one else is safe. Mum has to sleep with her purse under her pillow every night. I feel sad when I see her taking it upstairs but I know she's right. If she leaves her purse downstairs, I'll rob her. I can't help myself.

I'm almost never at home. The other kids in the street are a sort of family to me. I hang around in the school playground out of hours, knowing that sooner or later someone will appear, and today it's Trevor.

Trevor comes from a nice family: his mum's a housewife with a lot to say for herself and his dad drives a boring car. Trevor's about five years older than me: he must be thirteen. He's tall and lanky with sticking-out teeth. I'm pleased when he talks to me. I feel important with older kids. He gives me a cigarette and we smoke together and he seems to be my friend and that feels good.

He says we should go over to the cattle market because it's really dangerous to walk along the top of the cattle pens. I like doing dangerous things and I've never been to the cattle market. I know that on market day it turns into a teeming chaos of mooing, bleating, and trucks reversing. But I've never been there when it's empty.

We go a long way round: Reynolds Street, past the cricket ground, right onto Chester Road. Some of Kidderminster is red brick but lots of it is modern and the houses and the shops and the factories go on and on. The green bits are the sports fields and the patches of waste ground and the nicest part is where the big chestnut trees line the cricket ground. I touch their smooth trunks as I pass. Every October I try to climb them so I can shake down the conkers but I'm never big enough. Now I'm eight I might be. Maybe Trevor will help me if he's still my friend. When we get to the cattle market we find a huge stretch of silent concrete emptiness. He's right about the pens. We can walk along the tops and jump across the corners and it's fun. Trevor's fun. We play for a while, until Trevor gets into a pen and I jump down in there with him. I think he's going to give me another cigarette but he does something else. He does it just as though it's all a part of our play and he does it so suddenly that I let him. He pulls down my trousers and my underpants too.

I am astonished. I wouldn't even show my dick to my mum when I had an infection. So why does Trevor want to see it? I stare down at the top of his head as he takes hold of my dick. He puts it in his mouth. I don't know what I'm supposed to do. I don't know what I'm supposed to feel. I don't feel anything. It's like when Dad hits me and I float up and watch a man hitting a boy from the branches of a great, green tree. Now I'm high above our heads, watching the top of Trevor's dark head as he takes my dick in his mouth.

He sucks hard. I watch him. After a few minutes he stops. I don't meet his eye when he stands up. I pull up my pants quickly. I hear my own breathing. It is fast and shallow. My heart is beating fast. I know that my friend Trevor has done a dirty thing. I have no idea why.

Trevor grabs my shoulders and shakes me so I have to look at him. I don't want to.

'You don't tell anyone, see,' he tells me. He doesn't sound like my friend now. 'Don't even think about it. Because they're never going to believe you.'

He's probably right. No one ever believes me.

'You tell and I'll say I never. And they'll believe me.'

I am bad and everyone knows it and I'm a liar and everyone knows that too. So there's no point telling. And what's to tell? I thought a dick is something you pee with but now I know that it's something other people put in their mouths. It's another one of the strange things people do, like birthday parties. Except it isn't. Birthday parties may be no fun, but they don't make me feel very small and very miserable the way Trevor has.

When I get home I'm invisible as usual. Kelly and Shane are fighting over the television channel. Mum's busy with Bethany. No one seems to understand that I'm different now. And even I am not sure how I'm different or why.

Chapter 5

My daffodils bloom and look fantastic and I am very proud of them and I take special care planting the small Red Hot Poker plug that has arrived. Mum doesn't seem very enthusiastic about the daffodils or the Red Hot Poker. When, in the summer, it finally blooms, the daffodils are long over and the Red Hot Poker is the only flower and I know it looks pathetic among the pieces of ruined paddling pool, the dog shit and the bikes without wheels. I am disappointed. Shane sniggers and Kelly isn't interested. Mum takes a picture but she looks at me strangely. I am relieved to get to the Allbuts' house and see flowers all over their garden. Brian Allbut is snipping some and tying back others and he's discussing next year's flowers with Jill and that makes me feel better because I know that Brian Allbut is not a poof.

When Dad comes home he goes out more and he drinks more than usual. My mum's angry with him all the time. She and Nan do a lot of talking in the kitchen in their low voices. One night, Dad is so drunk that he can't drive home from the Steelworkers' Club and my big sister Kelly does it for him. She is twelve years old and she drives his brown Capri all the way back to Reynolds Street. I wish I'd been allowed to do that. On another occasion, he arrives home with the Capri full of vomit. He offers Shane a fiver to clean it out but Mum's very angry and won't let him.

I haven't seen Trevor much but I'm hanging around in Reynolds

Street as usual one afternoon when he appears. I do remember that thing happening at the cattle market but it was a strange, isolated event and not telling anyone about it almost made it not happen. I'm shy to talk to him. I'm not sure if he's my friend. But he's nice to me today and says he'll give me some of his cigarettes. We go to the school playground. No one else is there. I start to feel nervous. We sit down on a ramp and smoke.

Then, suddenly, he reaches across to me and pushes me to the ground. In one deft movement he pulls down my trousers and my pants as well as his own and then he rolls on top of me. So now what is he doing? It doesn't feel as though we're going to fight, and my cigarette's still burning in my hand.

He pushes his body against mine. I shut my eyes. I float off up to the roof of the school, to the highest tree, and watch us from there.

He rolls around on me, our dicks together, and then starts a pumping action against my body. If I open my eyes I can see all the bones in his face. I shut them again and once more I'm looking down on two boys, their bodies pressed together. The one under-neath is so much smaller that he's almost hidden. Maybe that's how it is to be Jehovah, always looking. And He must be looking at us right now.

After a while, Trevor stops. His face is red. I pull up my trousers miserably.

'Don't tell,' Trevor reminds me, hard-voiced. 'Because I'll say I never and no one's going to believe you.'

I wonder what we were doing. My dad is always calling me a poof. Is this what he means?

We go to our homes and I don't tell anyone. Instead, I try it on a younger boy. I am Trevor and the boy is me. He's staying at our house after school because my mum is supposed to be looking after him. When we're up in the bedroom I roll him over just like Trevor rolled me in the playground and pull down his trousers and get on top of him and push myself around a bit. Like Trevor did. I don't even know why I'm doing it. I feel nothing. A glance at his face tells me that neither does he.

'Don't tell anyone, see,' I say afterwards. 'No one would believe you anyway because I'm older than you are and I'll say I never.'

He nods, distantly. I recognise that strange absence in his eyes.

But my interest has been awakened now. Trevor has unlocked a door for me and opened it. Not much more than a crack but I'm certain something's inside.

There's a girl who's often at our house after school and, still without understanding why, I take her out into the garden with a blanket to the dog kennel. We lie on the blanket with the smell of dog all around us and I feel inside her clothes. I take off her pants. Her body is strange. It is very different from mine, fleshier, with an interesting absence between her legs. My fingers explore all over her. She is soft like water. She is exciting. My heart is pumping fast. I want to touch her more and more. There are tiny strings deep inside me and something is strumming on them and it feels good. So now I begin to understand. This must be the feeling Trevor was looking for.

From now on, I touch girls whenever I can. I soon learn that girls my own age are less interesting to feel than older ones. As they get older, they get fleshier. And they nearly always let me. One of my sister's friends is thirteen or maybe even fourteen and she corners me in an alley behind Reynolds Street. She must know my age but she doesn't care.

'You show me what you've got,' she tells me, 'And I'll show you mine.'

I know what she's talking about. I stare at her smooth, brown skin and I'd like to touch it. I'd like to feel her all over. I let her lead me to the deserted playground and we go up the ramp to the fire exit where there are old brick arches that you can hide in. She pins me against the wall. I am a little bit scared when she pulls down my trousers and pants and then her own. There's something angry and demanding about her. But as we rub our parts together I feel naughty and excited. My body tingles, I can hear my blood pumping, my heartbeat sounds like a storming army. Then, suddenly, she decides that we've finished. We pull up our pants. We go back to the alley and carry on walking in the direction we were going. We've barely even spoken to each other.

I'm digging around with Matthew, one of my mates of the moment, in the nettles on some waste ground behind Reynolds Street when we find a bag of magazines and inside are pictures. Pictures of grown-ups. Completely naked. The women have enormous breasts which hang like fruit and the men are strangely pink and very hairy. Together they are doing the same kind of stuff I am doing to girls, only a lot more, because the men are actually putting their dicks inside, yes, inside, the pink women. The magazine has close-ups so you can see how they do it and their dicks are different from mine, more like enormous flagpoles.

'It's sex,' says Matthew knowledgeably. 'This is sex. Or it might be fucking. Or both.'

Matthew and I turn the pages and stare and we don't know whether to laugh or point or be embarrassed. The pictures are mesmerising. And they give me a new understanding. What I do with girls when I feel them is sex. It's what grown-ups do. It's what my dad does.

I know why Mum's angry with him now. It's not only his drinking, it's a woman, and not the tanned raven who was around a few years ago when Bethany was born but another one we've seen him with. Dad is doing sex stuff with her. And when Mum shrieks and yells about Dad's wickedness, she's talking about sex. It's something men do a lot with many different people while wives stay at home with children. This is clear to me. It's just a mystery why it makes Mum so angry.

Our house simmers. I smell fury whenever I walk in through the door. I try only to eat and sleep there. The rest of the time I am out on the street. Sometimes I go to the Allbuts'. They sit me in their living room and I put on headphones and listen to records of funny people like Marty Feldman. I roll on their settee laughing. Or I do some drawing. Once I bake some cakes with Jill. And I plant a pip from an orange. Whenever I leave I get that strange feeling again that I'm a nice, good kid. At night I lie in bed wishing I was their son.

Now I'm nine, almost ten, I can climb the huge horse chestnut trees by the cricket ground without help and shake down the conkers while the other kids wait below.

I get higher and higher into the tree's own private world of moss and silver bark and scurrying insects. I concentrate on where the next hand goes, on finding the next foothold, and this is so absorbing that when I look round and find I'm up a tree in Kidderminster and remember that I'm Mark, I'm surprised. I feel as though I've been away for a while.

I climb so high that I'm a bit scared but everyone's watching me so I lean forward onto my belly and slowly edge along a branch. All around me are leaves, turning brown. The leaves are arranged in bunches like hands. There must be a million green-brown fingers on this tree. Maybe they'll catch me if I fall. When I peer out I can see Kidderminster, the roofs and high-rise blocks and collapsing gas tanks and vandalised factories. I shimmy further. Beneath my feet I can feel the long emptiness.

When I get near the end of the branch I beat at the conkers with a stick. I can hear their small, hard bodies fall to the ground far below. I don't climb down. The others pick them up and shout for me to come but I say I'm staying a while.

The sound of their feet and voices soon gets lost in the sound of traffic. I'm alone now with the tree. I like it in horse-chestnut world. Maybe I could sleep here, stay forever. It's starting to get dark but I don't move. The tree wraps itself around me as though it loves me and cares about me. Little bugs scurry past. They think I'm part of the trunk. I don't want to go home.

When the cars below have their lights on and I can see stars above through breaks in the leaves, I climb down. My feet sting when they hit the ground. I gather the last conkers and put them in a sack and pull them home on my bogey made from pram wheels. Reluctant to go in, I lay the conkers on the front path and stamp on them until the beautiful, brown bodies, shining in the lamplight, emerge from their green, prickly cases like pearls.

Mum comes to the door. She whacks me around the head.

'Look at that mess all over the path!' she yells.

I try to scrape the green slime away with my foot.

Much later, I go in with my conkers. She's waiting for me. Behind her the house is still. She's not angry any more. Her voice is strange.

I glance at her and see that her eyes are bloodshot and her face is red and bloated. She's been crying and she looks revolting. I turn to go because there's no bubbling in our family.

But I'm not fast enough. Mum catches me and flings her arms round me, holding me tightly against her woolly sweater. I can't breathe. She's suffocating me. My conkers fall on the floor. I try to get away but she won't let me. And now she's sobbing, dropping wet tears on my head, I can feel them. I gasp for air. I am repelled. I am sickened. I want to hit her, cut her, vomit on her, headbutt her, do anything that will get me away. This isn't about Mum loving me. It isn't even about me at all. She's clinging to me in her despair, but that isn't right because I'm only nine and hugging isn't supposed to be this way.

I struggle for my life and eventually I pull away, sick with disgust. I pick up my beautiful, shining conkers and leave her sobbing on the sofa, the way my dad does when he's just hit her. I go straight upstairs.

Shane's there, lying on his bed, listening to music, living in his own world. He barely acknowledges me. I lie down. I remember how, when I was smaller, I was always trying to get Mum to hug me. And now she has and it was horrible.

Chapter 6

Jill and Mum and Bethany and I go to London. We are visiting Jill's auntie Betty in the suburbs but we're to spend the first part of the day in central London. I have never been to London before and from the moment I arrive and feel the buzz on the streets, the way the people move faster, their many colours and accents, the constant parade of signs and faces and shop windows, I love the place. I stumble as I crane my neck to see the top of buildings, I watch the changing of the guard, I climb on the mighty lions in Trafalgar Square, I hear Big Ben chime, I eat sandwiches beneath the wheels of Boudicca's chariot by Westminster Bridge, I see Eros, god of love, with buses and taxis circling him at Piccadilly and when I get back and people ask me what I liked best about London I say: the statues. I tell Jill Allbut that I am certainly coming back one day.

Auntie Betty is impressed by my enthusiasm and from now on regular parcels arrive full of London information and souvenirs. I have a London scrapbook and stick everything in carefully. I like being alone in my room doing this. Or I like being out on the street with my mates. I'm never around the house because now Dad is always here.

Our new prime minister is Mrs Thatcher. This is a time, says Jill Allbut, of mass unemployment in Britain. Our dad has become a statistic. He has no work and money is short. Mum rushes round cooking and cleaning wherever she can but the biggest crisis is that Dad doesn't have any drinking money. And the only thing worse than Dad going to the pub is Dad not going to the pub.

It's Sunday and he's desperate for a drink. He must have a drink because it's Sunday. He roars around the house, a big, dangerous gorilla in a cage. He tells my mother to give him a fiver. She refuses. She needs the £5 to buy food. He ignores her and makes for her purse. She intercepts him, trying to snatch it away. The gorilla pins her to the wall with one massive paw and with the other he extracts a fiver from her purse. She protests and that makes him really angry.

We watch in horror as he shoves the thin blue note into her mouth and, with two fingers, pushes it violently down her throat. Mum stops struggling. She turns red and gasps for breath. We stare. We don't do anything. We are powerless. We are watching Mum die. She stops gasping. Her body is going floppy. Then the gorilla suddenly reaches into her throat like someone unposting a letter and retrieves the note. Probably it is wet but he doesn't care. He snarls and swears in gorilla language and then he goes off, slamming the door, to the pub. Mum is going to start crying now. I escape as soon as I can.

I go over to the canal with some mates and when I get back I find that kids are gathering on our street. I join a gang of them and our gang masses with others in the empty school playground. There's an atmosphere. People shout at each other. Fights break out. I wander around, watching for a while, and then I notice, in the thick of one of the fights, a tall, bony, dark-haired boy, older than me, fists flying. Trevor.

As soon as I see him I know, without even thinking about it, that I want to fight him. I want to beat him. I want to turn him into pulp.

I stride towards his jostling group and elbow my way in. The other kids see the look on my face. They step back. A few shout: 'Go, Marky, go!'

When he's standing right in front of me, he looks frightened. He sees a mad dog, all teeth and hackles and hair. I set on him. Within a few moments he's on the ground. I pummel his face with my fists and then I pummel him again. My hands land on his stomach and sink in deep, then his chest, then his chin. His eyes are closed. I bang his head against the playground. I smash the expensive screw-in teeth he's been boasting about in our street. And, just to make sure, when he's lying there still dazed, I get a brick and shove it in his mouth.

The kids stare at me in amazement. Everyone's watching now. There aren't any other fights, only ours. Then cheering breaks out.

Slowly, Trevor gets to his feet. He feels his mouth. He runs his fingers along the place his teeth should be. When he looks at his hand he finds blood. And he knows his teeth are broken.

He is furious. He shouts at me and then he makes his way up the street to my house. I follow him. I'm really scared at what my parents will say. I tell him not to go in. But he splutters: 'You're going to pay for this.'

I wonder how much his teeth cost. I wonder if Dad has spent his fiver and got home from the pub yet.

Trevor pounds on our front door and Mum answers. She sees a boy with blood pouring from his mouth, me standing behind him. Her face goes white.

'Your Mark did this,' roars Trevor from his bleeding mouth. 'Look at me!'

Mum stares. I don't say anything. Trevor starts demanding that Mum pay for new screw-in teeth. I can see that she is about to apologise and agree! Trevor is livid, he is shouting. And then, suddenly, Dad appears at the door behind her.

'What's going on?' he says. Trevor tells him, spitting blood.

Dad says: 'How old are you?' His voice is dangerous. It is quiet, too quiet. Does Trevor know that it's Dad's dangerous voice or do you have to be a member of our family to pick up the signals?

'Fifteen! I'm fifteen and my screw-in teeth are all broken and you'll have to pay for them!' yells Trevor. I shudder. I wouldn't yell at my dad like that.

'Fifteen . . .' Dad's voice is an undertone now, and loaded with threat. 'Fifteen. And my lad's ten. And you're here complaining about him. Take yourself and your blood off my doorstep and piss off back home. You little poof.'

Trevor stares, broken-toothed, open-mouthed. Then slowly he turns and goes.

Before Dad closes the door I give him a cunning grin. Dad mutters: 'Frigging poof, that boy.' And it is one of those moments when I really love him, even though he doesn't know what he's done for me. I follow Trevor down the road, taunting him. 'Fuck you, Trevor, just fuck you.'

Next time I go to the Allbuts', they give me bad news. We are having a snack in the kitchen and everything seems normal enough. Then Jill says they've got something to tell me. I stop eating. I look at them both suspiciously. Their kind, even faces are creased with concern. Jill tells me, very gently, that they're moving.

My first thought is that I want to move with them. I want to leave Reynolds Street too. Then I think that maybe they're only going to the other side of Kidderminster. Brian shakes his head. They're going to another town. Redditch. I've never been there but I don't like it already. In fact, I hate Redditch. They're moving because they're changing schools.

I don't finish my snack. I can't chew any more. I can't swallow. But I say nothing. I ask no questions. I make no comment. I don't tell them that they are my sanctuary and that without them my life might be unbearable because I can never be that other Mark, the Mark who loves painting and talking and who is spoken to kindly.

I don't visit them again. On the day they move they come to say goodbye and to tell me they'll arrange for me to come to Redditch as soon as possible. I nod but I don't say much. My last view of them is two sad, worried faces. When I close the door I go up to my room and I don't come out for a while because I don't want to see the removal van outside their house, taking away the Marty Feldman records and the radio where people talk to each other, I don't want to see men carting out all the conversations and pictures that used to be there. At night when I go to bed I feel as though someone died today.

Chapter 7

When I'm at home there's nothing to do. The atmosphere is stifling and I hate it. But when I'm out on the streets with the big family of local kids I've grown up with, then the whole town is a playground for us to vandalise, to rob, to run around.

My best mate is a streets mate who doesn't even go to our school. Daniel is from a large, noisy family and he's very clever at devising new bad things to do. He's baby-faced and his build is slight so he's not much good for fighting but he's into everything, he wears the right clothes and he uses his brain where other people use their fists. As soon as we meet, we become firm friends.

At home, there are more kids. They've colonised our house. Not only does Mum mind children after school until their mothers get home from work, but loads more kids from the children's home follow her back to Reynolds Street when she's finished her shift in the kitchens there. We're at school with these children's home kids so we know them all. The boys spend their clothing allowance on cigarettes and dress themselves from charity shops in old suit jackets and ragged jeans. Shane and I think they look terrible.

Clothes are important to us: Shane's a mod and I'm a suedehead. A suedehead is somewhere between a skinhead and a mod. That means I have a crewcut Number One, which is as short as it gets. I wear a suede jacket and a bright red Fred Perry polo shirt and jeans

with Doc Martens or moccasins. That's the look. The music is The
Beat, The Selecter, The Jam and UB40. As a mod, Shane wears a
blazer, as though he's just about to go out boating, and a bright
button-down shirt.

'I was hip when I was young,' Mum informs us. We look at her
round body and lined face in disbelief. Our house often throbs to the
sound of her Johnny Mathis records. Surely that never could have
been hip. She gets out a picture of a beautiful young girl.

'That's me,' she says, 'when I was seventeen.'

It's hard to see any similarities between the girl and our mum. The
girl in the picture looks as though she has a few dreams. But Mum
is married to Dad.

She tells us that she used to hang around in north-eastern clubs
that were 'in'. They were the 'underground'. She heard The
Animals, Gerry and the Pacemakers and The Who, she says, and we
pull faces. Were Gerry and the Pacemakers really 'in', let alone
'underground'?

'Oh yes,' says Mum. 'They weren't mainstream music. They were
hip. Especially The Animals; there was a Newcastle sound and they
were right in the middle of it.'

And Mum was there. It's hard to believe looking at her now,
leaning on her Hoover.

She tells us that Dad used to be a Teddy boy and that sounds even
funnier.

We ask: 'Did you ever see The Beatles?'

She nods and looks dreamy. 'I camped all night outside the City
Hall in Newcastle to make sure of getting in. And I did.' She
smiles. 'When they came on stage, I thought life couldn't get any
better.'

We look at Mum. You can see from her face that she's been married to Dad all these years and that she's been miserable. Her hands
are wrinkled from doing other people's cleaning and taking care of
us. She looks tired. Probably she was right that her life wouldn't get
any better after seeing The Beatles. But we don't feel sorry for her.
We don't much care if she used to be young and pretty and have
dreams. We're living in our own world of friends and music and

we're leaving her behind. Mum and Dad are losing us. And that's when they find Paul.

He's one of the boys from the children's home and he spends a lot of time at our house. He's four years older than me. Everyone likes him. Even Dad likes him. They laugh and joke together. I'll never be able to do that, even when I'm Paul's age. I see Shane watching them too and I know he's thinking the same thing. We're thinking that Dad wishes Paul was his son instead of me and Shane.

So when Mum starts to talk about adopting Paul, we're not surprised. Mostly I'm surprised that Paul would want to join our family. My fantasy has always been to live at the children's home, especially since the Allbuts went, so maybe we should swap. I could become an orphan and Paul could become the son Mum and Dad always wanted.

The adoption process begins. Paul is staying with us most of the time. He sleeps up in the attic room with me and Shane and now that it's nearly Christmas he's going to stay for the holidays. Money is tight. Dad tells us that he has almost no money left after buying us all Christmas presents but he will hold back a few quid so that he can have a pint over the festive season. That's the sort of thing he says when Paul's around, stuff which makes him sound like a normal dad.

Dad puts aside a fiver. He places it carefully in a small silver-coloured butter dish, which he leaves on a shelf in the lounge. Everyone knows that leaving money anywhere in the house when I'm around is an unsafe thing to do. Probably Dad thinks I'm so scared of him that I won't steal it. But from the second he puts that £5 in the butter dish I become obsessed by it. I must get it. Even though I'm sure to be caught.

In a matter of hours, I seize my opportunity. Tea's over but Mum hasn't cleared away yet. Paul, Kelly, Shane, Mum and Dad are still sitting round the dining-room table together. My parents behave better when Paul's here. They fight less and everyone talks more.

I saunter off as though I'm bored. I go into the lounge. I turn the TV on. But I don't sit down and watch it. Instead I stealthily climb onto the brown arm of the reclining chair. I have to pause to balance or I'll go crashing down onto the record collection beneath and that would be the end of Johnny Mathis. My heart beating and my eyes all over the room, I reach for the butter dish and very, very quietly I lift the lid. I take the fiver and stuff it into my jeans pocket. I replace the lid. Then I sink down into an armchair and pretend to watch the TV. My heart is beating so loudly I can't even hear the programme.

After a decent interval I go upstairs. I stash the fiver under the carpet under my bed. Later, I show Paul the money. He is quick to take charge.

'Hang on to it and we'll spend it at the weekend,' he instructs me.

At the weekend we buy sweets, lots of them. Sweets for Paul's brother at the home, sweets for Shane and Kelly, sweets for our mates and ourselves. Nothing for spoilt brat Bethany, of course, who trots off to Jehovah's Witness meetings holding Mum's hand. She's not having any of my sweets.

On Boxing Day, it is Mum who finds that the butter dish is empty. She tells Dad. No one has any doubt who took the fiver.

'I never!'

'You frigging little bastard,' snarls Dad in that dangerous voice of his. 'I'll frigging kill you.'

And, while he thrashes me in the dining room, I continue to shout that I never and Dad continues to tell me how much he hates me and it feels as though we've always been saying these things. But only one of us is telling the truth, and it's Dad. He really does hate me. I'm never comfortable when he's at home. I keep out of his way and that's how he likes it. He doesn't want to see me, he doesn't want to hear me and he'd prefer it if I wasn't there at all.

'And what,' demands Mum after the thrashing, 'did you buy with Dad's five pounds?'

'Sweets,' I admit.

'Sweets! Did you eat them all?'

'No! I bought them with *him*,' I say, pointing to Paul.

There is a terrible silence as everyone turns to Paul. He reddens.

'Did he know where the money came from?' asks Mum. Her voice is small. She is hoping I'm going to say no. Dad looks at Paul and then back at me. He doesn't want this to be true either.

'Yes!' I shout, and there's triumph in my voice. 'Yes! He knew it was your fiver!'

And that is the end of the adoption and the last night Paul spends in our house. Mum goes up to pack his bag and he is returned immediately to the children's home. After that I glimpse him at school sometimes but he is no longer one of us. There is talk about sending me to the children's home, too. I just wish they would.

Chapter 8

I'm a social drinker. I get drunk at parties with older kids, especially my big sister's parties. I'm the life and soul, at least until I've drunk myself into a stupor. I don't know what I do then because I can't remember. But when I first get drunk everyone thinks I'm funny and sharp, except for Kelly who's almost always angry with me for getting off with her friends. Personally, I'm amazed at the number of sixteen-year-old girls who'll snog an eleven-year-old boy, even one who looks older.

Kelly hates me mixing with her mates but she disapproves even more when she sees me spending time with Pete and his crowd. Kelly wants to join the police force one day. She has a round, pretty face and she behaves herself and she thinks she's a rung or two up the social ladder from us. She's the opposite of Pete. He used to be a skinhead and he was one of the lads I first got drunk with on Strongbow. Now he's a punk and he lives in a squat.

Kelly's a bit scared of the squatters but I'm fascinated by them. Pete doesn't seem to have any family, just other people who come and go from the squat. It looks like an ordinary red-brick house from the front but inside the walls are painted with swirling hippy pictures and the back garden is weedy and full of bike parts and the fence is falling down. The people in this house don't follow any of the rules. They get up when they like, sometimes not until evening. They take their clothes off when they like, even if other people are around. One has tits that are so big and heavy I can't stop myself staring. How does she carry that lot round with her all day? No one else takes any notice.

Now the Allbuts have gone, the squat becomes my chaotic new sanctuary. I feel comfortable here. There are tin cans for lampshades and mostly mattresses instead of beds. I like to talk to Pete and his mates. Everyone accepts everyone else for who they are. And no one asks questions like: why aren't you at school? Sometimes I steal food from our kitchen and Pete cooks it while we talk, or we chat while Pete washes his socks in Dettol. Sometimes I help him mend his old motorbike.

Pete's introduced me to lots of new things and one of them was gas sniffing with a butane lighter. That was a few years ago and I often do it at home now. Unlike drinking, gas sniffing isn't a social activity for me. It's a ticket to another world and I like to travel alone. One sniff and I escape. I never notice Mum's pot plants normally but when I sniff gas I can find myself right inside their pot talking with the stems for twenty minutes. Or I'll sit on a dust molecule having a chat with a piece of brick. When I wake up I find I've been drib-bling and my head's pressed against the wall but I don't care. I've been in the living room and all the time I haven't been in the living room so it's a great way of getting out of the house without ever opening the door.

I find my sisters' company unbearable. They're both so well behaved and Dad's so different with them. But I only hate my sisters. I don't hate all girls. That's because I know what girls are for now. I'm finding these discoveries very exciting. And it's the Italians in our neighbourhood who are showing me the way.

Kidderminster has a big Italian population. They come from Sicily, which is a very hot island where people eat tomatoes all day. They have Catholic schools and their own shops with sausage things hanging from the rafters and baskets of olives under every table. When these families left Italy, some of them came to Kidderminster and some went to New Jersey in America and the two branches are always flying backwards and forwards to see each other.

I am good mates with some of the Italian lads. My friendship with Antonio is based on insult trading and fighting. At the Catholic youth club (me and my brother and my mate Daniel have been thrown out of all the other youth clubs for bad behaviour but the Catholics will put up with anything), it's Italians versus English. Antonio and I beat the shit out of each other and call each other names every Saturday night but we're still good mates.

With boys, I do gang things. As for girls, they are for fucking. You are supposed to fuck as many girls as you can as often as you can. And then tell your mates about it. Ever since Trevor I've messed about with a lot of girls, snogged them and felt them and fingered them but I haven't completely fucked one yet. But now I am eleven. And there is Bianca.

At the Catholic youth club, everyone's doing it. We boys sit around talking while Daniel and I pass each other cigarettes. The girls are across the room. There's no contact between the boys and the girls except to shag. We lead up to this by eyeing each other all the time.

I spy Bianca. She has bobbed black hair and olive skin, big eyes and full lips. She is tall and slim but not too slim. She looks great in her trendy skirt and black top and her black woolly tights. And she is so, so beautiful. She must be at least fourteen.

I'm eleven but I'm developed for my age and I catch her looking at me. She glances away quickly. And then I try it. The approach.

'You all right?'

'Yeah.'

'Wanna come for a walk?'

This can only mean one thing. She understands what.

'All right.'

We walk out of the youth club hall, past the pool table and the bar football. We step outside and, although we have our coats on, the cold hits us. It's raining and the rain feels cold. I hold her hand. We don't say anything. I lead her around the hall to the plastic porch of the convent. Probably she walked this way a thousand times when she was a kid here, taught by nuns. But now she's here for something different.

I start by kissing her. She lets me. Then I run my hands inside her clothes and, when she offers no resistance, I throw down my coat and pull her to the ground. Since it's so cold tonight, I keep my gloves on. She keeps her coat on.

Overhead, the rain pounds on the plastic corrugated porch roof. I lift her skirt. I can't feel her skin because of my gloves so I run my mouth all over her. She is very beautiful. She smells Italian. It's not an unpleasant smell, it reminds me of the back of the Italian restaurants in town, onions and garlic and spices. I start to pull off her thick tights. At first she knocks my hand away but I put it straight back and in a few moments I know for sure that she is going to let me. She's going to let me do it!

She lies still. Her body is wood as I enter her and lose my virginity. She does not move or make a sound. Maybe it's the first time for her too. She gives no indication of pleasure and I don't expect her to. It doesn't take long.

There is no conversation afterwards. I don't want to talk to her or be with her. I want to get away and fast, back to the youth club and my mates. I pull her up and put my coat on and soon we're back in the hot, throbbing club. Only I'm different now. I've really fucked someone.

The first thing I do is tell Daniel about it. He smiles at me with his big baby smile. Then I tell all my other mates. I tell them everything except that it was my first time.

In the summer holidays all the kids for streets around congregate in the Reynolds Street school playground. It's an old, red-brick primary and, apart from this patch of ground, there's nowhere else to gather, certainly nowhere else to play football. All I have to do is hang around and soon there'll be lots of other kids and we'll have a cigarette and agree what we're doing today.

And someone says, let's go swimming.

We disperse and come back with our towels, our bathers and a bit of money to pay for the pool and a bag of chips afterwards. In a gang of about ten or fifteen lads, English and Italian, we cross town to the swimming pool next to the dole office, knocking on doors, kicking over bins, shouting rude things. Antonio and I are the youngest, Carlo's probably the oldest. He's seventeen and out at work now.

He orders everyone around. 'Come here, you little cunt, you got to fucking do what I say.'

And we do because he's our hero. We call him the Granny-Shagger because he went to Butlins one weekend and fucked an old lady and took the toilet chain out of her chalet to prove it. He walks round with the chain in his pocket.

Carlo fancies my big sister but she doesn't fancy him. When he puts on his swimming trunks you can see handfuls of flab hanging over the top.

At the pool we break all the rules. You're not supposed to dive and we do. You're not supposed to hold your mates' heads underwater and we do. You're not supposed to run, dive-bomb, fight or push people in and we do. And all the time I'm keeping an eye on Carlo and his younger brother Gianni.

Carlo finds a girl who is probably the ugliest girl I've ever seen. She has a huge face and a horse's mouth and half her dinner's still plastered round it. There is no way Carlo can have an interest in this girl for anything apart from sex. He is talking to her intently, one arm behind her along the pool rails, the other stretched right across her to the rail on the other side. God knows what he's saying but she's giggling. When I look at her closely I see that she isn't just ugly, she's a nutter. She's about fourteen and she's probably at a special school.

A few yards away Gianni is doing something similar with the girl's friend. This one is a bit prettier but you can tell at a glance she's at the special school too. Gianni is making the girl nervous. She doesn't look at him and she keeps pushing him off but he grabs her again. He's being dominant and insistent but she's not trying hard to resist him. Next time I glance over their way he's got his legs wrapped round her in the water. And soon afterwards I can see that he's groping her all over.

We come out squeaky clean with our fingers wrinkled and our hair tousled. Antonio and I go to the car park to wait for the others. It's below road level and in one corner is a small, square pump house. There are older lads wandering over to this pump house so we follow them. They're forming a queue. We see people arguing. As we get closer we hear what they're arguing about. They all want to be next. Next for what? We go round to the side of the pump house. The road is high above us. The concrete is broken here. Weeds grow out of it. People have shoved shopping trolleys over the road's edge and the broken metal skeletons are scattered about. And between the pump house and the road's high retaining wall, there's a wrestling match.

I stare. Carlo is wrestling the horse-faced girl. No he's not. He's fucking her. He's holding her leg up while she stands against the wall and his body is banging rhythmically against hers. I can hardly see her because another lad's working on her top half. He's started to snog her horse face off now and his hands are all over her tits. Then Carlo finishes what he's doing and the other lad shuffles round to take his turn at fucking her and the boy at the front of the line moves in to take his place.

The prettier girl is a few yards away, up against the wall being worked on by two other lads. I can see her face. It's expressionless. Blank. She's not protesting or enjoying it. Her head sways a bit in time to the boy's rhythm. I'm not sure she's really there. Maybe she's looking down on herself from some high tree. So, is this what everyone does?

There are about ten lads in each line so the girls are going to be busy. We watch for a while, fascinated. Then we wander off and have a cigarette while we wait for the big boys. I feel sad. I don't know why.

Finally everyone emerges. The boys are in front, laughing and talking and jumping about. The girls wander behind, pulling their skirts down. No one talks to them and they don't talk to each other. We go for a bag of chips. I see the girls head up towards a tough housing estate which is full of old mattresses on lawns and burnt-out cars. No one says goodbye to them.

At school, the biology teacher, strangely embarrassed, gives us sex education lessons. He shows us weird, clinical diagrams of dicks and uses words like vagina and penis. He talks about relationships and he keeps getting coughing fits. We know it's all about fucking. But we can't square the language, the diagrams or the relationship stuff with anything we're actually doing or anything we saw at the pool.

Chapter 9

I visit the Allbuts at their new home in Redditch. They give me the usual warm welcome and then show me what's behind their house. Trees. Woodland criss-crossed by streams. Most of my tree experience has been confined to apple trees and the big horse chestnuts near the cricket ground but these are different.

At first Jill and Brian slip through the fence with me and we all explore. The trunks are thick but they are low, and wispy growth erupts from them like hair. Brian explains they're mostly willow that has been pollarded. That means they've been cut back, so although the trees aren't high they are very old. Dry, curly leaves crunch underfoot. I like the sound they make. I crunch about for a while, examining the trees, climbing into the strange cradles of their broad trunks, twanging at their sappy little branches. I get so absorbed in this new place that I hardly notice the Allbuts have left me to enjoy myself here.

I go the whole weekend without a cigarette. I mostly spend my time in the woods, making dens in the dense tree growth, racing little stick boats down the river. Sunday morning is relaxed, the opposite of the pub/church misery back at 89 Reynolds Street. Jill listens to *The Archers Omnibus* while Brian and I take a walk behind the house. We talk like we used to. Conversation. At first I'm rusty but then I start remembering how to do it.

On this clear, fresh day the sunlight is sharp. I can see my own breath. We go through the woods and out into the fields beyond. One of them is ploughed. The light bounces off the top of each red-brown furrow as if there's gold in the soil. And I see a hare. It runs across the shining, freshly turned earth with speed and joy. I am almost overwhelmed by the beauty of this scene. I stare after the hare when it has vanished because it gives me so much pleasure to see the spot where it ran. I will never forget its beauty.

Brian is watching me. I wish he would explain how an animal in a field can move me close to tears.

'You're an artist, Mark,' he tells me.

I almost forgot that. I've almost forgotten about painting and drawing and all the other things I love to do. They've been squeezed out of my life. You do those things in the calm, quiet spaces, and for me there aren't any calm, quiet spaces any more. I fill them all and I fill them with trouble.

I'm always being cautioned by the police: for stealing, for running riot with my mates in the shopping centre, for fighting, for climbing up onto the roofs of buildings. At home, the punishments get worse and the next time I'm caught stealing I don't want to go back to face the shouting. I head for Pete's squat instead.

He's not there and I don't recognise any of the people who are. They're grown-ups but they let me in and I wait patiently for Pete. They're playing punk music. They're smoking. They're sitting on chairs or kneeling on the floor and there's a sense of anticipation. They're passing round a torn-off piece of kitchen foil with a brown blob on it. The person after you in the circle holds the foil in one hand and a cigarette lighter beneath it with the other until the brown blob is running down the foil giving off smoke, and you inhale this through a tube.

I'm sitting waiting for Pete but it happens that I'm a part of the circle. So when it gets to me, the man on my right holds the foil and lighter and I copy everyone else and smoke it.

I inhale and a moment later something very, very warm is filling my body. It is penetrating to my toes and my fingers like liquid. I inhale again and when it reaches the back of my head I become aware of a great kindness wrapping itself round me and making everything all right. I take some more and my worries stop nagging. My fears evaporate. Nothing much matters. I just release it all. It's like putting on six pairs of gloves on a cold winter's day, gloves which fit neatly over my brain and keep all the thoughts in there warm and safe.

The brown blob comes round to me three times. Then I go into Pete's room. I lie down on his mattress on the floor under a grey, itchy blanket. The light bulb is covered by an old tin, slashed to let some light through. I lie there staring at it all night, vomiting. It's the nicest vomiting ever because it is an expulsion without pain.

When Pete finds me much later he is furious with his mates. I hear him shouting. I don't know why. I don't care. That brown blob has convinced me that everything, everything, will be all right.

The next day I get up and feel strange. Sleepy, my senses dulled, but with last night's warmth still inside me. I go to an arcade and hang about and one of my uncles is there. He tells me that everyone's been looking for me all night, including the police. Still feeling weird, I wander off to the police station. I'm no stranger here. Usually they take me straight home but this time I am led to a detention cell. They lock the door behind me. I don't like it. I'm alarmed by the sound of the keys. I'm always in trouble but I've never been locked up before.

There's nowhere to sit. The room is bare. High up are thick blocks of glass that admit a little light. The walls are nicotine-coloured. They make me want a cigarette. I slump down on the concrete floor and wait.

My mum picks me up. She isn't angry. She's very white and she looks terrible. We go home and she doesn't shout or hit me but the sterile, deadly atmosphere in the place feels like a punishment anyway.

I see Michael Jackson's 'moonwalk' on TV. Everyone does. Everyone wants to do it too. Evenings, in the school playground, we mess around moonwalking. Then we watch *Top of the Pops* and Jeffrey Daniel on *Soul Train* and it's obvious to me and my mates that there's something going on out there and we want to be part of it. The music is hip hop, the movement is break-dancing, and it's come all the way from the ghettos of America to Reynolds Street.

Some kids, like my big brother Shane, prefer The Ramones. But a small group of us, English and Italian, gets hooked. We study the moves on TV and in films like *Break Dance* and *Beat Street*, then we try them ourselves. At first we're slow. It seems we'll never learn anything but the simplest hand waves. Some of the moves look impossible: turning on one arm or walking like a crab with your legs behind you and spinning on your head. But we can do a lot of the other moves if we practise. And that's what we do. Practise hourly, daily, week in, week out. Interest turns to obsession. Our standards rise as our legs and arms start to follow our instructions. We don't appear on the streets with a move until it's perfect.

To break-dance you need to be very powerful and very supple because every movement is highly controlled. The top half of your body has to be strong because your arms so often support your weight. I'm learning to defy gravity with my body. I'm learning to fly.

In America, breaking evolved out of gang warfare: the boys with the best fighting muscles turned into the best breakers. Here in England, it keeps us out of trouble. I'm so focused on breaking with my crew that I don't have time to steal and run riot in the shopping centres any more. We start carrying our own pieces of lino around with us, rolled up under our arms. We can stop anywhere – on the pavement, in the school playground, at the shopping centre. Down goes the lino and out comes the ghetto blaster and we're away. A lot of people watch us. A lot of people admire us. And that includes girls. The harder the moves get, the more we practise. We learn windmills, with our arms on the ground, our bodies straight and our legs in the air. We perfect a three-man helicopter. We jump, we spin, we're in perpetual motion and sometimes, when crowds of kids are watching and the music's thumping and my body's almost weightless, I feel as though I'm leaving Kidderminster behind. I'm on the streets of America in a break-dance movie, and that's where I want to be.

The clothes are important: for us, the right tracksuit, the best trainers, they say it all. I am submerged in hip hop and being a break-dancer gives me the strongest sense ever of who I am, stronger than stealing Mark, drunken Mark or even fucking Mark.

Chapter 10

I am thirteen when Shane and I get home from school one day, knock on the front door and see a strange shadow approaching. It isn't Mum, or Nan. Dad's around; we've seen him driving past. But the shadow isn't his because, after a huge row, he's not living at home. I know at once that something's happened.

The door swings open. Standing there is the long-nosed, thin-cheeked Maureen, my mum's Jehovah's Witness friend and hated donor of THE WORLD'S GREATEST STIRER! She eyes us unpleasantly. No greetings are exchanged.

'Where's Mum?' Shane asks.

Maureen pauses. Her face is flushed. 'She's in hospital.'

We stand on our own doorstep, staring at her, peering past her into the hallway, looking for Mum.

'She's took some pills. An overdose of sleeping pills is what she's took.'

So Mum is dead. She was supposed to live with the animals in Paradise forever but instead she's dead and I suspect body-snatcher Maureen has killed her.

'She's still alive,' says Maureen after a long pause, because she doesn't want to rush with the good news. 'But she's in hospital and you're to pack your bags and stay with me.'

I run over the news headlines again in my head. Mum's in

hospital. She's overdosed on her sleeping pills. The words don't mean anything.

'She's tried to kill herself,' stresses Maureen.

We go into the house and find that Dad is there, and Kelly and Bethany. Bethany's crying. Dad hasn't been around since the last big row but we express no surprise at seeing him because we have no surprise left in us. He doesn't know what to do with himself. He keeps getting up and sitting down again.

Kelly explains that Nan knew Mum had been to the doctor's to pick up her sleeping-pill prescription and she was worried when she rang the house and got no reply. So she came straight over and found our mum out cold on the bed. An ambulance came with its lights flashing and took Mum away. I listen to her words without feeling anything. I am cold and metallic, like a real robot instead of the robots I get dressed up and pretend to be when I'm break-dancing.

Kelly assures us that Mum is going to be all right: 'They're pumping her stomach now.'

'Fuuuuuucking hell!' we say.

Maureen indicates that Mum has done something very wicked in trying to kill herself. Jehovah's Witnesses, although they are always predicting the end, aren't actually supposed to bring this about. God will deal with the unsaved in his own good time. Although we suspect it's the kind of thing Maureen might try on God's behalf. Ever since she converted Mum she has had some sort of power over her, like a malevolent auntie.

Dad saves us from Maureen by assuring her he can take care of us himself. She gives him a searching, beady-eyed look that says it's all Dad's fault Mum has overdosed and then she turns the same beady-eyed look on us and that means it's our fault too. She gathers up her big handbag and goes.

Just fuck off, you old witch, I think. Because my dad's the boss around here, not you.

The house is quiet. I don't ponder on what's happened or why or what the consequences might have been. I don't think about anything much. I wonder if it's okay in the circumstances to change into my breaking clothes and get outside with my ghetto blaster and my lino. The rest of the family is sitting around, not even talking. Shane's upstairs playing music. So I get changed, but when I'm outside it's obvious that everyone's already heard our news. Adults in the street greet me then look away quickly. The kids stare. A few ask questions which I ignore. And the dancing's no good today, either. My body hasn't got the lift. My movements aren't fluid. I try some robotics and I know I don't look like a robot, which is very strange because I feel more like a robot than ever before.

The next day, Mum's back. She looks pale. She doesn't say much. She offers no explanations but goes straight up to bed. We turn on the TV. Bethany goes up and lies beside her on the bed. Then Dad takes Mum in a cup of tea and there's a lot of talking but for once their voices are quiet. Nan appears and shakes her head and says Mum was driven to despair. But we all know the truth. We've known it for a long time, from Mum's wild shrieking and crying and her constant warnings that life's coming to an end. Well, now the whole of Reynolds Street knows too, maybe the whole of Kidderminster. Mum's mad.

In September I'll be going to the high school now I'm thirteen. But before that there's the summer holidays and I'm to spend them with Dad to give my mum a rest. Dad's going to work at Blythe power station near Newcastle. We're to live together in a caravan by the sea.

On the first day in our caravan Dad goes off to work, leaving me a pound for some milk or crisps. I lie in bed and roll myself a cig-arette using Dad's liquorice roll-up papers. I switch on the radio and, while I lie back and smoke, I listen to the love stories on Simon Bates, laughing because the men are so soft and poofy. When I go out there's a gang of lads over in the woods and I join them. They're gathering wood to light a fire on the beach. That sounds okay to me. Over the next month, these lads and I light fires, go swimming at least three times a day, catch fish and cook them, get drunk, smoke a lot and shag girls in the sand dunes. It's a great life.

The most surprising thing is Dad. Every morning he goes off

and leaves me a pound. Every night he comes home with pie and chips and that's what we eat. Our diet never varies. Dad's drinking is limited to cans and he doesn't get drunk. We have one cup and one plate each and these we rinse and leave on the drainer. We have one dishtowel which lasts the whole summer without a wash and we don't care. It's so simple. I love this life and I love my dad.

But all good things must come to an end and eventually Mum arrives with six-year-old Bethany in tow. As soon as Mum and Dad are together again, the air in the caravan turns sterile. Dad's all over Bethany as usual and that's annoying, but Mum's presence is the real disaster. We hate her. We resent her. And Dad says so: 'We were all right, weren't we, sonna, until she came along?'

In September a lot of things change. Dad gets a job on the North Sea gas rigs. It's two weeks on and two weeks off and the pay is incredible. For the first time ever, we have some real money. I start at the high school and am sent to Auntie Tanya for half term. She and Uncle Steve moved up to the Lake District a few years ago when one of the Kidderminster carpet factories closed. Kendal's a small town and it's boring and there's no one to break-dance with. That's what I tell Mum when she asks me what I think of the place, as though my answer really matters.

A few days later, I get home from school and find a For Sale board outside our house.

I am very, very shocked. I don't want to go to Kendal. No one wants to go. Kelly is eighteen and has been living with her boyfriend since she found she was pregnant and Mum kicked her out, so she certainly isn't going. Shane will soon leave school and start work for a scaffolding company and there's no way he's going; he announces that he'll live with Nan instead. But none of my reasons for not going, like missing my friends, seems to count.

A few people come to look round the house and it is sold almost instantly. And then, while Dad is off on his North Sea gas rigs, we move.

Our goods are packed into the back of a van and Bethany and I get in. I sit in the brown reclining armchair without reclining and

Bethany sits on the settee. To stop them smashing, Mum's cottagey pictures from the dining room are placed on Bethany's lap and I hold the big mirror. I look down Reynolds Street, its red houses stretching off on either side until they turn a corner. Kelly and Shane say goodbye and their faces are the last thing I see before the doors are slammed shut. We sit in the dark and listen to more farewells outside. Then the lorry starts and we rumble off in the dark in what could be any direction but I know is north.

We arrive. Someone opens the doors. Now I'm looking down another street of terraced houses but this time it's grey. The small, stone houses are grey. Rain is falling and the rain is grey. In the distance there is green. It's a hill and on it is a grey castle and above that the sky is grey. I don't want to get out of the van but a man has started to move things now and Auntie Tanya's voice can be heard outside. My mum is bustling about. Bethany helps as best she can.

I go for a smoke in the rain. I walk from one end of Kendal to the other. It takes about five minutes. The streets are silent. There are no kids anywhere. I can't see any covered shopping centre where they might be break-dancing out of the rain. If I pass anyone, they're white. No black faces, no Italians, no one who even looks interesting. There are no pedestrian underpasses or railway bridges or canals or any sort of place where I'm used to messing about with mates. And there aren't any mates. Kendal is another world. It is dead. Or maybe I am.

I walk in silence and then I enter the new house in silence.

I go to my new room and I barely come out for weeks except to visit Auntie Tanya. Her young kids bounce around and she lets me smoke and there's a bit of life here. I ring Shane but we don't know what to say. Probably we've never said much to each other but we didn't notice when we lived in the same house. I phone Daniel. He tells a few stories. Just hearing him makes me long to be there.

My new school is modern and rectangular on the edge of town. I enter on my first day feeling sick with nerves. I am led to my class. It smells just like my last school, a mix of chalk, putty, disinfectant and kids, only the Kendal school smells of rain as well. I have taken the trouble to look good. It's important for these redneck, back-of-beyond kids to know that I'm a tough urban boy so I'm wearing a pair of trousers that are dark grey with red, cotton-lined pockets. The trousers have a slight sheen to them, which should indicate to anyone who knows anything that when I'm not in school I'm a break-dancer. Of course, the Kendal kids notice the trousers but they don't pick up the right signals because break-dancing hasn't hit bumpkin land yet.

'Must be some kind of poof,' remarks a boy quietly as I pass his desk on my way to the front of the class where my new teacher is greeting me. To the teacher's surprise, I halt in my tracks. His welcoming words falter and his eyes open wide as I spin around. I walk up to the kid with the big mouth and I punch him. The class is silent with disbelief. Even the teacher doesn't know what to do. Then he sends me out. And I haven't even sat down yet.

After my big entrance, my school career goes quiet. My whole life is quiet. It's so quiet I wonder if I really could be dead. I gradually get to know some other kids and we sniff glue by the river together. Tripping, I smell the water and then I disappear into the run of it and I am the river and then I become the land. It's a good experience and there are many like it but nothing can lift my mood. Except the news that Dad's coming back for the Easter holidays and we're all going down to Kidderminster for a couple of weeks. I live for those weeks, asking Mum over and over again if I can stay there and live with Nan. She says no.

As we get close to Kidderminster, I smell the old smells and see the old sights and I'm smiling for the first time in months. Nothing's changed. My mates are the same, the dancing's the same and I slip right back into my old slot. I live my two weeks at breakneck pace, trying to cram a year into a holiday.

I'm kicking around the town centre with Dan and a few others when one boy starts to talk about the prostitutes at Balsall Heath. You can shag the woman of your choice for a tenner: he knows because he's been. We're all fascinated but one lad, who's already out at work, is more than fascinated, he's obsessed. He asks so many questions that in the end we decide to go. Now this is going to be the kind of experience that you can't have in Kendal. In the car on the way into Birmingham the working lad, overcome by excitement, gets out his wages. He gives us each a tenner to spend.

We get to a street where undressed prostitutes sit in windows under red lights. They look surreal. Some are under green lights and they look like aliens. Men who probably don't wash very often are loitering around; others look clean but furtive. Cars drive past, turn round, and drive back again. Locals march along the pavement without bothering to look right or left, wearing expressions of pained resignation.

We lads are excited by the variety of women, by their sizes, shapes, colours and ages and the way they beckon us in. We are like kids buying candy but we try to sound manly.

'Fucking hell, look at that!'

'Yeee-hah!'

'Shit, God and wank!'

Some of the prostitutes are young and beautiful. A few are disdainful, most rearrange themselves in seductive poses as we pass. Some are repulsive old women. They must be fifty years old. They are wearing fishnets and their make-up has bled out of their lips to cover half their hard, weathered faces. They sit smoking, their legs open. The whole street is like a circus freak show.

The lad who came here once before explains knowledgeably: 'You ask them how much. That's what you do.'

He shows us how. You have to look directly at them and nod. The women smile seductively and hold up ten fingers or maybe fewer.

Finally we select one. She is of a womanly age, perhaps even thirty, well rounded and beautiful, and we like the way she looks at us. Her smile is full of promise. She's attractive and experienced and she'll show us a good time, that's for sure.

One by one, we go in. The lad who's given us the money is first. He disappears into the doorway and the woman pulls the curtains. We smoke dope while we wait. A few minutes later he reappears making manly, appreciative noises. His hand shakes as he takes the spliff.

Daniel's next. He comes out smiling. Now it's my turn.

I am nervous. I don't want to notice the way the paint's peeling and the letterbox has been taped over as I enter. When I get inside, she's waiting for me. I look quickly round the room. The curtains are drawn. There's a chair. The stained walls are bare. In the red light the smoke of the prostitute's cigarette circles slowly. She's draped on the bed, her weight on her elbows. Her knees are together. And there's this door. It's near the bed and it's ajar. I am immediately alert. What's behind it? Who's behind it?

I look at the prostitute. She looks at me. She opens her legs to reveal an expanse of dark hair. I'm scared. I'm not horny. I'm only a kid and this woman is an adult. She's bigger than me and she's looking straight through me and she clearly has no intention of stubbing out her cigarette when we get down to business.

She instructs me to take off my clothes. Suddenly feeling very shy, I start with my jacket. She waves a hand to stop me and a thin trail of smoke follows her fingers through the air.

'Just yer trousers,' she tells me.

Just my trousers? I pull the coat back over my shoulders and I take down my trousers and now I feel really stupid. Ridiculous, in fact, with my scrawny boyish legs under my big, thick jacket. Aroused? Sex is the last thing on my mind. I can't possibly do it with this woman in this place, knowing that anyone could be behind that door, watching me, maybe preparing to stab me. This is a dark, hostile environment and I want to get out of it. I pull the tenner from my pocket and I see her eyes glint.

'Look, it's all right,' I say, 'just, er, take it, okay?'

She smiles, not the same sort of smile she was wearing in the window, a knowing, humourless smile. She accepts the note. I glance at the open door. I think I detect very slight movement behind it. I put on my trousers as quickly as I can.

'Well . . . bye then,' I say to the prostitute.

She ignores me. It crosses my mind that all the other lads have done the same. This whore's sitting on a single bed smoking while we walk in one by one and each hands her a tenner for doing absolutely nothing. This thought sends me back outside smiling. I light a cigarette and the next lad goes in. All the way home in the car we boast about what we did, how she moaned and how we fingered her. We smell each other's fingers. There's no smell at all.

A few days later, it's back to Kendal. The return is terrible, worse than the first time because now I know what's waiting for me up there. Precisely nothing.

Chapter 11

A few months later Dad comes home from the gas rigs looking very pleased with himself. He has an announcement to make. We're moving.

I've started to teach break-dancing at the local arts centre. I've got a group of new friends. I've had girlfriends. I've won a few fights. Yes, I'm finally getting settled in Kendal. And now we're off again. Where to this time?

'A farm,' says Dad.

A farm? We don't want to move to a farm, we aren't farmers.

'We are now.'

But we come from the city, we belong in the city. It was bad enough moving to this small town. Surely Dad doesn't want us to live in the country?

Dad says: 'I've always wanted a farm and now I can afford to buy one and I've found it and I've bought it and we're going there.'

But we don't want to go!

'We're going. It won't hardly affect you because it's only ten miles away.'

Ten miles!

'You'll still come in to Kendal for school,' he says. He thinks that's reassuring.

No point arguing. No point even for my mum to protest. Dad's made up his mind. And he's the only person round here with a choice. He talks about the farm incessantly and when I complain to my mum she says quietly: 'He's obsessed.'

I thought Dad and I got quite close last summer in the caravan. After last summer, if Dad was looking at a farm and thinking of buying it, I'd expect him to take me to see the place. Or even just talk about it. But we're not in the caravan any more and he's become the same old dad.

So one day we pack up and pile into a van again and when, after about half an hour, we stop and the doors open, the first thing we see is rain. It's raining so hard that you can hardly make out anything but low cloud and green valley.

'It's beautiful,' Dad says. 'House is sixteenth century.'

We stare at the beautiful sixteenth-century farmhouse. It is long and low and divided into two houses. Dad has bought one side and he's planning to buy the other, so soon all this will be ours. Inside, the silence in the rooms has real depth because the walls are many feet thick. It's like the silence inside me. This place is desolate. I am desolate. From my bedroom at the back of the house, something red flickers past so quickly that by the time I'm at the window it's gone. What was it?

The rain eases a bit and I wander outside. I see sheds and, stretching into the distance, fells made green by the constant rain. At the end of the valley is grey sky. And close to the house, there's even more water. A river.

'We've got three miles of it,' says Dad proudly. 'And it's some of the best freshwater fishing in England. That's what everyone in the pub says.'

I take my cigarettes and go to the back of the house and wander under a bridge and up a hill and suddenly there's a roar like thunder, so immense, so loud, so shocking, that I duck. Then I see the red flicker again. It's a train. A high-speed train. The bridge is a railway bridge and the track passes right behind the house. I carry on walking up the hill. I can hear a distant drone and it's not from the railway line. When I look down and across the valley I can see, in one sweep, the farmhouse with Dad wandering about in the yard surveying all that he owns, the railway and, past the railway, the motorway. The M6 winds along the side of the valley like a great, grey snake. The distant drone I can hear is the trucks and cars going north or south, going somewhere else. For a lot of people, the presence of the London to Glasgow high-speed railway and the M6 might mar the landscape. For me, they make it. Because they lead somewhere else.

Dad soon goes off back to his gas rigs. I go to school over the fells in the morning and when I get there I'm constantly in trouble. I'm always being sent to the headmaster. Sitting outside his office one day, waiting for my pep talk, I meet another naughty boy who's doing the same. It's one of those friendships that begins instantly and you know it's going to last a long time.

Ian has jet-black hair and eyebrows that meet in the middle. He's big and if it wasn't for those rounded baby cheeks, he'd look like a man. In many ways, he has to be a man, because he has a small brother and sister and his father's dead. His mother's a hopeless alcoholic who pisses the bed. They live in a house that's dirty and untidy with beer and cigarette stains on the carpet. Ian can do whatever he likes because no one really cares about him except his nan and she's not always around.

We soon start skiving together. The teacher takes the register and then we look at each other and we're off, across the school playing fields. The teachers stand, watching, while we disappear.

We go to the fields or the river and lie low in long grass and smoke, usually cigarettes but sometimes weed. And we talk. We talk about all the things we're going to do one day, the places we'll go. For me, it's London. Ever since Jill Allbut took me, I've wanted to go back.

We talk about our fathers as well. Although my dad's hardly ever at the farmhouse, when he's around he's scarier than he used to be. He's drinking a lot and, at the least provocation, or sometimes with no provocation at all, he hits me with serious, grown-up punches, the sort he throws in the pub when he's fighting over a woman. And whenever he's angry he reminds me, in that hissing, threatening undertone, how much he hates me.

With Bethany, he's completely different. She's a sweet, open-hearted kid and she loves Dad and it's obvious that Dad loves her. He has already bought her a horse that's kept at the stables up the road, and two more that live on the farm. The nicer he is to Bethany, the nastier he gets with me and Mum. I resent Bethany a lot for this. And, even though Bethany's a good girl who goes to Jehovah's Witness meetings, it seems to me that Mum might also have started resenting her. Then, when Dad goes away, everything's all right again and the three of us reach a kind of balance together.

Ian tells me that he would give anything to have a dad. His died when he was young. I tell him that I would give anything not to have a dad. At least in his memory there's a father he can respect. At least he can say that he used to have a good dad.

My mum has been earning herself a bit of money lately. Since they've bought the next-door house, she's used it for holiday lets. People touring the Lakes stay there for one night or longer. It's self-contained and Mum leaves them everything they need to make their own breakfast. With the money she has bought a little car, a red Renault. Each day she drives it over to the back entrance of the motorway service station, where she has started a new job working in the restaurant.

Dad is due back today but the first thing I notice when I get home from school is the Renault 5. It's standing in its usual place but it's different. It's been destroyed. There are huge slash marks and its bonnet is hanging off, the roof is collapsing onto the seats, large chunks are missing from its sides, the lights are broken, the glass is shattered and lying in splinters all around. I examine the car in disbelief. I can't guess what kind of collision would produce this sort of damage.

Inside the house, I recognise the silence at once. I recognise it from Reynolds Street. You can smell the anger, the pain, the misery. It means Dad's home.

I find Mum. She is a red-eyed, red-faced, quivering mess.

'What happened?' I ask. 'Did you crash the car?'

She shakes her head. 'Your dad did it.'

'Did that? To the car?'

She nods. I look out of the window at the destroyed Renault.

'With an axe,' she explains. 'He just slashed it all over. He even got up on the roof.'

Then I ask that question about Dad it's always hard to answer.

'Why?'

She fights tears. 'My new job.'

'At the motorway services?' Of course, Dad's come home to the news of Mum's job.

'He doesn't like me working there.'

'Why not? You've worked other places.'

'He says there are a lot of people from the pub who work there and he knows all about it. He says I'm a truckers' moll. He wants me to hand in my notice.'

This is followed by a fresh round of sobbing. I've seen too much of Mum's sobbing to feel sympathetic. But I'm shocked. Her car has been hacked to pieces by a maniac.

'Where is he now?' I ask Mum nervously. 'At the pub?'

'Down the stables with Bethany.'

I am silent.

'He's bought her a new horse. A palomino. All the girls want palominos.'

There's nothing to say.

I take a walk up the hill and look at the sunset. The sky in the west behind the fells is a blaze of fire and in the east the motorway reflects its red light. The tarmac curls lazily round the edge of the valley like a long, red cat. On it, barely discernible, is the unseeing traffic, all of it going somewhere for some reason of its own. I think it is the most beautiful road I have ever seen.

I'm crossing the yard, passing the smashed-up Renault, feeling the still night air, when I hear screams inside the house. I find my mum on the hall floor. She is lying on the flagstones, shrieking. I don't know if Dad has hit her. He seems bewildered. He is standing over her looking too helpless for a man who has just punched a woman. She writhes at his feet. I don't absorb her words. I never do when my parents fight, I only try to take care of my own skin. I know she's singing some kind of emotional, accusing, angry lament. It's mostly incoherent. It's probably insane. I don't listen.

Dad looks at me and shrugs. I remember the axed Renault outside. I stare at Mum screaming on the floor. This house is a lunatic
asylum.

'Help your mother, will you?' Dad mutters to me. 'I mean, just
sort her out.'

He goes away and I see Bethany peeking, terrified, round the
door.

I'm suffocating but I kneel down by the sobbing, screaming mess
that is Mum. Actually she appals me. I want to kick her. Instead I
offer her a hand.

'Come on then, Mum,' I say. My voice sounds uncertain even to
me. I know the tone you're supposed to adopt with crazy people,
sort of firm and bright, but I can't do it and for a while her wailing
continues.

Eventually she struggles to her feet and I sit her down in the
lounge. Bethany makes her a cup of tea. Mum stops crying but she
still looks completely mad. She tells Bethany: 'You'd better go and
pack your bag. We're leaving.'

'She's always telling me to pack,' Bethany says quietly. 'But we
never go.'

I decide I'll have an early night. I go to my room and am smoking fiercely when the express from Glasgow to London suddenly
lights up the night and then is gone.

I watch Dad and Bethany the next day. I see the way he jokes
around her, making fun of her in a nice way. He makes fun of me,
too, but it's not so nice. I've already decided that I want to go to art
college and he keeps calling me a poof. But when he's with Bethany
he acts like a big, docile horse for her to pet. He's quite tactile with
her and the only time his big hands are gentle is around Bethany. It
seems to me that the two of them have their own world, with its
own problems, which they share in whispers.

Chapter 12

Mum gives up her job and replaces her Renault and Bethany rides her horse and Dad goes away and the house is quiet again. This summer I can leave school and I intend to. My first aim is to get away from the family and the farmhouse and now I've got a place at art college, at Stourbridge, back in the West Midlands. I just have to pass a few exams and then in June I'll be free.

But when Dad gets back from the rigs, he finds I've stolen some of his tobacco. I still can't help it. For years my mum has slept with her purse under her pillow because she's known that I'll steal when-ever I can. I protest that I really did mean to replace Dad's tobacco, only I forgot. Dad won't listen. He's angry. He says he's going to deal with me and then he goes out to the pub and I know what that means. He'll need some vodka inside him to punish me.

I am tense all evening. We all are. Bethany goes reluctantly to bed. I stay by the fire with Mum. Much later, I hear the door open. I can tell from the way it slams, from his footsteps, that there's a big bully in the house and he's going to choose a victim. Of course, it's me. I've been waiting for him, waiting for the door, the footsteps. He doesn't come straight in. He bangs around, winding himself up. He doesn't deserve a family like this. How the hell did he get a frigging thief for a son? Why has he had to put up with me all these years?

There's a storm and it's building, layer upon layer of thick, black cloud.

And then, here he is, a massive dark presence in the lounge. I look up at him. He crosses the room, grabs me and starts to punch me.

His hairline moves back and his eyes blaze with hatred and there's vodka on his breath and spit coming from his mouth. He punches me hard with his right hand. I see its crucifix flash towards me. His left hand, the one with LOVE tattooed across it, holds me tight, too tight, round my throat. I can feel the immense size of his fingers. I am terrified. I experience pure fear. There is nothing else in me but fear as I am confronted by his hatred until suddenly, in that transcendental way, I am looking at us from a high, green tree, watching this man hate me, asking myself not why he's doing this to me, but why he wants to.

Bethany has appeared, sobbing, in pyjamas. Mum is screaming. Dad's enormous arm is drawn back again and again and each time it straightens his fist pounds against my face.

I see his knuckles in slow motion. I hear the crack of my nose and taste metal in my mouth.

Then, when he has been punching me forever and ever and I am floating high above us, high above the house, he pulls me to my knees. My neck in his hands, he forces my face towards the fire. I feel the resignation that comes with extreme fear. This is now completely out of control. Anything could happen. The fire already has slack on it for the night and it is smouldering. I resist with all my force but I am no match for a man made of steel scaffolding.

I glimpse Bethany, standing on the settee, red-faced, wet-faced, screaming. My mum runs around in hysterical circles. And I know from the strange shape of her mouth, from my sister's yells, that this is going to be bad. I shut my eyes as Dad shoves my head on the fire. I can feel its heat pressing against my cheeks, starting its penetration of my skin to all the soft, vulnerable places inside me. He's going to kill me. I can't see where else this can end.

I hear Mum on the phone. The police. She's asking them to come.

His grip loosens suddenly, without warning, and I grab this

moment to slide away from him, wriggling like a trapped wild creature. I scramble round his big body. His huge hands dive at me. He is stronger but I am faster.

I run out without any shoes. All I can feel is my own panic. I'm not going back to this place, to this house of craziness ever, not ever. Because nothing can be the same again. Apart from this deep instinct, I know nothing, I think nothing. I'm not anybody any more.

The police find me walking up the side of the motorway in wet socks. They put me in their car and take me home. Dad does not come out. Mum talks to the police officers and then she goes to the next-door house and tells the bed-and-breakfasters that she's using one of the bedrooms. I am deposited in a room there.

I stay with my auntie Tanya as long as Dad is around. When he leaves for the gas rigs I go home. Bethany greets me warmly and her welcome makes my eyes sting. I walk into the hall and hear the familiar dense silence and smell the home smells and suddenly, surprisingly, shockingly, I start to cry. I go straight to my room before my mum or Bethany notices and I remember those ropes from my childhood, how they were wrapped so tightly round me I couldn't move or breathe. Well, they're back.

At the window the express train appears and disappears like an apparition. I try to control my tears. I make my eyes follow every angle of the graffiti art I've painted all over the walls. When that doesn't work I try damming my tears, bracing my body as if for a fight. Then I close my eyes tight until my body shakes with the effort. But it's no good. I give in to the power of my own tears. I cry and cry and I can't stop. I cry for days. Not minutes or hours but weeks.

My mum says she understands. She says I'm depressed and she understands that because she cries a lot herself. I look at her and think: you've got yourself into this situation. And you've dragged me in with you.

I'm better when I'm in Kendal. I'm always anxious to go there. But when I'm back home in our farmhouse jail, the tears start to flow again. And, like Lake District rain, once the deluge sets in it doesn't stop for a long time.

I must be a poof, I'm bubbling so much.

Dad comes home. I stay out of his way. Then the worst thing happens and he catches me crying. His face curls up in disgust the way it does when my mum sobs or shrieks or turns into a wobbling blob of jelly on the floor. There's no kindness. I see only hatred. He despises me. When he looks at me his eyes are freezing blue ice.

It's that blue ice that leads me to some cool, clear decision-making. I'm in my bedroom with its walls so thick you can't hear the high-speed trains. I'm lying on my bed, outsize graffiti art all over the walls. The silence is so heavy here I can almost see it, almost touch it.

I decide to stop crying. No more hot tears for me. I won't cry any more. Ever. Dad hates me and there's a reason for that: I'm hateful. I hate myself. He despises me because I'm despicable. I despise myself. Dad wants to destroy me because that's the best thing to do with a kid like me. From now on, I'll destroy myself.

As soon as exams are over I pack my bag. I'm sixteen and I'm leaving the farmhouse behind me forever. I'm going to art college. I'm going to become an artist, no matter how poofy Dad thinks that is. As I leave, Mum looks relieved. Dad isn't there. Only Bethany cries.

Chapter 13

Art college doesn't start until the autumn. It's June. I don't have anywhere to go so I head for my sister Kelly's house. My big sister's living in a semi-detached council house in a nothing sort of area of Kidderminster. She has a baby and she mothers me a bit as well. I like it. When I look back I realise that she's sometimes tried to play mother to me before now but all I did was hate her because she was my big sister and Dad's favourite, at least until Bethany came along. Now she becomes more like a friend.

Despite always being such a good girl she's hooked up with one of the most violent and feared lads from our old neighbourhood. He's friendly to me at first but he's soon tired of having me around and starts to show it. I'm sorry for her. And I know it's time for me to go.

I spend the summer sleeping on the sofas of anyone who'll have me: Nan, aunties, Shane, Daniel. And I land the perfect summer job.

I've always had a soft spot for the West Midlands Safari Park, ever since we got stuck there years ago in Uncle Mike's Mini. I remember how we sat laughing in the steamed-up car as the world turned into a red skyscape. And now I'm working there. In the fairground, on the ghost train. I've always liked fairground art: in the curves and swerves there's something of the graffiti I've learned to love. The ghost-train colours are so bold, its purples and reds so deep and immediate, that it's easy to miss the high level of skill that has created it.

My job is to run the ride and take care of it and I do this energetically. And, I pick up girls. Something about the music, the noise and colours makes everyone let go a bit. I stand by the ghost train chatting to the prettiest girls as they queue.

'There was this big bloke last week, tough, Geordie accent, enormous hands with tattoos right across each knuckle and up his arms, probably a steel worker, dressed like a cowboy with a big moustache . . .'

I look at them. I'm surprised they're not scared yet.

'So, he went on the ghost train and he was terrified. I mean, you could hear him yelling for mercy right over in Kidderminster. Finished the ride and his hair was white. Pure white. And his moustache too.'

They climb into their cars, wide-eyed.

'Be brave, girls,' I say solemnly.

If I like the look of them, I switch off the power when they're halfway round. They scream. Their screams aren't like Mum's: there's no real fear, just a mixture of delight and excitement. When their car appears at the end of the ride, I'm standing there to assist them. I'm smiling.

'Enjoy it?' I ask, casually.

They point to me. 'You switched off the power in there!'

And the game's begun. They decide to go on the ghost train again and maybe again and by the end of the day I've got their phone number.

Before term starts, I go looking for a bedsit in Stourbridge. I'm independent and free and grown-up. Except secretly, so deep down I can't admit it, I'd like my mum to help me. She doesn't, of course, but at least she's organised an income for me. She's explained to Social Services that, although I'm only sixteen, I can't stay at home because of my father's violence and now they're paying me £30 a week.

I feel different from the other students. The majority of them are still living with their parents. College ends and they get on their buses and go home to a hot meal and some love. I'm younger than most of them but it seems to me I'm much, much older.

I'm glad I still have my old mates to ease my loneliness. The Social Services' £30 comes on Monday morning and on Monday night I go out to clubs with the boys and we spend most of it getting wasted. Later on in the week, when my mates' dole or wages come through, we get wasted again but this time they pay. We know who we are when we drink and take drugs. We're bad. We're in charge of our lives. There's no one to stop us and we can do what we like. So what if there's no money left for food? Food doesn't matter and no one's around to tell us that it does.

At first, I attend my college classes every day. It's horrible getting myself up and going out in the morning. Did I really want to be an artist? Maybe I only wanted to escape. I've never thought much about what I want to create and how and why.

I do a series of six self-portraits using inks. I know all about inks because they were favoured by my art teacher back in Kendal. He was a precise, traditional Lakeland artist who'd paint detailed land-scapes and then scratch the sheep's wool in, line by line. He disapproved of my interests, graffiti and abstracts. Now I try to use traditional materials like inks in a more abstract way. And I develop a love of Oleopasto, a sticky, putty-like medium that I can use to layer my work.

I like some of the teachers but my heart's not inside the college walls. It's outside in the world of people and ideas. Gradually I meet other students who stimulate those ideas. Most are much older than me and some are real artists, working with integrity in various media. They are gentle, kind people. Some are punks, a few are hippies. We talk. I've never talked about art before, except as a kid with the Allbuts. But here everyone has ideas to express about art, and about politics. Where I come from you're expected to be inarticulate. And now, suddenly, people are talking to me and I'm finding I have a lot to say. They take me to Stonehenge in an old bus where the women breastfeed their babies. It's like Pete's squat: another chaotic family I can kid myself I belong to. But I'm from Kidderminster. I couldn't introduce them to my old mates. If

Dan heard any of our conversations he'd never stop taking the piss.

Becoming an artist isn't going to be easy with Daniel and the others around. One evening a group of lads is driving into Birmingham. It's sunset. The sky in the west's on fire. Unnatural reds, oranges, yellows and blues rip behind the clouds like layers of silk.

'Look at that!' I say.

They glance out of the window. They wonder what I'm talking about.

'The sunset! It's beautiful!'

They all turn to stare at me, even the driver.

'What?' they say.

My best mate Daniel punches me. He says: 'You fucking weirdo.'

Well, I won't say that again. They can't appreciate beauty, or they won't. I must remember to be less art school when I'm with them. And I'm with them a lot.

The only thing the Kidderminster crowd and the art college crowd have in common is drugs. The rough lads use drugs because they're the fastest route to obliteration. The college crowd are look-ing for some artistic stimulation in the way drugs can alter and expand boundaries. The older, more serious artists incorporate these transformations into their work. I always mean to do the same and I find drug-taking a really creative experience but then the ideas slip away from me like fragments of dream. And I head for obliteration because inside I know I'm a rough lad from Kidderminster.

There are just a couple of people at college who are like me: rough boys who want to be artists. They become special friends. One is a stonemason who found he liked carving so much that he's here to study other media. He's ten years older than me and he introduces me to blues, the illegal black drinking clubs of post-riot Handsworth. They are filled with reggae and the sweet smell of hash. Once, we go home from Handsworth to his Black Country flat with a small bag of brown powder. I'm very excited to try it. This stuff is the devil's own drug. It is stigmatised and feared. It is heroin.

Watched by me and a collection of half-finished stone sculptures, he folds silver foil on his kitchen table as though he's making a small paper aeroplane. Then he wraps it round a pen to create a tube. He folds more foil, splits the bag with a kitchen knife and pours its contents into a channel. He reaches for his lighter and a flame flickers beneath the foil. The powder bubbles until it isn't powder any more; it's become a blob and, with his head on one side, he holds the tube to his mouth and inhales. The heroin is fluid now and he chases it down the folds. There's a strange smell in the room I recognise at once. Where from? How do I know the bitter, chemical odour of heroin?

He passes it to me. At first I just get a nasty taste at the back of my throat. By the time I've chased the blob down three lines of foil, a pair of warm woolly gloves is tight round my brain and I know with a certainty that everything will be all right, it will be all right. And I know that I've used this drug before. The smell, the effects, the foil, I first met them at the age of eleven. In Pete's squat back in Kidderminster, the night I ran away and he wasn't there. I sat in a circle of strangers and they passed it round. That was heroin. That was why Pete yelled at them when he got home. Because I was eleven and I'd been chasing the dragon.

I have girlfriends at art college and one of these is a hairdresser called Kirsty. She likes hanging about with funky art students. Together we discover rare groove. We go to a club called Salvation Disaster in Birmingham where everyone makes an effort to dress outrageously. All the Sharons and Kevins are in their shiny clothes queuing for the big mainstream club downstairs, the Power House, while Kirsty and I stand in a thin line of weirdos winding up the adjacent staircase. We are dressed for pure psychedelic funk. There are girls in huge hats with frills all over their enormous dresses, men in jodhpurs with riding crops, Kraftwerk fans with their fringes cut at neat right-angles looking futuristic in straight pencil skirts, black men in wide brim hats wearing leather and leopard skin. I'm in my mod-influenced black and white checked trousers with red socks and brogues, a red hat, red braces and a white shirt.

The Kevins take the piss relentlessly. We don't care. We secretly look down on them, on their bigotry, their lack of imagination, the way they're all fighting when we go to catch the night bus in our crazy clothes. I'm an art student and I'm not like them: we're into rare groove and our drug is speed, not only the alcohol that is soon going to make them so violent.

When Salvation Disaster closes, Kirsty and I get over to an all-night club at Aston University called the Jug. This feels exciting and different, more like a huge dancing party than a club. There's a record called 'Future Acid Tracks' by Future, and others like it, which I sense are signals. They're signalling that something new is about to happen musically, socially, but I don't know what. We're too busy being now with our funk.

Amphetamines make it easy to keep going all night. Speed enables you to drink a lot and after taking it alcohol isn't so dulling. You dance or talk shit all night and you talk rapidly and whether your friends are listening or not, you'll talk to them for four hours with-out expecting them to reply or ask a question. On speed, you can speak to a wall and after a while you'll have talked it out of being a wall and persuaded it that it's really a fence.

A life without drugs is unthinkable for me: it's the only way I know. Thirty pounds a week doesn't buy me much but by now I've tried or regularly used heroin, opium, amphetamines, acid, cocaine, magic mushrooms, hash and my old friend, alcohol. These last two I take daily. I must have a drink. And I must have at least one spliff. I can't sleep at all without it.

I'm not the only person who can't afford enough drugs; neither can the Kidderminster lads. And we know the answer. Stealing. We generally steal together. Stealing is the thing that keeps me in with the rough crowd. Stealing is what makes me one of them: it's not an art college thing. And deep down, I feel that's the way it has to be. Because maybe I'm just pretending to be an art student. Along with all my old mates I'm on railway tracks and I can't get off, however hard I try. Everyone brought up with me is on the same tracks and they lead to drugs and crime. Leave school and that's what's waiting for you at the next station. When I came to art college I wasn't only trying to escape Dad, but the railway as well. Then, when I remember the flickering London to Glasgow high-speed service, swishing along the valleys of the Lakes, fast as a time-traveller, I know for a fact that no one can get off it.

One night, I'm with some Kidderminster mates and we've taken speed and drink and it happens we've had some magic mushrooms too. We're tripping but we're sure of one thing. We want more to drink. There's only one way to get it. A lad holds some canvas up against the off-licence window and my cousin and I, buzzing with excitement, drop-kick the glass, run in and grab some bottles. We are incompetent: we fall over. Bottles smash on the floor. The lights spin and the whole thing happens at about a hundred miles per hour.

We feel like master criminals although we know that unplanned, grabbing crimes are the least successful. And sure enough, within minutes, we are surrounded by police cars. Apparently our raid was caught on a dozen shop and city centre cameras. We were so obliterated that it hadn't occurred to us to cover our faces.

I already have a history of petty teenage criminality so this is not my first charge but it's the first time I've been bound over to keep the peace. An impossibility, when I'm with my mates.

It's a Monday near the end of the college year and, as usual on a Monday, I'm with Daniel spending my social security money. We're meeting my brother Shane, our cousin and a couple of their mates. Shane's not into funk. He's a smart football hooligan. The lads he's hanging around with these days are quite middle class in their ironed shirts and Kouros aftershave.

We meet up at a yuppie wine bar in Kidderminster that isn't my kind of place but there's a lot of them around these days. They've sprouted up suddenly, as though Mrs Thatcher's been all over the country scattering wine-bar seeds.

'What's that up your jumper?' asks Daniel.

I reach inside my clothes and produce something I was using in my last lesson today. I didn't have anywhere else to put my French curves: it's a Perspex shape you use for sign writing. The lads pass it round. It's come from art school so it must be daft and poofy.

Across the wine bar a group of out-of-towners is leaving, and they've shoved a pregnant woman out of their way. She's objecting and so is her boyfriend, and so are a few other people but this is a wine bar, not a pub, so no one's fighting. And the lads responsible, who sound as though they're from up north, aren't apologising.

I've been drinking and taking speed. They're the same drugs I take at college parties but here I'm that other Mark and they have a different effect. When Shane and our cousin and their mates get up to follow the troublemakers outside, I stow my French curves back inside my jumper and Dan and I go too.

We trail the northerners through the shopping precinct until, finally, we fight. I feel my elbows bending and straightening like pistons, I feel my fists smacking into flesh. There's a pause when my French curves falls out and, as I shove it back up my jumper, the man I'm fighting runs off. It's all a blur of boots and fists and street lamp and kerb. I glimpse Dan, who's too scrawny to be much of a fighter, hovering over someone another lad is punching, waiting for a clean kick. At the end there's blood in the street and men all over the ground and my brother kicks the head of one of them and the man starts to twitch. Then we run.

That night, the police come round. They take an unhealthy interest in the cut on my knuckles. I explain that I've been mercilessly attacked by a can of beer I was opening. I invite them in to see the can. I tell them I hope it won't resist arrest. They're looking at me very closely now. They want to know what I was doing this evening, where I was. I lie. And, just to prove I'm not the sort to fight, I add that I'm at art college. They look so surprised that I produce the thing I shoved inside my jumper at the end of class today.

'What's this?' ask the ever-curious police.

'French curves,' I explain. 'Use it for sign writing.'

The policeman picks up my French curves gently with big hands, studying it. He turns it over. There, on the back, is blood. And now I remember it falling out during the fight and my stomach gives a lurch. I try to blame the blood on the beer can but the policemen are already handcuffing me. They tell me, since I'm insisting I don't already know it, that there was a fight after an incident in a wine bar tonight. At the end, there were two men in a coma and a trail of broken bones. I remember the way the man on the ground twitched when Shane kicked him. I feel sick.

One by one the six of us are hauled into police cells. Somewhere, far off, a radio plays. The song is a current hit: 'Don't Worry, Be Happy'.

Over the next three days of questioning I gradually stop bothering to lie. One of my brother's middle-class pals has grassed us all up, so there's no point. Also, the police have found out how much we had to drink that night and, on the grounds that our collective memory of the fight must be dim, they're throwing the book at us. We are all charged with a rioting offence, Violent Disorder Section 2. I am seventeen.

Chapter 14

Our solicitor tells us that we'll be going down for certain. There is seething public anger about football hooligans and lager louts and the government is keen to make an example of cases like ours. Since not one of us can give a coherent account of what happened during the fight and some of us have no memory at all, we are assumed to be guilty. Therefore we'll be sentenced, without trial by jury, to perhaps a few years in jail. The solicitor asks us if we want to put off our sentences for as long as possible. We do.

I leave my bedsit. My life is going to change now. Art college is over. Probably I've been pretending since I got here anyway. I've been pretending to be artistic, pretending to be one of the college crowd, pretending to belong when I'm just a rough lad. The train's stayed on its tracks and I've pulled in at the next station along with all the others. I'm going to jail. I'm going to jail for an offence I can barely remember committing.

At least I won't have to pretend any more. I can stop trying to be different. I'm bad. I'm rough. I'm hard. And I'll shortly have a jail sentence to prove it.

In the long summer months between the fight and our inevitable court appearance, I give up. I hand myself over to a life of drugs and crime, and in this Daniel and I become inseparable comrades. We have nowhere to go so we live rough, sleeping in fields like tramps.

Or sometimes we take over other people's flats. These flats belong to girls or weak lads and we move in and shove them out like cuckoos. We fuck girls, teenagers who let us do what we like to them and then, in their sad, soft, girly way, ask for more. They're drawn to us like magnets. They think they deserve guys like us.

We break into garages, houses and cars and afterwards struggle to remember anything about it. We cheat anyone who comes near us. We roll drunks who stumble out of the yuppie wine bar where our big fight started. If they resist we take them round the corner and beat them up. I'm not an instigator of this crime and I don't even enjoy it but I'm one of a group of lads and that's what we do. And we mix with people who are older and rougher than us. Secretly, I'm scared. Is becoming like them the next station on the railroad?

The most terrifying are brothers, Jake and Greg. We are sitting in a filthy, bare room in a filthy, bare flat in a high rise. The flat is full of people who've had so much to drink they've all reached blackout stage. Jake is scratching his face. He can't help it. He scratches his face over and over until it bleeds. He's injecting speed and drinking vodka. He finishes the bottle but he continues to put the glass to his lips. It's a minute or two before I realise that he isn't drinking from the glass but actually eating it. He's bitten a chunk off and now he's chewing it. His mouth is full of blood. Scrunch, scrunch, scrunch. I try not to stare at him. What I really want to do is run away.

His brother Glen is even scarier. I'm in his flat when a black guy comes to buy some hash. He starts off with his black bravado and Glen begins by encouraging him. The black guy thinks he's made a new friend and he sits down on the dirty settee and smokes a bit and drinks a bit and as he gets drunk he keeps on boasting and I know, I just know, that Glen is going to turn on him. The atmosphere is thick. It's awful waiting for it to happen, like waiting for my dad to come home from a binge. The black guy is oblivious, happily bigging it up, laughing and joking with Glen. And then it happens. Glen stops mid-laugh and his voice turns cold and he says: 'Who the fuck do you think you're talking to? I hate you, fucking nigger, and I'm going to take everything you've got.'

I stand there powerless and repulsed, pretending this is normal as he beats the black guy up. I even pretend, at Glen's request, to punch his victim. After that, I need a sanctuary. I go straight to Vanessa's.

Vanessa is my first real girlfriend. There have been a lot of girls, of course, but Vanessa's different. I met her with a crowd of her friends when I was with a crowd of lads and I knew at once that she was better than the others. I want to show her that I'm different too. I may look like a hoodlum and act like one and talk like one but I want this girl to understand that there's someone else inside. And, bit by bit, she believes me.

Vanessa's small and very pretty with never a black hair out of place. She works in a clothes shop. Unlike most of the people I know, she gets up in the morning and goes to work. She lives in an immaculate house with her attractive mum who can chew up hard men and spit them out. But Vanessa's not like that.

Girls are always talking about love and Vanessa's soon saying she loves me. That's a licence to treat her like shit. But I retreat into her arms whenever the mayhem I've caused gets too much even for me. She's always there, loving me, understanding me, giving me money and meals and a warm, ordered sanctuary from the madness. And I think I love her. Whatever love is.

In September, it's time for us to appear at the Crown Court in Worcester. Daniel's mum drives us. In the car, we agree that we've made the most of our time since we were arrested. We've enjoyed our freedom. We've had lots of fun. If what we did slopped over the edge of fun into a new, ugly reality, well mostly I was too obliterated to care.

We need a spliff before we can go in so Dan and I are late in court and we are stoned. I am wearing my sheepskin coat with the rips in the back: we've been sleeping rough and we look rough. My brother's here in his fine shirt and smart trousers. Now there's a lad who's sorted himself out. He's working in scaffolding during the week and at the weekends he becomes a football hooligan. My cousin and his mates are all looking respectable. They're drinking lads but they're not like me and Daniel. Only for us has drug-fuelled criminality become the norm. It might have been a streak in the lives of the others. For us, it is life itself.

The courtroom is Victorian. It is huge, high-ceilinged and brown-panelled. In the dock we are raised an absurd sixteen feet off the floor and the judge is higher still, and this gives the proceedings a cartoon flavour. There's no sign of Mum or Dad or our sister Kelly. Or Nan, even though three of her grandchildren are in court today. We didn't expect anyone to come. But it makes me feel good that Daniel's mum's here, a warm-hearted soul who sometimes gives me clothes or lets me sleep in her house. That woman was born to worry. She's watched whole generations of her family traipse through the courts and into jail. And now this is Dan's coming of age.

We stand handcuffed in the dock and the wigged old judge starts talking. I can feel my ears burning. I can't take in the actual words the judge is saying but I know they are awful. He must be talking about someone else. He can't mean me. Doesn't he know that I'm not really violent inside?

As the sentences are announced, everyone reacts differently. The two middle-class lads, my brother's mates, crumple: the one who grassed cries and the other collapses then, unusually for a violent crime, he's sent to an open jail. My brother, my cousin and Daniel all laugh as they hear their sentences. I stand, transfixed, unable to laugh, unable to move.

I get nineteen and a half months.

I am numb as we are led from the dock, out of the room and downstairs in a long, shuffling, handcuffed line with police on either side of us. I think: stop the train, I want to get off. But it's too late.

Outside there is a coach waiting to take us to jail and, with our handcuffs still on, we board it.

Chapter 15

We are to stay in Gloucester Jail until they can allocate us places in other prisons. I share a cell with my brother. I'm scared, but there are no surprises. A bed at each end. A small window. Scratched surfaces. Right-angles. No secret places, nowhere to hide. The yells of other prisoners. The sound of keys nearby or far down the corridor, always locking, unlocking, locking. And that smell, like school, only the disinfectant's stronger.

We are given prison clothes to wear and our own kit is handed back in a pillowcase. My brother tips the contents of his pillowcase out on the bed and there's something that doesn't belong to him: an enormous pair of Y-fronts. He holds them up. They're ripped and covered in blood. We look at each other in horror. We've heard a lot about prison bullying: is this what's waiting for us? Or is it some kind of joke the screws are playing?

Within a day Shane and I are arguing and we're both demanding a change of cellmate. Shane goes off to share with our cousin and Daniel joins me. He's tall now, but he still looks anaemic. His body's painfully thin with blue veins at the side of his face and he still has the big baby eyes he had as a kid which make him seem about four-teen. All summer we created a crazy, drug-filled world of crime: others may have visited it, but we lived there together. So what if Dan doesn't appreciate sunsets the way I do? We're closer than mates, we're brothers.

For one hour in twenty-four we can walk round and round in a high-walled courtyard outside. A lad with a scarred face walks with us one day and gives us some advice when he learns that it's our first time. He explains that tobacco is a unit of currency here in jail.

'If you want to get on top of people, don't smoke all your fucking tobacco allowance. Just smoke half and at the end of the week all the other lads are desperate for a fag and you've got a quarter-ounce to lend the wankers. And, whatever you give, you get back double next week. See? Double.'

That's a wicked rate of interest. We sit thinking about it when we're back in our blank cell for blank hours with our potty to piss in. We agree that if tobacco's money, it's the key to power here.

We're allowed to choose a book from the library every day and I read everything Orwell ever wrote, even though the essays are mostly boring. I'd read the back of a jam jar if I could, to let my mind out of the cell for a few minutes. The library gives each prisoner a book-mark that has a picture of a man climbing over a wall and the words Escape With Books.

I gain acceptance. Acceptance is knowing that you're in jail and you're not getting out soon. I live my life within a few small walls and I live it to rules others have made. However, I can't settle because I know I'm not staying here.

Within a fortnight we're on the move again to Pucklechurch where prisoners meet from all over the country to be separated into groups for their destination jail. I never knew there was this vast human cargo system, silent and unseen, shuffling men around Britain all the time. And now I'm a part of it.

Daniel and Shane and I are going to Portland in Dorset.

'Portland!' say the other prisoners.

'What's wrong with Portland?' we ask. They shrug.

Finally someone says: 'It's got a reputation, see.'

We only know it is a Good Order And Discipline jail. That means it's a borstal. It feels like a long, long way, and when the bus approaches the south coast it is evening. The sun is sinking in the west and throwing its red light across the water. Another one of those beautiful sunsets, but I'm not stupid enough to mention it to Daniel or anyone else. The beach is a big dune of stones that stretches away into the distance and the bus is heading straight for it. I wait for the crunch, then I realise that we're actually on a road that runs along the spit. There is red water on both sides of us, filled by the sunset.

Portland looks like an island. It looms ahead, a grey mist hanging over it. Where it joins the sea, there is the desolation of industry: naval buildings, gas tanks, big storage buildings and any number of great grey, square places that might be borstals. But the bus doesn't stop here. It climbs the steep hillside, weaving in and out of dismally grey houses, its engine roaring in low gear. Then we get to the top of the hill and we look back and see that we are surrounded by ocean. Far below is the straight pencil line of beach that connects Portland to the mainland.

Suddenly the bus halts against a high cliff face. Everyone simultaneously takes one deep breath as we realise that we're really at the top and that the cliff's below us. In front now are walls. Massive, imposing, grey-white walls.

A huge gate in the walls opens and the bus drives in. I feel sick. The gates slam shut behind us.

The mist stretches right down to ground level here. We get out into clammy air and deep shadow.

As soon as my foot touches the ground in this ageless, timeless place, a voice roars: 'Get into fucking line!'

So I've arrived in borstal.

A big, angry-looking screw glares at our ragged line and yells: 'Whatever you knew before you came here, you can fucking forget it!'

We are given uniforms: red waffle ties and blue striped shirts, denim jeans and round-necked denim jackets. Then we are dispatched to our cells.

Portland isn't technically an island but it feels like one when I'm alone in my cell in Hardy block with my sea view. I watch it through my small, barred window as it changes moods, from angry to calm to threatening. So this is really jail. Gloucester was sociable in its way and the screws were relaxed. Now I am completely alone in a small room with an uncertain future. It's been like this for prisoners since the beginning of time.

Back in Gloucester Jail, Daniel and I asked the other inmates questions whenever we could and now we know that jail is a system and we have to learn to play it to our advantage. We have to rise to the top instead of being down there among the weak, bullied individuals. We've already understood that, on one level, there are a mass of rules and regulations. Break them and you're sent to a place called the Block, which scares even the hardest lads. On another level, the day-to-day, there are no rules. It's a jungle.

Daniel and I want two things: to be together and to work in the kitchens. It hasn't taken us long to learn that the kitchen wing is the best place to be, and, at £5.60 a week, the best paid.

We tell the screws that we are cousins and Dan has a problem reading so he'll need me to read his personal mail to him. And I say I'm a chef. Our scam works. We are both going to the kitchen wing, away from the sea. Shane is to be moved to the works wing. We're on Parade, that's what it's called when we march round and line up, and they shout Shane's name and he's marched away. I watch him from the line. His ears still stick out and, although he's grown-up now, he's really still that scruffy, unloved little kid. I remember how he used to beg our dad to watch him play in school football matches and our dad never showed up. I wish Shane would turn back and look at me now. But he doesn't. I feel that pain again, the pain of acute sadness that is reserved only for Shane. I watch him cross the courtyard until I can't tell his denim-clad figure from all the others.

On our first day in the kitchens we learn that Dan will be cleaning and I'll be cooking breakfast.

The kitchens are huge and shiny with a massive wooden table down the middle. We are watched over by a screw in a glass box. I'm given a while to settle in and then, when break time comes, the lads down tools and announce: 'Initiation!'

It's Kangaroo Court time. I'm going to have to prove myself in some way, and with my fists.

They glance towards the office, where the screw is working behind his glass divide. He can't see into the toilet recess but we can all see each other in there because there are no doors on the cubicles. Something about the way the screw's bent over his work, with a conspicuous degree of concentration, convinces me that he knows what's about to happen.

The lads give me a choice. I can pick someone the same size and weight as me until one of us bleeds. Or else they'll all beat me up.

I choose a Welsh guy who is a little bigger than me with tattoos up his arm and on his face. The lads hand me a thin pair of oven mitts for boxing gloves. I remember the boxing lessons I had as a kid. Yet again, I silently thank the school psychiatrist.

We go into the toilet recess, out of the screw's eyeline, where there is a smell of piss and some spit and blood on the floor. We square up to each other in our bakers' whites with our oven gloves. I am scared. I murmur an offer: 'Listen, mate. Let's just have a knockabout. I won't hurt you if you don't hurt me.'

But the Welsh guy isn't playing shadow puppets and I've barely finished speaking before he cracks me hard, right in the face. And now I'm angry. I'm livid. So I fight. I fight hard. I fight my way right out of fear and through a deep fury I didn't know was in me. I can feel my punches through the oven glove, feel the skin of his face and his bones beneath my fists. I recognise the glazed look of fear in his eyes. The muscles in my arms contract like a thousand rubber bands every time I pull back and with every blow they turn to steel.

'John-son,' yell the boys. There aren't any first names in jail. But gradually this turns into 'John-o, John-o', and to the rhythm of their chant I pummel the Welsh lad's face until his whole body crumples beneath me. I jump on him and continue to beat him. A demon has leapt out from deep inside me, a demon of pure, white-hot anger.

My fury remains until there is enough blood to end the fight. His bakers' whites have his blood and piss from the toilets all down them. I've won. I look up. The lads are cheering. The screw is apparently deaf. I step back. Most of all, I'm surprised. Where did that angry John-o come from and where has he gone? I don't feel angry any more. I don't feel anything. I help my victim to his feet.

For the rest of the day, everyone chants under their breath: 'John-o! John-o!' So I've passed my initiation and I'm one of the boys. That's a reassuring form of protection. I'm only seventeen and the borstal takes lads up to twenty-one. Most of them are rough boys from rough places like me. But some are extremely dangerous: you can tell which ones at a glance. There's a massive lunatic from the army who's in for rape. He was sentenced just before his twenty-first birthday so he's still here at twenty-two. He's tough and he'll jump anyone weak or anyone who stands up to him. I'm not going to cross him.

In the first week, Dan and I remember that here tobacco is money. We smoke half our allocation and loan out the rest and before you can say jungle we've got lads all over the block in debt to us, and so deeply in debt they can never repay us. They're in our pockets. Soon there's so much tobacco coming in that we can't smoke it all and we're telling lads to give us biscuits or squash or shampoo instead. And make sure it's Timotei. That's power.

When Daniel's mother comes down she tells the screws she's here for both of us. In the visiting room are lines of tables but no table is going to come between her and her boys. She throws herself across it. We're pleased to see this long-suffering, rough bundle of love. Brushing the tears from her wrinkles, she reaches into her mouth and produces a small gift. Dan already has his trousers undone ready. He snatches the parcel and then rapidly shoves it in the only hiding place he has, his arse, an area he has already prepared for its arrival with baby lotion. We spend the rest of the visit in a mixture of anticipation and paranoia.

Dan's mum tells us in a whisper, 'I'm never fucking smuggling hash into this place again, never!'

The men in her family made her bring it. They've all done bird. They all know.

'I'll be back in a fortnight,' Dan's mum assures us. 'And I'm not bringing in none of that stuff again.'

But we know she will. She may be a hard-faced, bottle-blonde to other people but to us she's a princess. We are jubilant when we manage to get the hash safely back in our cell. We keep it all for ourselves. And then, when the screws have locked up for the night, I can once again relax with a spliff and know I'll sleep.

From this time on Dan's mum keeps us well supplied. And when the loving Vanessa says she'll visit, I persuade her, too, that bringing us some hash isn't such a dangerous thing to do.

I like baking and I'm good at cakes. We get up at 4.30 in the morning, about ten of us. We all have breakfast together in the kitchens at the enormous table. We eat our bacon sandwiches and drink tea and there's a big bucket of milk in the middle of the table we can dip our mugs into. It's a slobs' tea party. When I've finished my shift I sneak cakes and cornflakes out and pay the orderlies to take them back to my cell. I sleep all day. Then, by the time I wake up, it's Association, which means we can socialise and play snooker. Finally, I get stoned. I get stoned a lot but always before bed. And as I fall asleep I can find a kind of happiness in the small rhythms of my day. Jail's not so bad, as long as you stay out of the Block.

But I do miss the outside world. Because I know it's changing, and changing without me. When new prisoners come in, they're talking about the new music and the new drug and the new scene. The drug everyone's taking out there is LSD, or acid. The music is called acid house. And the scene is raves. Raves are massive parties, usually held outside or at some enormous indoor location like an air-craft hangar, where thousands of people take acid and dance to the music.

I remember dancing all night at the Jug. It seems to me that place was a bit like the raves everyone's telling me about, only on a smaller scale, and the music was rare groove. As for acid, I've tried it, of course. It's an interesting drug, expanding boundaries, challenging structures, giving you wild trips, but I'm not sure why people are suddenly taking it in their thousands.

Lads talk about the raves they've been to and they lend me tapes of acid house music. I listen to it over and over again. I listen care-fully. But I don't get it. I don't understand how the music, the drug and the scene are all fitting together. I can't wait to get out there so I can find out what's happening.

Chapter 16

One morning, someone tries to smuggle a sandwich out of the kitchen. The screw finds it hidden in the lift shaft and he's furious. We're all in trouble. He tells us that we can't have any breakfast today. But we want our breakfast, we're hungry and we want it.

We go into the recess, the one where I beat the Welsh guy with oven mitts for boxing gloves. After a few minutes' angry discussion, we reach an agreement. We will refuse to work.

The screws knock on the glass of their office and tell us to get on with our jobs. We say: 'Fuck off!'

They knock harder. Their faces change, suddenly: they're redder, broader, more shadowy.

We say: 'If we can't have breakfast, we're not working.'

A couple of screws come out of their office. They tread towards the recess with firm steps, their chains and keys clinking as they move. They try to open the door. We put our feet against it. A barricade. Actually, we're just ten kids who want their breakfast, but as far as the Portland authorities are concerned, we're a riot.

The screw hits the riot bell and suddenly there's the sound of big feet in big boots at the door. It caves in and all at once they're on top of us: boots, helmets, shields . . . full riot gear, in fact.

We are pulled out of the recess one by one with agonising force and thrown onto the floor. When it is my turn, my knees are folded under me in one brisk, violent movement and a stick's rammed into the fold. Another stick is run painfully across my back and between my arms and I am carried, a few inches from the floor, back to my cell. They tell me I'm going to the Block.

I throw all my stuff in a mattress cover to be locked away. I'm not even allowed a toothbrush or toothpaste in the Block. Two screws come for me. They're isolating us, dealing with us separately. I'm alone and I'm terrified. I don't know what's waiting for me but I know it's going to be bad.

They take me to the Block and it's like going to the dungeons because this is the most ancient part of the jail. There's a groove in the step where it's been rubbed away over many years and the sign outside is blank, because so many busy hands have polished it off.

I have to step down to go through the door. I see a line-up of screws waiting.

'Come on then, you little bastard,' they shout. The door is closed behind me and my feet do not touch the ground. The screws carry me in by my thumbs. I am thrown into a cell and slammed against the wall. I slide down it and they yell at me to get up and when I do I find there are about six of them in my tiny stone cell. They jump on me and pull my shirt over my head and my cuffs over my wrists. They pull my trousers and my underwear down to my ankles and when I'm naked and helpless they beat me. And it is a real beating. They use their fists and knees and elbows. Once I look up and see a familiar screw. He's a Christian; at least, he's always spouting Christian stuff. But now he's smirking, the holy little cross on his tie glittering. He's enjoying it, maybe even getting sexual satisfaction out of watching a naked and humiliated adolescent suffer. I close my eyes. Anything could happen because now I understand that I am far from the ordered regime of the rest of the prison. I'm in a jail within a jail. Some screws have created their own warped, secret world, run to their own rules, where they can do what they like to me and no one will know. I keep my eyes tightly shut. I am in the branches of a high, high tree, looking down on six big men beating up a frightened lad far below.

It goes on and on. And then, when at last it stops, they give me my instructions. The floor is covered in rubber tiles and they tell me that I have to stand on the two tiles at the back on the left whenever I hear them opening my door. I have to stand to attention with my thumbs down my legs as though I'm on parade and I must say my name and number and house.

Then they go away and leave me naked. I shiver. It's December and the small, high window is wide open. It is covered by a cage and, no matter how hard I try, it is impossible to get a hand through that cage to close the window.

The walls are blocks of grey-white Portland stone. And, apart from a potty, a floor rag and some cardboard, the cell is empty. The cardboard's in there because there's probably some human rights law that says every cell must have a chair and a table. And the cardboard is certainly folded into the shape of a chair and a table. But you can't sit on a cardboard chair. And what can I use my cardboard table for?

I can't smoke. I can't do anything. And when it's dinnertime – I only know it from my stomach, there's no other way to measure time passing – I hear the door and leap to attention on my two squares of tile.

'Johnson WM1702, Raleigh House, sir!'

'Dinner!' bawls the screw. He marches in, grabs my head, pushes it back and squeezes on my temples until I think his thumbs are coming through my brain. He carries on yelling although he's about an inch from my face.

'Get your dinner! Now!'

I try to leave the cell but he stops me at once.

'Right, when I say run, I want you to run. And when I say run I want to see it in your fucking face, you fucking little bastard.'

I go back to my two special squares of tile and prepare myself to run. My body says run. My face says run. He shouts and I run for the door but I am halted almost immediately.

'Stop! I didn't tell you to run out of the fucking cell, did I? You run to me. You run right at me. As hard as you fucking can. And remember, I want to see it in your fucking face.'

I hesitate because I don't know what kind of game this is but I've had my instructions and I don't want another hiding. I am terrified.

I go from nought to sixty on the spot and I hurl myself right into him, my face snouty and my teeth bared. He catches my body and throws me, using the force of my own momentum, out of the cell. Bam, I bounce off the wall and I run again, run like a maniac, up the ancient passageway to another screw who bounces me again, and then another. At the end of this sprint is dinner. A screw throws it at me and now I have to run back with it. The dinner goes everywhere. It slops all over me, over the floor, but I keep on running. I am naked and the screws are laughing at me.

'Look at the size of his dick,' they yell. 'Ha, little dick! Little fucking dick!'

Then they lock my door behind me and I sit naked, eating what remains of my dinner.

It is dark outside now and I am very cold. I try and fail again to close the window. There is a hot pipe in the cell, running across the back wall under the window. I push my body up against it for warmth. It can only heat a few inches of skin at a time but it's something.

They come in later and see the red marks the warmth has left. So they beat me up again. You aren't supposed to get warm.

Later, the door opens once more and I get on my tiles and say my name and number and by now I'm shaking with fear as well as cold. Whenever they open the door you just can't tell what's going to happen. But this time a smaller figure comes in, cautiously and quietly. The padre.

He sees my terror. He's seen it all before, in every cell, every night. 'It's all right,' he says. 'I'm not going to hurt you.'

He looks at my bruises, studying me with concern in his eyes. By now they've given me a pair of gym shorts, otherwise I'm still naked. Even the padre is shivering. He asks if I'm okay, if I'd like to talk, whether he can do anything. Maybe he can pray with me? I say: no thank you, Padre. He leaves, still looking worried.

The screws throw in a mattress and a blanket. The mattress is only a couple of inches thick. I lay it out on the floor and then shiver under the blanket, massaging my bruises. There is a deep silence. It is broken occasionally by screams. Someone is being beaten up further down the corridor. Later, far away, I can hear what sounds like a wounded animal or a small boy whimpering. But I don't cry. I know that it will soon be Christmas and that must mean I've had my eighteenth birthday.

There is slopping out in the morning, a disgusting process because I have to rinse out the rag they've given me for toilet paper.

'Bed-pack, you little fucker!' shouts a screw. I have to fold everything, including my clothes, into a perfect square with razor-sharp edges. 'Book!' roars the screw and I have to run down the corridor to the bookcase, grab a book without time even to see its title, then run back. The books are all novels and I swear that, without exception, they all have the last ten pages ripped out. Bastards.

Every time I sprint down the corridor, I have a micro-second to marvel at its cleanliness. I only have to look up to see that even the copper pipes on the ceiling are gleaming. It takes me a while to work out that, silently, busily, outside my cell, an army of orderlies is scrubbing and polishing. They are the nonces, the sexual offenders, who are kept in the Block for their own protection but given freedom within it. And they like to keep the place sparkling.

Apart from brief interludes of running or violence, I'm left in my tiny cell alone all day without clothes. After a few days I can't even read the book I fetched in the morning. I can't concentrate on anything. I count the stones in the walls over and over (142 each side). I run around singing every song I know and then making up some more. I shout, I dance, I chant, I skip. I break-dance. I body-pop. I do robotics. I sing some more. Then my mind gets too numb even for that and I just jump about in silence to keep warm. I keep trying to close the window. I am unsuccessful.

One day they let me write letters. I usually receive a lot from Vanessa and I try to write back, not letters telling her I love her and asking her to wait (I'm too hard for that kind of thing). But Vanessa's one of the few people who knows there's another Mark and when I write I try to show her I'm more than a thug. I tell her how I want to change. And she seems to understand. Today I write to her as openly and honestly as I can. And I write to Kirsty, the girl I knew at art college. Our relationship was brief but now in this small cell I need to communicate. Kirsty's not just a hairdresser but a hair consultant, with bright red lipstick and snappy clothes. She lives with her wealthy parents in Wolverhampton. I don't declare undying love to Kirsty either but I do talk about seeing her when I get out.

Of course, the screws read my letters. And they play a little trick. They put Vanessa's letter in Kirsty's envelope. They send Kirsty's letter to Vanessa. I know what's happened because, almost immediately, I get two Dear John letters, brought to me by a happy, smiling screw. I come close to crying. Now I really am alone in this cold, bare room. I've lost Vanessa.

My mother visits with Bethany. I've barely seen them since I left home but since I'm in the Block, we're not allowed more than fifteen minutes together. Mum and Bethany have a one-thousand-mile round trip from the Lakes to Portland and they're given fifteen minutes with me. Shane's already sitting with them when I am led in. Mum and Bethany stare at my cuts and bruises and black eye. They start to cry. I try to explain about the Block. Shane knows about it, of course, but he's shocked too.

My mum says, through her tears, that she's going to write to the Prime Minister, Mrs Margaret Thatcher. I ask her not to, as it would make things even worse for me.

She has time to tell me that Kelly's left her boyfriend and moved up to the Lakes. Oh, and Mum and Dad are formally divorced at last. I nod. I already learned, about a thousand years ago when I was at college, that they'd finally agreed to stop torturing each other. And not because Mum threw Dad out but because Dad has a girlfriend and she's pregnant. He asked Kelly to tell Mum that he wasn't coming home. Now he's with his new partner in Durham. Mum says that the farmhouse is sold and she and Bethany are living in Kendal. Then it's time for me to go back into isolation. I don't look at them as the screw leads me out.

In my ten days on the Block I am given ten minutes in the tiny exercise yard by myself. It is raining. The rest of the time I am banged up. The silence is infinite. The boredom and depression, the sadness and the fear, they're infinite too.

My happiest moment is when a screw appears with a bag of sprouts for me to peel. So it must be Christmas. I am grateful because he's given me something to do and it feels as though he's being kind. But mostly the screws are cruel, sadistic and unpredictable. They terrorise with the constant threat of violence. It feels all too familiar.

When at last I am allowed back into my old block, I find Daniel has swung things so that I'm in the cell next to him. The new cell feels strange and ill fitting. At first I am uncomfortable. I am disorientated. Any change in prison is traumatic, even a change to a better cell, because it upsets the routines that keep you sane and reminds you that you have no control. Someone else stuck their pictures on the walls with toothpaste and you can see the ghosts of their presence and you have to learn to live with them.

When a screw appears carrying the mattress cover with my stuff in it, I start to make myself at home. I get out my little radio. I switch it on and lie back on the bed. They're playing Sinéad O'Connor singing 'Nothing Compares 2 U'. I close my eyes. I relax. I feel as though I've just been released from jail.

Chapter 17

I am going to be different. I am going to change. I am on the coach to Weymouth, where prisoners are released. I am going to be different. I am going to change. We flash along the beach road and I stare to the horizons in disbelief. Was Planet Earth this big before? Were the colours so bright? The immensity of the sea reminds me how small my world has been for the last eight months. I take a deep breath and I smell freedom.

There are about six of us in the minibus and we all have brown envelopes in our pockets with £30 in. I look terrible because I'm wearing the clothes I was wearing when I was sentenced: that ripped sheepskin coat and some tracksuit bottoms.

We are dropped at Weymouth train station. I feel weightless. I've been carrying a heavy load for eight months and suddenly I'm not any more. Most of us head immediately for the conveniently placed off-licence across the car park. I buy Special Brew. I close my eyes and feel the cool, cool liquid slipping down my throat. It's never tasted this good before. It's like getting back to your oldest friend, your long-lost love, your most comfortable clothes, your favourite place. My body relaxes. I feel a familiar and welcome fuzziness spread through my body and into my head. And I get on a train to Birmingham.

I've had a lot of time to decide where to go when I'm released.

Dan's already back in Kidderminster because my sentence was lengthened after the kitchen riot. But if I go there, I know what will happen: I'll slip right back into the crazy life I left behind. Probably the right thing to do is return to Mum and try to settle down with a job in Kendal using my new baking skills. But first, I'm going to visit a girl. Vanessa's still angry with me after she read my letter to Kirsty. But Kirsty's forgiven me and promised to show me what I've been missing. And she's going to help me find the new look, the hair, the clothes I should be wearing.

It's 1989 and I feel as though I've been in jail all my life. We have a lot of sex but it's not good sex. It's awkward and uncomfortable because I don't really remember her, or remember her body. But when I sink down into a real bed with soft covers and a soft pillow, I feel as though my life just changed from monochrome to colour.

Kirsty cuts my hair in a trendy style, to the front with a flat fringe. We go shopping and buy a green frog coat with a frog hood. And flares. I must have some baggy flares. Finally, when I've got the kit, I'm ready for my first rave. But by now Kirsty and I are miserable. It's obvious to both of us that our relationship ended a long time ago and we don't know why we're doing this. I head for Kendal.

Mum and Bethany are living in a house in a tiny cobbled alley called the Shambles. They're pleased to see me. Bethany's twelve but she still seems like a little kid, jumping over me with excitement. I don't like all this affection. We don't show it in our family and when Bethany hugs me I feel ill. I look at her, a powerless kid, and she reminds me of how it was years ago for me and Shane and Kelly. I visit Kelly, who's also in Kendal. She's on her own now and has two kids, one of them new-born.

I tell the family that I'm going to change and I start looking for a job at once. My mate Ian's moved away with his family but there are other friends, and when we notice flyers around the place for a rave in Blackburn we have to go.

As soon as we get near Blackburn we hit gridlock. Every kind of car, from Mercedes to Beetle, is jam-packed into the town. Sound systems boom, people stand on car roofs or rave right there in the street, some take off their clothes, the sweet smell of spliff circulates faster than the traffic, there are whistles and singing and shouting and hugging as the traffic lights change from red to green to red without anyone moving. We're having the party right here.

The police are bewildered. No one told them there was going to be anything happening in Blackburn tonight.

Finally we get to a vast, dark field. We aren't asked for money. I've never seen so many people, all of them young like me and all of them taking acid and dancing to the music. I like it. I love it. I join in.

When I take acid, everything I thought I knew becomes unknown. My life has been nothing more than trivia and boredom, it has been dominated by the silly, small routines of jail and now that is replaced, wonderfully, vitally, by a primeval, colourful world. It seems to me that truths are being revealed, that after all those months of jail-think I'm entering a new state of mind with new possibilities and new hope. I get caught up in the music, with its primitive, repetitive beat. The experience is hypnotic. At times it feels transcendental. Drinking and fighting and shagging someone you can't remember in the morning are part of the old culture, and from here all that seems disgusting and shallow. Now I understand about raves. They're new, they are now, they are a revolution.

After this, it's hard to settle down to job hunting. But I soon find one. I'm going to be a baker in a hotel. Each morning I get up early and then I drink my wages until late. I drink a lot. I get very drunk. One night I piss in the bed. Mum's had enough.

'You've turned out like your dad,' she says sadly. 'And she asks me to go.

For a few nights I sleep in a car and wonder if there's more to life than unfolding my aching body in the morning and staggering off to a dull job with other grey-faced people. Then I think: fuck it. After all, I was in the Block so I must be really bad. Too bad to change. I catch the next train down to Kidderminster where my friend and brother Daniel is waiting for me to resume the mad life that got us into jail.

Dan's mum is pleased to see me and lets me stay. She seems to understand that Dan and I are real brothers because we've shared a cell. And from now on, we're always together.

We start stealing and dealing all over again only now we're harder, much harder, and our crimes are more cynical. I've changed and I know it. Art college? That mad idea I once had of becoming an artist? Well, that's been beaten out of me. In jail we've learned to live on our wits, manipulate people and use violence and retaliation as a routine means of survival. And I have the Block to thank for making me an expert in brutality. What a great training ground Portland was for a life of crime: it's much easier now to do these things and not feel a qualm.

In just a matter of days I'm in with the crazy brothers, Jake and Glen, and their friends again. I feel hopeless. I don't want to be with these people, I don't want to behave like this. My own powerlessness threatens to overwhelm me.

The best thing is that Vanessa forgives me. I look at her sweet symmetrical face and say I'm sorry and once again she sees through Mark the thug to that other Mark who needs her but can't admit it. She smiles. She still loves me. Once again I find some sanctuary in her house. But mostly my sanctuary is drugs. The drugs of choice are Special Brew and amphetamines. The speed enables you to drink vast amounts without actually getting paralytic, plus you get a separate buzz off it. The downside is that this can be a psychotic combination. You're not a happy drunk. You twist things up in your mind, get paranoid and do things you wouldn't normally do.

One day we're drunk on Special Brew and high on speed as usual, when a man we know comes up to us in the park. Michael's very old, older than thirty, and he's wearing a suit and smart cufflinks. He's a well-known local conman and he says he wants to talk to us about a business proposition. Our minds race as he tells us he knows of an insurance broker who will be in Kidderminster today. He'll be carrying a lot of money, credit cards and some very useful business chequebooks that Michael will find easy to turn into money.

We nod. This is sounding fine already. We're bad and we have to fund our drug-taking so we're certainly up for some easy crime. We've been to jail so we know we're criminals.

Michael says he needs a couple of quick, bright lads to separate this insurance broker from the contents of his pockets. If we take on the job, we'll be rewarded.

Full of energy and bravado we follow Michael to a pub near the town centre and he tells us to wait while he goes inside. Later he comes out and gives us a signal, nodding at a man walking down the main road. Tall, upright, blue blazer and grey slacks, hair just greying at the edges.

We follow the insurance broker along the road. We're very excited; the speed is making our blood pump harder in our bodies. Daniel keeps giggling: he always laughs when he's scared. The broker is walking downhill and we walk behind him trying to look normal, trying to look as though we aren't buzzing. The man goes to the pedestrian underpass at the big roundabout. I remember sliding down the steps here on a tray as a kid.

When he's under the roundabout, he goes into the public toilets. We follow him and the atmosphere changes. It is cold and echoey and dingy. It is the right sort of place to do what we're going to do. He walks over to the urinal and, as soon as he reaches it, we are there too, behind him. I put an arm round his neck and a foot round his legs, a move I've used often in the past. The man struggles. I smack his head against the wall, hard, and then he is still. I hold him fast, his expensive blue blazer pressing up against me so I can see the weave. I say: 'If you don't move you'll be okay.' He says okay, okay, and he doesn't move while Daniel rifles through his pockets and gets his wallet. The whole thing only takes a few seconds and it is exciting like a roller-coaster.

As soon as I let go of him the man swings round and tries to grab me. Daniel gets him and produces a knife. I didn't even know Dan was carrying one. There's a flash of blood and suddenly it's everywhere, colouring the toilet floor red, covering the walls, splattered on my clothes. The man crumples. He isn't standing up any more. He is sinking onto the floor in front of the urinal and we turn and run back through the underpass and into the park. A woman is walking through with all her shopping. Dan pushes her against the wall and her bags drop and her shopping goes everywhere. Dan is laughing like a psycho.

We run to the park. Under a tree we take the cash out of the wallet and keep it for ourselves. We don't go looking for Michael.

We get home and lay low with the wallet and when the buzz wears off a bit I begin to feel a deep-down, gnawing fear that we've killed the insurance broker. I'm scared. And something else scares me too. I've hurt and possibly killed a man and I didn't feel a thing. It was as though someone else was doing it, not me. That's how it was when my dad or the screws in Portland hit me. It was all happening to someone else.

Michael appears the next day. We hand over the cards and he takes us to shops and buys us a lot of stuff we want like clothes and gold jewellery. I get a bright T-shirt, yellow trousers, some tan Kickers boots. We've started going to raves at a Birmingham club called the Humming Bird where the music is acid house and the drug is acid and everyone's wearing bizarre, colourful clothes.

A couple of weeks later Michael gets arrested for trying to pass one of the insurance broker's cheques. He sings like a bird. At the police station, I learn that the so-called insurance broker was a pensioner. Well, he didn't look that old. Thank God he isn't dead, although apparently Daniel did slice part of his ear off. So Michael had made up the story about targeting an insurance man: he just went into the pub and chose any affluent-looking victim. Michael was a conman and he certainly conned us.

I deny all knowledge of the crime over two days of questioning but by the second day I've come to terms with the fact that I'll be returning to jail. When the police say they're going to the shops where Michael bought us the clothes, I give up. I know we were caught there on CCTV.

I tell the police everything that happened but I leave out the drug use. I've already learned from my last conviction that if you admit to a degree of incoherence then they'll try to pin anything on you. It's a system and I'm playing it.

The charge is Robbery with Violence and we are hauled up before three magistrates. The OAP in charge is a very old lady. She must be at least ninety. It's like a film because I feel as though I'm watching someone else instead of actually being there. The magistrate tells me that I've been charged with a hideous crime and the streets aren't safe with me out on them. She says I'm a violent person. I look at her in disbelief. I think: But you don't know me!

She says that the court isn't big enough to deal with our crime and that must mean we're going down for over a year: the police have been talking about five years. Suddenly, breathing's difficult. There's a long pause before I can step down. Dan's with me and he gains his composure first. When we turn, we muster our old bravado. I hear someone laughing and telling the magistrate to fuck off, I don't know whose voice it is, Dan's or mine. Inside, I am desolate.

So I'm back inside less than two months after being released. The remand centre is in Redditch. The last time I went to Redditch was to visit the Allbuts and I played in the woods all day and saw that hare running across the ploughed field. The beauty of that image gives me pleasure even now. I wonder if the Allbuts still live here. They're a few miles away, but they might as well be on another continent.

After four months I am sentenced to two and a half years. The judge says it was a despicable crime.

Chapter 18

I am allocated to a young offenders' jail in Rugby. I have a cell to myself and I rely on visits from Vanessa, my brother Shane and Dan's mum to keep me supplied with a spliff every night. It is a good jail with decent screws and sometimes even flushing toilets. But towards the end of a year, incarceration starts to get to me. I feel edgy. I can't settle. I no longer find a spliff a relaxing experience: it just produces anxiety. I have panic attacks and sweat in terror in my cell. I am anxious about my release. I don't know how I can change. Vanessa's my girlfriend. Will I go back to Kidderminster with her? If I do, I'll be straight back inside.

I ask all of these questions when I am interviewed by a probation officer at the end of my first year here. She's middle-aged, middle class, a civil servant. She leans forward.

'Admit it, Mark, you've got a drugs problem.'

I stare at her.

'No I haven't.'

'You committed a crime you can barely remember. You were out two months and, high on drugs, you committed another crime. Your drug-taking has cost you two years of your youth. Can't you admit you've got a problem?'

I swallow hard.

'Well.' I cough. There's a long pause. She waits. 'When you put it like that, I probably have.'

'And when you get out it could all happen again. You need help, don't you, Mark?'

Something in her tone suggests that she's about to make some kind of offer. I smell something. I scent a swerve.

'Yes,' I say. 'I need help.'

'What were you doing before your first conviction? Did you have a job?'

I tell her I was at art college. I want to laugh at myself, laugh and cry, when I admit, shakily, that I'd hoped to become an artist.

She listens. Then she suggests that instead of completing my sentence in jail I go into a drug rehabilitation centre in Birmingham. This woman is saying I can leave prison. I can hardly believe my ears.

'There are conditions,' she warns me. 'You can't drink or take anything while you're in rehab. If you do, you'll be sent straight back here to complete your sentence.'

I say: 'I want to try.' And I mean it. I don't just want to get out of jail. I really want to change. I need to go somewhere where I can have a life that is far from the railway I started out on. The probation officer is offering me a safe house.

As soon as Dan hears about this he tells the Probation Service that he has a drug problem and is badly in need of rehabilitation. They ignore him.

My anxiety on leaving jail is acute. I am nervous on the train. I stare out of the window at the world's amazing freshness. Everything in jail is stale and out here the colours are so vivid they jump at me.

A probation officer takes me to a huge and beautiful house in Edgbaston. The house has recently been refurbished by a drugs charity called Turning Point and it was opened by Princess Diana. It has high ceilings, windows from floor to ceiling, terraces and gardens. Someone tells me that J. R. R. Tolkien wrote *The Lord of the Rings* in the garden and when I walk outside I see strange, ornate old lights under overgrown bushes.

Intimidated by the sheer size of the house, I go back to my room and lie down on my bed because it feels like the only safe place to be. On the other bed lies a man shaking and moaning, clutching his legs, rocking and talking to himself.

I know what this is; I've seen it before. He's a heroin addict and these are the symptoms of withdrawal. It's called rattling.

'Haven't had any for a week,' he says.

My key worker, Hugh, appears and I leap to my feet guiltily and start folding my sheets into a prison bed-pack.

'Whoooooooa,' says Hugh, smiling. He's about ten years older than me with a trendy curtains haircut and jeans. 'Just relax – this isn't jail! I'd like to talk to you about the kind of art you're interested in. I've recently got a BA in art myself, actually.'

I sit back down on the bed.

Hugh explains how the centre works. All the staff are social or mental-health workers. They believe that drug addiction is a result of family and environmental conditions.

'Addiction is a learned response,' he tells me. 'We think that, with the right treatment, it can be unlearned.'

That sounds simple enough. Except that I don't see myself as a drug addict. Joe, lying rattling in the next bed because he can't get his hands on any heroin, now Joe's a drug addict. I've used a lot of drugs, probably more than most people, but I'm not like him. Plus, I have no intention of putting a long-term brake on my drug use. Living without drink or drugs would be like living without my legs or my fingers. Unthinkable. Beyond my imagination.

Hugh was right when he said that this place isn't jail. There are no locks on the doors. I can go out. They give us money instead of making us work for it. There are outings, life story groups, and groups to discuss how you're feeling. I am given a questionnaire to fill in with a list of words along the left side. On the right side I have to write what these words mean to me. The words are Powerlessness, Hopelessness, Dishonesty . . .

I am confused. I don't know what they want me to write about Dishonesty. I turn to the bloke on my right and use the exam-cheating techniques I developed in school to throw a quick glance at his paper. I scribble a modified version of his answer in the box. That's what Dishonesty means to me.

For the first months I remain anxious. The adjustment from a jail regime to this liberal world frightens me. I've been eating alone in a cell for so long that I'm scared to take my meals in front of other people. I'm not sure how to behave. And I don't know how to relate to the other inmates without jail behaviour: that is, manipulation, threats or violence. Plus, for a long time now, it's been Dan and me against the world and now it's just me.

I gradually begin to relax and join in the life of the house. The social workers are like amiable if dysfunctional parents. But inmates' relationships are complex. Most are sleeping with each other. There's a complicated pattern of girlfriends and boyfriends and then, after a few weeks, it all changes round and some inmates are hurt and some are angry and the dynamics of the house are different for a while. Then we settle down for the next change. Vanessa, who has kept me supplied with hash through most of two jail sentences, comes to see me often. We even manage to sleep together. But I have girlfriends in the house as well. And the greatest of these is Jodie.

Jodie is a stunning black prostitute and crack addict. She is funny and cheerful and she laughs a lot and is nice to everyone. She is five years older than me but I quickly discover that underneath that giggling, easy-going Jamaican exterior is a deep sadness. Something about that sadness connects with an inner sadness of my own.

Jodie presents herself in a very sexual way: practically everything she says and does has a sexual subtext. She has been severely physically and sexually abused throughout her life and, now that she is addicted to crack, prostitution is the only career opportunity that will yield the kind of cash she needs to fund her habit. She is in rehab because, like every addict ever, she really wants to stop. Or just to take a break from the daily miseries of addiction. But everyone can see that Jodie's chances of recovery are slim. In fact, this place is more like respite care for her. Although she doesn't use in rehab, like most of us she's waiting for the day she gets out so that she can take drugs again.

Apart from Jodie, the best thing about rehab is the art block. I'm in there most of the time. Hugh works closely with me, discussing ideas, suggesting media. I do sketches, paintings and some work in clay but my new love is photography. At Hugh's suggestion I apply to The Prince's Trust for a grant to buy a good camera. With it I take pictures around Birmingham and some are accepted for an exhibition. My favourite is three tramps leaning against each other on a bench with their dog and their cider. You look at their faces and each one tells a story and you wonder how they got to be living out on the streets. Did they make a series of choices or a series of mistakes?

I am offered a photographic job. There is a big charity fashion event in Birmingham and I'm paid to take the official pictures. Jodie comes with me. She wears a black dress with tiny beads and looks fantastic. She is soon surrounded by alpha-males in black ties. I take pictures of the models and then a few snaps of the wealthy punters at the champagne reception afterwards. They're all dressed like the characters in *Dynasty*. When I've finished I go straight back to my darkroom. Jodie doesn't come with me. She stays there knocking back glass after glass of the free champagne. She reappears in rehab the next day, looking dishevelled and stinking of alcohol. Drunk is what we don't get in rehab. They throw her out.

When it's time for me to go, I head straight for the off-licence. We all do it. We've spent rehab discussing what we're going to take when we get out and not one of us has considered giving up for good. The kind-hearted but misguided social workers have tried hard to persuade us to change but, so far as I know, they haven't succeeded with any of us. We all regard our drug habits as manageable. For us, drugs are not a problem that needs to be solved.

However, I can't say rehab has been a complete waste of time. It's been a lot nicer than jail, I've met Jodie and I've done loads of artwork. And it has given me time to decide that I don't want to live like a bandit with Dan in Kidderminster any more. I know I don't want to spend the rest of my life hanging around the ugly housing estates where I was brought up, drinking and stealing. I make a conscious decision to get off the railway and change train.

I write to Daniel, who is still in jail, saying that I'm staying in Birmingham and changing my life. We'll certainly always be friends but my life's going to take a different course now. And I explain to Vanessa that I'm leaving her. She cries. Her sweet face crumples. She's spent the last few years visiting me in prison and now I'm out I'm telling her that I'm moving on.

'Why?' she asks, her face wet.

I can't look at her. I don't know how to explain that her destiny is one way and mine's another. I can't say that I don't want to be on the same train as her any more, that it's time for me to move on from a good, conventional shop assistant to someone much more exciting: a crack-addicted prostitute.

Chapter 19

A housing association offers me a flat in Birmingham. I like it here. I love the buzz of the city all around me. And, after my long period of abstinence, I'm ready to consume large quantities of drugs.

I make a beeline for Jodie, who has been out for a few weeks. I know that one of the first things we'll do together is smoke crack.

She has a tacky bedsit in a falling-down house on Murdock Road in falling-down Handsworth. The staircase has a thick carpet that smells rancid and the bedsit is dingy and almost empty. I can't say she actually lives here because the conventional idea of having a home doesn't fit in with Jodie's lifestyle: crack keeps things too hectic for that. She might sleep in crack houses, on the streets, in men's houses, cars, anywhere.

The bedsit seems to be where Jodie works. There's a pile of used condoms in the bin. The bed has a cover but no sheets or blankets. The walls are bare. The light bulb is bare. Otherwise there is just a fridge and a stereo.

Crack is a cocaine-derivative. It's a little stone, white, yellow or grey. I watch Jodie, naked, black and beautiful, make a pipe. She has a cigarette burning on top of the fridge at the end of the bed, and when there's enough ash she puts it onto the pipe. The pipe is a complicated little arrangement of broken mini-Bacardi bottle, Blu-tack, rubber band and foil. She flattens the ash and very carefully puts the crack on the top. Then she stands against the wall and lights it. She holds it with caution and great respect because this stuff is precious, more precious than gold, more precious than diamonds. She inhales. Her cheeks puff as she tries to hold the smoke in her mouth. Some of it escapes through her nose. Her head goes back against the wall. Her eyes are shut but I can see her eyeballs slide back, watch her twitching and fluttering inside those eyelids. She swallows the smoke in small breaths. Then, after two minutes, she comes back.

She is still high when she moves over to the fridge. I sit, naked, on the end of the bed, watching, waiting, anticipating, as, with great precision, she gradually remakes the pipe with ash and cocaine. I carry it slowly, slowly to the wall and turn round and lift it, carefully so that nothing can fall, to my mouth. I hold the lighter upside down and the pipe makes a little cackling sound, like a toothless laugh. I watch the crack melt like hot glass and the pipe gradually fill with brilliant white smoke. My eyes are fixed on it. Then I lift my fingers from the foil and inhale.

As I take in the smoke, my chest explodes. My hair stands on end. My pupils dilate and roll back in my head. My hands twitch. I can feel it all. I can feel my heart, my blood, I can feel a channel open up at the back of my head to my brain and then there is pleasure. Not like any other pleasure ever. It is the best sex, it is flying without an aeroplane, it is the joy of birth, it is a trip to the moon, it is winning the Olympics, it is a symphony, it is love, it is the most extreme happiness you can experience and then some more happiness besides. It is incomparable and to make it last I have to keep the smoke inside me, I have to breathe with my ears so none of it escapes through my mouth, I have to make sure I don't lose, dislodge or spill any of the crack in the pipe because losing it would be worse than losing life itself.

After about three minutes, when I'm blue for lack of oxygen I begin to feel the come-down. First it is just a small fissure in my happiness.

Then it gets wider and wider until there is an immense hole in my crack experience and I am a man falling without a parachute, flailing in the air, hanging, hanging onto thin air, trying to make the drug last a second, a moment longer.

But the come-down has begun and I am plummeting into utter despair and deep misery. Anxiety envelops me. Something awful is going to happen. The police are going to come and take me away. The devil is waiting for me. Disaster is around the corner, a disaster the size of a tidal wave, the world will end, my world will end, I hear voices telling me so. Anxiety becomes terror.

So this is the famous crack paranoia. Well now I understand everything about this drug. Crack is cruelty, crack is crime, crack can destroy everything. Take crack and you don't care about your spouse or your children or making money or your reputation, you don't care about anything any more except your high and you will rob, you will kill, you will commit any crime to get it.

We smoke some more but sooner or later, inevitably, there is no more crack. We face the come-down from which there is no relief. We are pranged. Pranged is the tuning fork that never stops vibrating. Pranged is the noise of two juggernauts hitting each other at speed on the motorway. Pranged is fingernails on metal dustbin lids. Pranged is your body and mind being cut open and exposed to everything sharp in the world.

Jodie gives me a Valium to help me cope with my misery. I am small and frightened like a baby and she holds me. She comes down talking, prophesying, doing her Jamaican ju-ju stuff. Then she gets down on the floor on all fours and begins to whimper. She is look-ing for dropped crumbs of crack, obsessively picking up anything that could be, might be, crack. God help her, she is even trying to smoke the fucking carpet. Finally, she washes out the pipe and pours the liquid onto a mirror, lights it, then tries to recycle the crack but the pathetic ghost she produces gives a tremble more than a high and maybe halts the come-down just a little and just for a minute after we've smoked it.

To manage the come-down I try sleeping, I try lying down, I try standing up, I try showering. The water cascades over me and feel-ing its touch as it runs down my body distracts me and for a moment it blocks out everything. It takes about ten minutes to get back down and then all I can think about is doing it again. And we do it again often. Soon, smoking crack with Jodie becomes a way of life.

It's a sexual drug but it is not an intimate drug. The only real intimacy is the clinginess of the come-down: I'm so on edge that I need a friend, and so does Jodie and we are bound together by this need.

But I have another life as well. I'm barely twenty years old and I've been put away for a few years and now I want some fun. Smoking crack with Jodie is an intense experience but you couldn't call it fun. Fun is what clubs are for. No sooner am I out of rehab than my brother is introducing me to the new underground club scene in Birmingham and to a group of his mates who love it.

The lads aren't exactly posh but they come from stable homes in Staffordshire. They're a good-looking bunch, the clubbing elite. They wear their hair long and designer clothes. One of them, Mark Downes, becomes a good friend immediately. He sells classic cars. Another, Neil Macey, is a DJ. He was running a record company when he was in his early twenties and he knows more about music than anyone I've met. He looks wild and dark but the others have jobs, real jobs, designing or selling, which means they actually go to work from Monday to Friday. I've never had mates who do that before. And they own nice cars and some have even started buying their own homes.

As soon as I meet them, I'm aware that my clothes don't look right. Since I'm just out of jail and then rehab, I have no idea what the look is and no money to buy it anyway. I wear a jumper I found for a few quid. It's dark, which is good. It has one stripe across it, which is bad. In fact, from the way the lads glance at it, I know it's very bad.

We go clubbing together. We sit somewhere close to the club's warm, beating heart. I am given a small, grey, speckled tablet called a dove. My first E. I take it. I hit the fucking roof.

Someone's unzipped my head and lifted my skull out. It's so powerful that for a minute my jaw locks and I can't move. Then I run out to the back and start to projectile vomit because what's happening inside my head is so amazing.

I am in a cloud of ecstasy euphoria. I love everyone. I love everything. I want to talk with Shane and all my new mates, I want to talk to everyone whether I know them or not, I want to socialise with at least one hundred people and I want them all to know that I love them. And the music is the 4:4 beat, which is primeval. It's been there all through history, that hypnotic rhythm. Acid house had the rhythm but now that ecstasy's the drug, acid house is diversifying into techno house, uplifting house, garage . . . Ecstasy music builds on the 4:4 beat. It's so solid that it catches you up and drives you along, keeping you stamping, keeping you enveloped in the warm base like you've come home. It makes me feel I can dance forever with my new mates. Because I love them. I put my arms up and sweat and close my eyes and feel nothing but love and I am practically having an evangelical experience. Does it matter that my dark jumper with the white stripe is not the look? No it does not, because I love everyone. This is brilliant. Where the fuck have I been? I should have been here! I love you! And you over there, I love you too!

I want to dance all night. I look at the lights on the dance floor, and take delight in their whiteness. I look at my brother and I am happy because I have a brother and we're all right, tight like we should be. Mark Downes is here. My friends surround me. Ecstasy is a celebration of life, unlike all the other drugs. It enhances the world. It is a social drug. It unites people, it ends gang warfare and football violence, it reminds us that love is what it's all about. It is something just for us, the Thatcher generation.

When the club closes we move on to another one, and then to a party and then it's almost Saturday afternoon. We sleep. When we wake up, it's time to get ready for Saturday night. We do it all again. And on Sunday night, it's over. The lads all have to be back at work on Monday morning.

My life soon fits into the Staffordshire lads' rhythm. Weekends are for partying and taking recreational drugs but when the others get back to their weekday jobs, my mind slowly dissolves on the comedown and I start on weekday crack with Jodie. She provides the drugs and they are so good that I am able to ignore the fact that she's slept with lots of dirty married men in order to buy them. I don't care what her job is. I don't care that the come-down is a miserable experience that robs life of its meaning. I don't care that we smoke it in sordid, dingy places. I don't care about the dangerous people we buy it from on the street. I only care about having more.

Back in rehab they told us that crack isn't a physically addictive drug like heroin. Your body doesn't need to keep taking crack. But it's psychologically addictive. Once your mind has been there, it will want to return again and again and again. And mine does. Not, of course, that I regard myself as an addict. I look at Jodie and I know *that's* addiction.

I become a whole new Mark at the weekends and for my new life I need money. So I get a job in a city centre petrol station. It's an underground petrol station and I work overnight. I watch the madness of the nocturnal world from my glass booth and then, going home on the bus at dawn, I see the city wake up. I treble my wages by buying stolen credit cards from an Asian mob and ringing up cash sales to them.

So now I can afford to reinvent myself. My clothes go dark and tonal. I wear black Caterpillar boots and a pair of deep-blue canvas trousers and a blue rollneck. I throw away the jumper with the white stripe. Neil starts to make jokes about it and that makes me feel like one of them. Except I'm not. They all grew up together and I'm a recent arrival. They have good jobs and nice cars while I work in a petrol station and don't even have a driving licence. They have no criminal convictions; I've had two jail sentences. I want to be like them but I never can be because something in my world view, maybe the streak of creativity that took me to art college, makes me fundamentally different.

One weekend, I'm clubbing with the lads and when the club closes we all get into cars. Neil knows there's a party in the middle of a field somewhere and everyone is off to look for it.

It seems to me that hundreds of us are looking in fleets of cars. But only a few of us arrive. Everyone else travels round and round in circles and then goes home but we drive along lanes, up and down hills, into the darkness like people going nowhere. And then we stop and leave the car by a field. We've arrived in Nowhere.

In the countryside the air smells different: clearer and thinner so you can pick up every small scent – a plant, a tree, an animal that has passed this way. My perception is heightened. I'm looking, I'm listening, I'm straining, because I know that something is out there. Overhead it's dark, really dark, not city dark. I look up and see the stars.

We stumble on down the lane past some other cars and then we turn a corner and almost immediately we can feel the music through the ground. We can feel the bass line. It's exciting, as though something really special is about to happen. We walk towards the noise and gradually we can hear more and more and before I can even see the lights of the party I'm buzzing. There's something new and different about the music. It's based on acid house but it's deeper, fresher and more melodic than anything I've heard before. Its sound is literally hypnotic. I am so amazed by it that I have to stand still for a moment. This is something new. It is pure. It has a special clarity.

When at last we see the party it is beautiful. You can tell even from a distance. There's a big marquee in the middle of a field and maybe three hundred flickering shadows walking around. We are drawn to them, drawn like moths to the big, shining marquee, our eyes fixed on it. The sound is loud now. It throbs through my whole body, the bass coming up from the earth, the high notes penetrating my head. And when we pull open the flaps it surrounds us. I am in a new world.

Along one side is a bank of speakers. The DJ is tiny in a landscape of big technology that is square and hard and solid like gravestones. Everything else is moving. All the people are dancing together and they're all part of one huge organism, held together by the 4:4 beat. Their faces are distorted, their eyes are rolling, they've all taken ecstasy and they're dancing inside their own heads but together they're a sea of humanity, waving together, every tongue and arm and head and leg part of a whole, driven by the beat. We take ecstasy and join in and then we belong here too, we let the beat drive us, and it drives us to the edge of the earth.

I hand round some microdots. Microdots are acid, but they're about a quarter of the size of a lighter flint. They intensify what is already an extraordinary experience. I am welded to the ground. I am close to delirium. The light, the colour and the people are now transcendental in their beauty and I don't know where the party ends and my hallucinations start.

My arms are hurting. Why? I see a man making mysterious symmetrical arm movements over and over again as though he's painting a huge canvas, sending up small clouds of dust when he sweeps his fingers against the ground. He paints the air for hours, and I realise I've been doing the same. Later, my ankles hurt. Why? I look down and see that my feet are twisted inwards and I've been dancing on my ankles. How long for? Maybe five minutes. Maybe five hours. This is trance dancing. I'm in a trance.

There's a girl across the marquee. She dances with almost breath-taking beauty. I look at her and she's saying: Come over here. And I say to her, without moving my lips or speaking, just by thinking: No, it'll ruin everything if I do and I can't ruin this. She knows what I'm saying and smiles. We have communicated without speech. Ecstasy and acid enable you to see things you wouldn't normally see. And you can't hide anything. If you're hating, then your hate shows. If you're creative, then it's obvious. Sadness, joy, anger, it's all there for anyone to see because your mind's naked.

When the sun comes up, the light changes and the atmosphere is different. The pace slows and there is a new melody to the music. All the notes are separated. Each is attached to a vertebra on my spine so that if I move my head up or down I can feel different sounds.

Everyone here is like me. Young and beautiful, our faces shining with life. Girls' clothes fold around them with a special, easy grace. They dance wildly or fluidly or slowly but never awkwardly. They are travellers, punks, hippies and many of them would be complete freaks anywhere else but here their wildness is right and lovely.

Silk is stretched from pole to pole in the marquee in many different colours and, with the dawn light shining through the silk and around the dancers, the scene is sumptuous. I belong here. This is my place. I'm meant to be here. Not clubbing because clubs are exclusive but this place and these people are inclusive and they're including me. When a lad drives a tractor through the marquee, pretending to be a farmer, we laugh at him until we cry. Because he's no farmer, he's one of us.

The music is deep house, fresh from America, and after a day and a night the party is still so magical that I hate it. I wish the experience away because I know that it is going to change my life and not just change it but ruin it. And I know that this is my destiny and I have no choice.

Chapter 20

I'm on the bus into central Birmingham to find Jodie. It's a cold winter's Sunday night and I've been dancing at clubs and then a free party since Thursday. I've finished now. The lads have all gone back to their homes in Staffordshire for a good night's sleep and recovery before work tomorrow. As for me, I can't stop. If the recreational drugs are over, I'll find Jodie and smoke some crack instead. I want Jodie. And right now she's visiting her mum, a retired pastor, who lives on a hideous concrete downtown housing estate.

I'm not feeling too well inside my head. Maybe I caned it a bit hard this weekend. In the pub, Jodie and I bump into Beano, a big black drug dealer. He knows me because I was in jail with him so, to the astonishment of all the other Jamaicans, he greets the white man warmly.

I am surprised when he presses something into my hand. A big stone of crack.

'No really. Take it,' he insists. 'For old times' sake.'

I thank him and we go back to Jodie's mum's flat. Jodie is almost dancing through the concrete landscape. But I'm suspicious, angry even.

'Why would Beano give me this?' I keep demanding.

'Because he likes you! He likes you so much he's given you the sweetie!' cries Jodie happily, still dancing, half laughing. That's her word for crack. She calls it the sweetie.

I shake my head.

'No. Wrong. It's not because he likes me. It's because he wants me to get addicted. He's given me a stone to have power over me.'

'What power's he got? We're going to smoke it together, you and me!' says Jodie, taking hold of my hand. I put the stone in my pocket and shake her away.

She says seductively: 'We'll go back to your flat and . . .'

'No.'

She looks at me uneasily. I do not respond to her attempts to talk.

Her mother is watching television in the lounge, surrounded by Jamaican mementos and pictures. We ignore her. I go to the bathroom.

'What you doing?' demands Jodie. She is right behind me. She is umbilically attached to the stone.

'I'm going to show him who's got the power round here,' I say. I still don't feel good. I might be sick. My eyes are hurting. The blood is pumping so fast round my body it almost deafens me as it passes my ears.

'Stop,' screams Jodie. She doesn't know what I'm going to do yet, but her guess is right. 'Stop, stop, fucking stop that fucking mad thing, that crazy thing you're doing, stop, stop.'

Jodie grabs at the stone as I throw it into the toilet but she misses. Splash. It's in the toilet bowl. Jodie lunges at it. I hold her back. Then she tries to stop me from flushing it away and by now she's screaming and sobbing hysterically. I pull the handle and then I hold Jodie still so she won't dive after it into the pan, down the pipes, into the sewers of Birmingham. We watch it go, transfixed. I have an acute sensation of loss as it whirls round a few times and then disappears.

For Jodie, this is hell. It's a miser watching the wind carry twenty-pound notes away, it's a miner dropping gold nuggets down a chasm, it's the disappearance down the pan of life itself. She falls to the floor shrieking and sobbing hysterically. I look down at her. I want to kick her. Where have I felt this before? Oh yes. At home, when I was a kid. Dad stands still as a rock while at his feet Mum shrieks and writhes. I watch Jodie with cool detachment. I do ask myself how it is that I've turned into Dad and Jodie's turned into Mum. Then I look up and see Jodie's own mother standing in the door, her round black face confused, questioning.

After a terrible argument we catch the bus home. Jodie isn't talking to me. We smoke a spliff since we're on the top deck of the bus alone.

I start to feel terrible. I close my eyes and I'm not there for a few minutes.

'Are you all right?' asks Jodie anxiously. She's staring at me.

I put my hand to my face and it feels wet. I look at my fingers. They have blood on them. Where is it coming from?

Jodie starts giggling, nervously and uncontrollably. She keeps glancing at me then turning away again. I conclude I don't look right. I certainly don't feel right. I feel I could internally combust. The sense of something bursting out of me is so strong that if I could get the bus window wide open I'd jump out right now just to release it.

I stagger down the stairs, teeth rattling, face wet. The driver stops the bus. He climbs out of his cab and walks towards me, concerned.

'Listen, mate, you need to get to hospital,' he says.

Jodie assures him I only live half a mile away but she's a giggling wreck and he ignores her.

'The taxis stop over there for a fag and a tea.' He points to a small shack by the side of the road. 'One of them'll take you to hospital.'

But I know I can't go. Hospitals sound too much like authority to me and I avoid authority.

I stagger off the bus, aided by Jodie, who is still laughing uncontrollably. She's just nervous but her laughter adds another surreal element to a surreal world. However, she takes me into the taxi drivers' shack where a driver is roasting himself in front of a two-bar electric fire. I stare at my face in a small, cracked mirror. There's blood everywhere. It's coming out of my eyes.

The driver says he'll take me straight to A&E.

I protest and Jodie protests too amid whoops of laughter. So the taxi driver takes me home instead and Jodie rolls me up in a quilt and I remember nothing more until morning. I wake up and Jodie's gone and I feel sure that she's left me for dead. She didn't want to be here when I died.

My eyes are still bloody but otherwise I feel okay. What can have caused this problem? I've had ten Es between Thursday and Sunday, some weed and some coke. Maybe there was a bad batch of Es. You can never tell with ecstasy. It's made from a chemical compound called MDMA, which has hundreds of little brothers and sisters. Because of its complicated family tree you have no way of knowing exactly what you're taking and what it's been made from.

I am frightened enough after the incident on the bus to wonder, for the first time, what all these drugs are doing to me. I decide to give up Es. My resolution lasts a whole week. During that week, whenever I close my eyes, I see the hideous image of the great grey stone of crack circulating in the toilet and then getting sucked down the pan. Why did I do it? I am plagued by a sense of loss and regret, as though someone close to me died on Sunday.

Another weekend comes and another free party, and, of course, more Es. After that first amazing experience in the marquee in the field, I have gone to every free party I can and they're all as good as the first. The collective name for the group who runs the parties is DIY, although since the group is innately anarchic, no one actually runs anything. DIY means Do It Yourself, and that means make your own rules and do things your own way. Or maybe it stands for Devil In You. No one really profits from the parties: they are by the people for the people. They go on for days and have no discernible beginning or end. The music is electronic, spawned by acid house, but it has its own deep, distinctive qualities, especially its bass. Tens or hundreds of us congregate, and whatever binds us together thickens and swells into something that is identifiable and unique to us, right here, right now. DIY is for us. We are Thatcher's children, grown now and leaving the 1980s behind.

For an earlier generation, music was about live bands. For kids like me, the DJ is god. He must choose the right music at the right time. He reads the crowd and takes them on a journey. He is the Pied Piper and we are the children and we follow. A good DJ will make you dance, then slow you down, he will lead you to happiness and through doors into the dark, he will relax you and excite you and then show you the light. Each night is different and each night is a living work of art that cannot be replicated or reproduced: even if you record it, you can't recapture it because the art can only occur at that time and in that place. And some of the DIY DJs create art that is the best ever.

Gradually I get to know these people. There's Simon DK, the granddaddy of the set-up. He's thin as a walking stick but he's attractive, because you can see his character in his face, sweet and endlessly generous. Rick and Pete, otherwise known as Digs and Whoosh, have the same open-handed, anarchic attitude to money and life. Rick is very tall, a physics graduate, while Pete, also a graduate, is tiny, only about five foot. They usually play together, the contrast in their heights looking freakish. Then there's a Sheffield DJ called Callum, another called Jack with dreads who, amazingly, comes from Kendal although I didn't know him there, Cookie the redhead, Harry, who drove the tractor through the marquee at the first party and made us all laugh, his girlfriend Barbara and two girl DJs, Pip and Emma. They're mostly graduates, some from Nottingham University, and they're attractive, musical, creative, chaotic and clever. They don't ask questions or make judgements, they know how to live for now. My social life becomes centred round the free party scene.

Tonight DIY is playing a Birmingham club, something they do only occasionally. It is called Attic and there's a large gay contingent. We have taken microdots. As I dance I think I am a Zulu warrior with a sword and a spear. I clip the floor as I trip. I dance. I dance like a maniac.

Suddenly I smell something strange that shouldn't be here. Cow shit. Cow shit? The music intensifies and gains a new clarity that jolts me. I look up and I become aware that, behind the DJ and his bank of speakers, a huge dark figure is looming. The DJ is maybe six feet tall. The great shadow figure behind him is at least nine foot. I see the outline clearly. It is in the shape of a man, its hair curly. It has horns. I look all round, hoping someone else will have seen it, but the dancers are caught up in the intensity of the music.

I turn back to the stage and the huge shadow figure, part human with horns, is still standing over us all. I stare hard. It is a sinister figure but something about its presence comforts me. I think: I know you. I'm one of yours and you'll take care of me. He is old, as old as man, perhaps older.

When I look again, the dark shadow has gone.

Going home, I remember how, all those years ago, I crept downstairs and saw Jack Frost sitting on the garden wall, looking back at me from his ice crystal eyes. I never doubted it was Jack or that I saw him.

Who is the shadow in the Attic? When the others are all back at work, I go to the Birmingham public library. I find a book of Greek mythology because the librarian tells me these are among the most ancient of legends, and I know the shadow I saw was the most ancient of figures. I read about Pan, god of music and remote hillsides, who appears when clear music is heard, Pan's pipes. Pan used to frequent Attica, where the young men exercised their intellectual prowess and their brawn.

The connection with the Attic club and its gay followers, the way the shadow appeared when the music reached a certain clarity, the picture in the book of a man-like creature with horns, it all makes me sure that I have seen the god Pan and that he has a presence at our parties.

Later in the winter I am at a DIY free party in an ancient stone barn near Sheffield on the snowy dales. The throb of the bass seems to give the place a heat of its own. I am dancing, feeling the music, when suddenly it reaches a new pitch of clarity. Pan's pipes. I know it from the sudden intensity of the room and that melody which has bubbled up through the tangle of sound. I look up and there he is. His great shadow appears behind Simon DK, who looks like a small cardboard cut-out with his sound machines. Pan is faceless but I know it is him.

I have taken acid but I am not euphoric and I am seeing something that touches my heart. I look around. The whole room has reached a stage of delirium and intensity. Everyone is locked up inside their own crazy dance. The music is so piercing and beautiful that I could cry. I look back to Pan and for a few minutes he is still there, and although he is sinister and mysterious I know that he is smiling on his children and he is our friend and protector. And then he is gone. He leaves me feeling warm and cared for. I am part of something ancient that only a few people in just a few generations have experienced. I become sure that these wild, beautiful, border-less parties are from some timeless fable. I feel privileged to be here and I know that I belong, with these people, with the ancient god Pan.

Chapter 21

On Sunday night, back in Birmingham, Jodie is making a pipe. I watch her. My mind moves from that wild outdoor place where I've spent the weekend to the small, dark place I'm in now.

When we've had all the crack Jodie's brought, I need some more. I always need more, but this time my need is acute. I must have some more. After the incredible experience of the free party, I can't face the crack come-down. I try to withstand it but it's too much after the acid/ecstasy euphoria of the last few days that has made me feel whole again.

'Go on, then,' I tell her. 'Get some more.'

She knows what I'm asking her to do. Go out on the street and turn a trick or two.

She gets dressed. Jodie doesn't have to dress like a tart to attract men. She just pulls on her jeans and looks beautiful. She saunters out onto the street. She goes round the corner to the park. I wait. I shower. I wait some more. My throat is dry, coated with ash from the crack we smoked. The silence in the flat is aggravating the deepest fears and darkest thoughts of the come-down. Now I suspect, no, I'm convinced, that Jodie will cheat on me. She'll have three men and tell me there were only two, or she'll get into a car with someone and keep it a secret. Then she'll come back with a lot less crack than she can afford. Or she'll buy the crack and she won't give me half.

This possibility seizes me with a physical force, as though a police-man has crept up and arm-locked me. I swing round. No one there. I swing back again. No one. Just silence. I know this is the monkey's paw: my name for the crack come-down feeling that someone's going to grab you any moment. Into the silence drips my paranoia. My fear of the police. My fear of betrayal. Jodie is monstrous, greedy, addicted and a bitch. She is certainly planning to cheat me.

I'm about to go and check on her when I hear her downstairs. She has a punter. I listen, making sure he's not causing any problems. Then the man leaves quietly. Soon there's another punter. Then, a few minutes later Jodie goes out to score. Every part of every crack transaction is dangerous, and not only because of the police. Negotiations are dangerous. Handing over the money is dangerous. Realising that they've given you polo mints instead of crack and knowing there's nothing you can do about it because you'll be knifed, that's dangerous. Anyone taking a street drug is vulnerable, because they're buying it, because they use it. A lot of crack dealers, from old Jamaicans down to the young entrepreneurial type in his black BMW, try not to use it. They try only to touch the stuff when they're selling it. As long as they can hold out, they have an advan-tage. I hate them for their power.

When she comes back, I'm ready for Jodie, ready for crack.

She takes off her clothes, I cross-examine her on how much she earned and how much she spent and I count the condoms and when I'm satisfied that she hasn't cheated then she makes a pipe at last.

I wouldn't call myself a drug addict. Junkies are people who inject and live on the streets. But there are times when I notice I'm caning it harder than the other lads. I'm thinner than them, and paler, and I don't look like part of the same tribe. The Staffordshire crowd only take recreational drugs and they're partying a bit less these days.

Mark Downes looks at me closely.

'You want to slow down a bit, mate,' he says.

I blink back at him. 'Huh?'

I don't want to apply the brakes. I always want more. I want the party never to end. I don't manage my drug use, I don't want to, I want whatever's available. My new friends, travellers and party people, are similarly chaotic. Their lives have no order or structure. They are anarchic.

Increasingly, the trailers parked at some parties have crack in them. Heavy drugs are creeping into the free party scene. And now that we're smoking crack, some of us are smoking heroin to ease the come-down. Smoking, not injecting. We use heroin regularly, maybe smoking it for a few days until we get all the warning signals of a mild heroin rattle: the withdrawal shakes and aches. Valium or a few drinks usually sees that off, but not without pain. One way of getting through it is to promise yourself another toot of heroin in a while.

It is Christmas, a period I've never much liked. Here I am at my brother's house. Shane and his girlfriend had taken acid and were already tripping when Jodie and I arrived and now we're drinking and lounging around. What could be more normal at Christmas? There's a comedy sketch on TV: a turkey keeps jumping out of the oven and everyone laughs a lot. That's normal, too. Except one thing isn't normal. I'm going crazy.

I sit, gripping the arms of the chair, watching the screen, horrified by the jumping turkey, horrified by everything. My mind is diving into places it usually only goes under the deepest, darkest influence of drugs. But tonight, although I've been drinking as usual, I haven't taken any drugs.

Voices talk to me. They threaten me. They laugh at me. Something evil is here, it is sinister, it is penetrating my world. I start to shake. I shout. I scream.

Eyes swivel from the TV screen in surprise.

'What are you on?' asks Shane mildly. Jodie looks sulky: so Mark's been taking crack without me.

I can barely hold myself together, the feeling's getting stronger, it is taking me over, something wicked is fighting for my life.

'It's the devil!' I shout. 'Can't you see that the devil's coming to take me?'

They stare at me. Crack talk. They've heard it all before.

'Calm down,' says Shane's girlfriend.

She's certainly planning something. She's going to tell the devil where I am. I grab her and arm-lock her. Shane jumps up.

'Mark, what the fucking hell's wrong?'

But I'm too shaky and scared to answer. This is the worst crack come-down ever and I haven't taken any crack.

I shout at them all. I shout warnings and obscenities. When I go quiet for a while, everyone ignores me. I have to get out of here, the feelings are so strong now that I cannot contain them, cannot contain my fears. I go home to my empty flat, but this time it gives me no sanctuary. There is something monstrous and evil here. It is lurking, hiding, but it is here because it knows what I am. Screaming, shouting, I throw my belongings into black plastic bags. Sobbing, I yell at the thing to go away. But it's still here. And it knows what I am.

'You are mine, you are mine,' laughs the devil. 'Evil bastard. Evil bastard like me.'

And now I know what has happened. I have touched the sun and been burnt. At DIY, in the beautiful, crazy chaos which is so wild that Pan sometimes appears, laughing with approval, I touched the sun and now the devil has come for me because no one is allowed to touch the sun and live.

Paranoia grips me, it holds every pore tight, it both paralyses me and sends me skittering all over the flat. My head is exploding with fear and anger. I am crazy. Drugs have sometimes taken me here but now I have found my own way into hell without a pill or a snort or a smoke.

I need help. Someone must help me. Shane's tripping, Jodie's useless – look at the way she just kept laughing when my eyeballs bled – all my mates are doing family things because it's Christmas and I'm here by myself going insane.

My isolation makes me cry. I am scared. I am alone. I am mad. Who will help me? Then I remember. There's one person who's supposed to care about me more than anyone else. One person who's supposed to wipe my tears and calm my fears.

It's hard to get to a phone booth. There are diabolic shadows everywhere in the night streets, waiting for me, jumping out at me, trying to pull me into their darkness. I shout and swear as I walk. I run to evade them, sometimes I hide. The door of the booth feels too heavy, as if great forces are pulling against me.

Inside the air is unnaturally dead. My hands are shaking so much that it takes a couple of tries to dial her number.

'Mum? It's Mark.'

She is surprised to hear from me. It's a long time since we've spoken and when I explain to her about touching the sun she goes quiet. The devil, I say, has been trying to catch up with me all this time and finally he's succeeded. Now that's something she understands. Mum's been on nodding terms with the devil for many years and when it comes to ranting about him she's always at the ready.

Her voice is comforting. The old platitudes I've heard all my life, about Jehovah watching me and loving me, about eternal life for those who believe, sound good tonight. I listen. I believe.

When I make my way back to the flat, I open and close every cupboard again and again, check all the corners, make sure the devil isn't hiding behind the curtains or under the sink. I roll up the rugs. I throw more things into boxes. I cry.

I am very frightened when there is a knock at the door. I turn out the lights. Cautiously I sidle up to the window and peer out. Two black people in suits, a man and a lady, carrying books. They have the unmistakable air of Jehovah's Witnesses. My mum must have sent them. I let them in and they open a Bible at the sixty-first psalm.

'Hear my cry, oh God . . .'

They talk in low, soothing voices. When they are gone, I won't put down the Bible. I recite the psalm over and over like a mantra. The next day Mum arrives with a friend from the Witnesses. The friend talks to me quietly while Mum puts my bin bags in the car.

On the journey, my mother's presence seems strange. Who is she? She looks like the mother I remember, perhaps a bit older and rounder. Or is she really the devil? I shake and sweat. I need some drugs but I'm scared to take any because I'm having the worst drugs experience ever without touching a single one.

We head north-west. The city streets and tower blocks that have been my landscape for so long are behind me. The motorway stretches ahead endlessly. Then at last we are driving through Kendal, the grey town in the grey rain, and I am fourteen again.

We stop outside a small house. It is a gatehouse and from it a drive leads to a distant gothic stone mansion on the hillside where the devil might live, although Mum explains that it's her employer's home and she's his housekeeper.

Bethany is here. She's fifteen but she still seems like a little kid to me. Not that I notice her. Not that I notice Mum or anyone or anything much. I am, after all, mad.

Jodie and I have many anxious phone conversations. She misses me. She wants to be with me. She wants to stop being a crack addict and get clean, too. If I can leave drugs behind me in the Lake District, so can she. And within a few days, she is on her way.

Mum and Bethany are taken aback by the arrival of a black crackhead prostitute. There aren't many of them in the Lake District. In fact, there probably aren't any others. Besides, the house is very small. However, they try to be understanding. They know that we are strung out and withdrawing and, as good Jehovah's Witnesses, they see the distress of others as an opportunity. Whole groups of church members work hard on converting me and Jodie. Since we both had childhoods that were steeped in the fight between good and evil, they are speaking a language we understand. We clutch at the straws they offer us and agree to study regularly with the Witnesses and even attend meetings.

Life in the tiny gatehouse is hard for all of us. Jodie and I take the place over. We scarcely notice the presence of the original occupants because we are so obsessed by the absence of crack. We are on a no-crack diet and to cope with this we compensate by drinking and taking industrial quantities of sleeping tablets. We are angry, volatile, argumentative and sometimes violent.

'I don't know you,' says Mum sadly when I shout at her and shove her aside one day. 'Who are you, Mark?'

Bethany is bewildered by us. She and Mum are stuck to the walls. They turn into ghosts while we dominate every room. They are scared of Jodie and scared of me and they look white-faced and tired.

Each week I visit an elderly couple to study the Bible and talk about eternal life. They are kind. Their philosophy is comforting.

With the help of prescription drugs and the steadying influence of these Witnesses, I begin to feel safe again. The voices inside my head stop.

After a few weeks Mum comes back from work in tears. The GP who is prescribing drugs for us has turned out to be friends with her employer. Over a glass of port the doctor has let slip that his friend's housekeeper has a pair of drug addicts in the gatehouse. Mum is sacked. She has lost her home and her job.

We all move, Mum and Bethany to a flat in Kendal, me to a house-share on the edge of town, and Jodie to a bedsit in Penrith where she takes a job in a supermarket and continues to study with the Jehovah's Witnesses.

I am still not well enough to work. I try to paint. I sell a few pictures. I rig up a darkroom. And inside me is a deep fear, an uncontrollable sadness, because I know for sure that the devil is in me. I get drunk as a skunk, often finding myself in the morning on some cold hillside with a bottle of wine and no memory of getting there. But I am recovering, slowly. I can feel myself stabilising.

As soon as I am capable, I head south for a DIY free party. I immerse myself in the music, the drugs, the people, the freakishness. I am happy here. I am happy to see everyone. I don't want the party ever to end.

'Are you okay?' people say, looking at me uncertainly.

'Fine,' I tell them. 'Just fine.'

When the party's over and my head's out of order again, I go back up to Kendal and resume a regular life of prescription drugs and Jehovah's Witnesses. As soon as I'm feeling better, I head off for another party. But maybe because the drugs we're using are now stronger and more plentiful, maybe because music's moving on, even the free parties are changing. They were momentous but now their moment is passing. In my heart I recognise this but I don't want it to happen, I don't want time to pass, I don't want to get older, I want fun. And there is still a lot of fun.

I go clubbing with Neil in Liverpool and then Birmingham and we end up at a DIY free party in Sherwood Forest near Nottingham. Everyone is off their heads. For me, clubbing and partying has so far lasted three days and three nights. I am incapable of managing my drug use. Because I don't want to. I want to immerse myself fully in the experience of the party. Then I'll recover when I get back to Kendal.

By the time we arrive in Sherwood Forest, my head has disintegrated. In Neil's car on the way here I've had pills and coke and Special Brew and a whole handful of strong brown speed but I can still appreciate the beauty of the forest. Smokescreen, another free party outfit, has a tarpaulin stretching through the trees with lights hanging everywhere from branches. Their DJ is up on scaffolding. Deeper in the forest is a big circular pit with a huge fire in the middle. People sit on grass seats. On the hilltop is the DIY tent with a wall of speakers and an invisible DJ. People wander around between sounds.

Neil walks through the trees with me. He was probably born at a party. His life is parties. We see a couple of friends sitting on a fence like kids, talking.

'This place is amazing,' says Neil. 'I haven't tripped in ages, but tonight I'm going to.'

'I'll have one with you,' I say. Well, I'm not known for hanging back.

The girl on the fence holds out her hand and in it is acid.

'American,' she tells us.

It is arranged in a square on her palm. It is painted in Celtic knotwork with brilliant purples and golds. The design is both intricate and beautiful. I've never seen acid like it.

I look at this beautiful drug and, with speed-fuelled aggression, grab it out of her hand and swallow it.

She stares at me. Neil stares at me. Everyone stares at me.

'What you're going to get,' says the girl slowly, 'serves you right for being greedy.'

'It was four small squares, mate, not just one,' says Neil helpfully.

Within minutes, I am out of it. I can't enjoy the music, I can't communicate with anyone: speech escapes me. I sit on the hill between the two sounds, DIY in one ear, Smokescreen in the other, and somehow the two meet in the middle and I blow my mind. I can feel it. I have gone over the edge of sanity. I don't have arms and legs and I'm not Mark Johnson or a person at all, I'm gone, so far gone that I'm not even scared. I'm not anything.

The sun comes up and I scan the party madness. The flames of the fire, the hippies with dreads down to their knees, the elderly speed freaks dancing half-naked, the hanging lights, the travellers, the colours, the flowing dresses. And I know that, wherever the edge is, I've gone over it.

When I get back up to Kendal I am still numb. I've had ecstasy, speed, acid, coke, Special Brew, weed, MDMA powder. I've had sleep deprivation, virtually no food, plus an overwhelming party experience. And now I can barely function. I am referred to a psychiatrist by the GP when I explain that my eyes are headlights and I can't shine them anywhere but the ground. The psychiatrist gives me more legal drugs to help me control my illegal drug experience. I don't know how else to escape from myself.

I break all contact with my clubbing and DIY mates for a while. Jodie is my comfort and support, and my occasional contact with the Jehovah's Witnesses is my drugs rehab because this is the only kind of rehab here. Jodie and I see each other whenever we can. Neither of us belongs here. We are both exiles.

Chapter 22

When Jodie rings my doorbell and suggests we spend a weekend in Manchester, I agree. I know what she means. I'm a radio and my antenna is tuned to drugs. Jodie's an addict and she's been in Penrith obsessing about crack all month and now the obsession is seeping out of her pores, I can almost see it. She's just been paid and I know that we're going to spend her wages.

We catch a train, check into a hotel in Piccadilly and then take a cab to the parks in Moss Side that are teeming with crack dealers.

We score well because we have her entire month's wages to spend. Then we take the drugs back to the hotel with us and we binge. We smoke crack and come down with Valium, brandy or heroin from Friday until Sunday night without even stopping to sleep. And then, quietly, ashamedly, without saying a word on the train home, we resume our godly lives in Kendal.

Next month, we do it again. And the month after that.

We're in a big Manchester hotel and we've got back from scoring and the air is thick with anticipation. In our faceless, characterless room, Jodie strips off and gets busy making a crack pipe. We've lined the door with towels so that the sweet, synthetic smell of our smoke can't escape. And on the bed is all our paraphernalia, including some heroin that's been melted onto foil ready to chase the dragon when we're coming down later.

We each have a smoke. Jodie's busy making the next pipe. I'm in my shorts at the end of the bed. I'm still coming down, and am in that shaky, paranoid, nervy state when voices in my head threaten me. I try to control them by breathing slowly and keeping very still. Outside, I hear something.

I say: 'Listen!'

Jodie scowls at me. I make a sign for her not to move.

'Listen! Can you hear it?'

I'm sure I can hear whispering.

'Oh here we fucking go again,' says Jodie irritably.

'I'm not paranoid! I can hear something!'

Jodie's angry now. She pouts at me.

'Fuck off, you're pranged,' she says and she starts to smoke. I can understand her aggravation. Who wants their high ruined by someone else's coming-down paranoia? Except, this isn't paranoia. I can really hear something. Or can I? Crack fudges the line between justified fears and paranoid fears and you can be one hundred per cent wrong when you're one hundred per cent sure that someone's outside. Except, I'm sure someone really is outside.

I go over to the door to listen. Jodie's getting upset. If she wasn't feeling paranoid before, she is now.

She finishes her circular breathing and doesn't move as she comes down but I can see she's all-over edgy and angry with me.

'Someone's whispering out there,' I report. She doesn't believe me, but she's scared now.

It's difficult to hear anything because there's some kind of aircraft flying low outside. But I listen hard and then, in the corridor right outside the room, I hear it. An unmistakable indicator of police presence. I rush back over to Jodie.

'They're here. The fucking police. They're here, I heard their radio crackle . . .'

At that moment, the noise outside the window grows to a crescendo. Bff bff bff bff bff . . . It sounds like a helicopter. Jodie has turned into a statue but now I rush to the other side of the room where the curtains are billowing weirdly. In an insane show of bravado I throw them open and a huge white light shines down on me from the sky. The helicopter noise is deafening. The light is blinding. It's like a scene from a war movie. Fuck it, the police must think there's a couple of big international drug dealers in here instead of just Jodie and me.

We stare at each other. She's pranged. I'm pranged. This is paranoia run amok.

At that moment there's more noise. Bam bam bam bam bam. The door! I hurl myself back across the room past Jodie's motionless body, take a deep breath, pull away the towels and fling it open.

Not one, but an entire crowd of policemen stands outside. I am aware that the room behind me is blue with smoke and the distinctive, pungent, sweet aroma of crack. Jodie is naked, apparently frozen, with a crack pipe actually in her hand. And all over the bed lie enough drugs to land us in jail for a long time. So we're fucked now.

At least ten policemen are staring in.

'I'm sorry to disturb you, sir,' says one of them. 'An escaped suspect is believed to be on the roof outside your room.'

I'm so high that even my voice is high.

'Yeah!' I squeak.

'Would you mind if I come in and have a look through your window?'

I hold the door open and the policeman steps in. With incredible presence of mind I walk ahead of him and flick the bedcovers. It looks as though I'm modestly covering Jodie's nakedness but actually I'm covering all the drugs on the bed. I even manage to hide the crack pipe that is still apparently stuck to the fingers of the unmoving Jodie.

'I'm sorry, miss, for this disturbance,' says the officer politely. Jodie is unable to respond.

He goes to the window and throws open the curtains and surveys the roof, helped by the light of the helicopter that is still hovering deafeningly overhead. He says a few words over his radio and then turns to me.

'Okay, sir, thank you very much, we won't be accessing the roof from here,' he says after a minute. 'Apologies for bothering you.'

He joins his mates in the corridor, all of whom have been peering in throughout. I close the door behind him. The footsteps in the
corridor go away. The helicopter moves off. After a few minutes
there is silence. Jodie is still paralysed.

We don't talk. We don't look at each other. We don't do anything.

Finally I say: 'That's it for me. I'm finished. No more crack for
me, not tonight, not ever.'

I pick up the cockle, the foil with the heroin on, to calm down
the madness inside me. I smoked a pipe of pure paranoia and as soon
as I finished the police were inside my head and outside the room.
How can I ever take the stuff again without experiencing hideously
heightened fears? And if I have any more tonight, those fears will
escalate out of all control.

Jodie very slowly unlocks her body and her brain.

She speaks. She says: 'I'm not stopping.'

'But when the police have finished catching this escaped guy,
they'll be back. They all smelt the crack.'

'I'm not stopping,' says Jodie.

'You'll get more and more pranged and more and more paranoid.
Have some of the brown, that's what you need now.'

'I'm not stopping,' says Jodie. Well, she is a crackhead.

I fall asleep and she carries on smoking. She wakes me up frequently for reassurance.

'Leave me alone,' I tell her. 'I just want to get up tomorrow and
forget it all happened.'

But Jodie is terrified and getting more terrified every minute.
She keeps grabbing hold of me.

'Don't go to sleep, Maaaaaark. Pleeeeeease.'

'Stop smoking that stuff and you'll be all right and you'll sleep
too.'

'Please don't leave me!'

She pushes me and pulls me, sobbing and crying hysterically. I
open my eyes and stare into her face and I see that fear has turned
her into an old woman. She is no longer the beautiful Jodie. Her
terror has aged her by many years. I am disgusted as she lies weeping
on the bed. I push her away. Suddenly, as though someone has

handed me a snapshot, I see my dad, his lip curling with distaste, as Mum writhes and sobs on the floor at his feet. How did this happen again? It happened when I flushed the crack down the toilet and now, once more, I've turned into my hard man dad and Jodie has turned into a mum-like pile of jelly. Was she always this way or is it something I did to her?

Sickened, I try to fall asleep again. But I am waiting for the police to return. They don't. In the morning we check out. We get on the train and go back to our quiet lives.

I try to stabilise myself with more prescription drugs and by drinking heavily. I live from dole money and a bit of low-key drug dealing. In an attempt to stabilise my life further, I decide to take a regular job. Starting work in a supermarket bakery feels like a significant step forward. Mum has a new flat in Kendal, Bethany has gone to live with one of her mates and I am staying in Mum's front room amid all the packing boxes.

I wake up one Saturday and it feels like my lucky day. My first pay cheque has arrived. I pull back the curtains and the sun is shining. There's a park outside and in it is a pretty girl. I recognise her at once. Rosie. I was at school with her. Then, aged about fourteen, she ran off to join some travellers. And now she's back, looking lovely standing in the park with a small kid, the sun bouncing off her long, auburn hair.

I get dressed and cross the park and we talk. She remembers me. She explains that she's come back to Kendal for a while to get off heroin. I'm sympathetic because I am trying to sort myself out back in Kendal too. We agree that it's really hard to kick drugs. Then we get into her sister's car with my pay cheque in my pocket and her sister's little kid in the back and we drive down to Moss Side to score.

We return with a stash of cocaine and heroin that we take to Rosie's house. Her parents are out and she's supposed to be looking after her sister's kid. We put the kid in front of the TV, do the drugs and then sleep together in Rosie's single bed. It's our first date.

Chapter 23

Rosie comes from a stable but not wealthy background: her dad's a factory worker and she's the youngest of six children. She wears long dresses, plays the tin whistle and loves folk music. And she's a craftswoman: she's already hand-made a couple of wooden horse-drawn caravans in a folksy, canal-barge style. She travelled England alone in them. Rosie thinks horses are the only way to go. Later, she sold the caravans for a lot of money. Probably she's spent most of it on drugs.

Rosie's life hasn't been easy since she left home. There have been battles with the police, a terrible accident when someone drove over her as she slept in a field, and now she's addicted to heroin.

Our relationship becomes very intense very quickly. There's no room any more for Jodie in my world. Rosie is the true love of my life. We have beautiful times together. We move into a flat in Kendal and I work at the bakery and spend my spare time restoring an ancient camper van. Sometimes we take off in it. We park in a forest and fling the doors open to the night so that the stars seem to be right inside. They have a clean, peaty smell like trees and turf. We light candles by our bed and Rosie's beautiful body is bathed in their soft light. The drugs we take enhance our deep feelings for each other. She is lovely and the world is lovely and everything is right for us.

Rosie injects heroin: she can't stop herself and if she tries to live without it she is really ill. So when she's around, heroin's around. I've often used it before, but now it moves right into my life along with Rosie.

Heroin is a good drug, embracing me with a warmth that curls through my body like love. Soon, very soon, I don't just like it, I need it. I feel sick when I don't get it. But, unlike Rosie, I am not addicted. Addiction is for the weak and I am strong. And there's one mistake I never make. I don't inject it. I don't inject anything. I secretly despise people who shoot up. Don't they realise that once you start injecting there's no end to it? Sometimes, at people's houses for instance, I'll be surrounded by people injecting themselves and I'll smoke gear with them but I won't touch a needle because I pride myself on avoiding the needle trap.

Although, at the same time, I'm curious to know what it's like.

I mean, it must be good or they wouldn't do it.

It's cold and dark when I wake up at 3 a.m. to go to work at the bakery and I ask myself why I need to get out of bed. I push one foot out and the air has an early morning hostility. I pull the foot back under the covers. Rosie's asleep. The bed's warm. I close my eyes. I go to sleep.

When I wake up for the second time the sun is filling the window. The room is warm. I stretch. I feel Rosie next to me. When two people need a drug, the best way to get it is not by getting up in the middle of the night to work with dreary people earning a small wage. No, the best way is buying and selling your drug. Dealing ensures both your supply and your income. Who needs a regular job? Who needs flour on his hands all day? Fuck it.

Rosie and I take off in the beautiful old camper van selling drugs. We hope we look like innocent students, so innocent that no one will think of searching the van. If they do, they'll find it loaded with crack, heroin and ecstasy from the axles up.

We drive south, to Frome in Somerset. It is summer and cows stand knee-deep in pastures yellow with buttercups. They peer at us over hedges that smell of sweet dog-rose. Rosie knows the travellers' sites here and has friends everywhere. Demand for drugs is so high

that I have to keep rushing back up to Birmingham for more sup-
plies. When the market feels saturated, we move on to sites around
Bristol and Bath, Rosie going ahead of me, wandering among the
travellers, making friends, telling them: 'There's a Brummie coming
through selling gear, anyone want some?' You always know who'll
buy. Heroin addicts try to act like other people but their dead-eyed
look, deathly grey complexion and scrawny bodies give them away.

When summer's nearly over we go to Kent for the apple picking.
The apples are a thousand tiny, blushing faces hanging from row after
row of identical trees. In ancient orchards at the edges of the farm,
travellers gather. I love the way their lorries and buses and caravans
arrive disgorging people and their children. They are transient, following the harvest round from cherries to hops to apples. It's an old,
old way of life.

The gentle travellers work hard up ladders all day picking and
packing the apples into crates and when they come back to the site
in the evenings to ease their aching limbs they want a meal, some
relaxation and a smoke. How they hate me as they hand over their
wages for a couple of bags of heroin and some pills.

The farmer presides over his workers. He watches my camper van
every morning and waits for me to come out and climb apple trees
with the others: he doesn't understand that I'm already earning more
than he can ever pay me.

'Planning to start today?' he asks cheerfully, standing at the van
door, stealing glances inside for something that might explain my
behaviour.

'Got a bug. I should be okay by tomorrow,' I assure him. But I
have no intention of picking his apples when I can fleece his workers. The farmer looks at me suspiciously but he doesn't know what
to accuse me of. He lives in another world.

After Kent there's Wiltshire, then Gloucester, and then it's back to
Frome and by now it's winter and Rosie and I are arguing. Usually
over drugs. If we're splitting a bag of heroin, I'm never convinced
that Rosie's split it evenly. And I resent the way she expects me to
keep her supplied. But if she doesn't get gear she cries and moans.

Our lives are ruled by her crap veins: she's always trying to steam them in the bath to bring them up, or she turns the heating on full until I'm nearly suffocating. She'll do anything for those veins. I watch in disgust at the bloody, messy, antisocial business of injecting drugs. Outside the van, the old hippie earth mother who runs the site is cackling away toothlessly while her kids run everywhere. She's talking to someone who's waiting for me while I smoke heroin and watch Rosie miss a vein. Then, when she manages to pull some blood, it takes her so long to do the business that it starts to congeal. She's going to miss her hit.

You just don't want to be around a heroin addict who's lost their hit so I get up and go out and there's John waiting for me. He's a tall, blond West Country lad who bulk-buys from me and then sells on to the end-user. He's like me, a man with a manageable habit he supports by dealing. At Glastonbury Festival he was one of a team who sold my drugs, wandering between tents calling: 'Es, acid, speed, buy it here!'

In my old, clubbing days, I dealt in Es and speed because it was fun. Now I'm dealing because I really need the drugs and the money. And I'm getting good at it. I can rapidly judge how dry a market is and charge accordingly and I have enough supply sources to ensure that I can quickly get all the drugs I need. I was never much good at maths at school but now I find I'm very good indeed. I have a useful memory: I shouldn't be writing down what people owe me but I do anyway, scribbling it on tiny scraps of paper that I hide all over the van. I don't really need to. When people owe me drugs or money, I almost never forget it.

We keep on travelling and our rows get worse. We resent each other. We're always accusing one another of cheating, of hiding bags, of dividing them unfairly, of not sharing at all. We fight. We split up. We travel in different directions. I sell drugs everywhere. I fuck other women. I keep moving. I invest myself in a lot of different places but not all of myself in one place, and the same goes for the people I meet. But no matter what happens, Rosie and I always find each other again because we need each other. Sometimes I wander around traveller sites calling her name.

'Rosie, Rosie, are you here? Come out, I love you!'

Together we head back up north. It's cold everywhere but it's colder here. The skies are an unremitting grey. In Morecambe the sea crashes like a series of great grey walls crumbling down. It's a wet, windy day. The dealer has just one bag. One bag between us. We go into the public toilets.

We look at the bag and we look at each other.

'If you smoke it, you won't get a hit,' Rosie warns me.

I close my eyes. I need that hit.

She says: 'You'll have to bang it up if you want to get anything out of it.'

I need heroin. She injects it, I smoke it, but heroin is the chemical that binds us together.

'It's up to you,' she says, waiting. Her nose is running, her eyes are watering because her body knows it's close to that hit now. 'Come on, make your fucking mind up!'

It's a fact that injecting's more economic. Smoke the stuff and half of it disappears into the atmosphere. Inject it and your body gets it all.

'What do you want to do?' asks Rosie. She's shaking now, she's so close to a hit. She puts down the toilet lid and sits on it.

But didn't I always say I wouldn't do this? Didn't I always say I wouldn't inject?

I watch Rosie as she prepares to inject, getting out the citric that she buys from Indian shops and her bottle of water and her dessert-spoon and her lighter. How many times have we been spoonless when Rosie needed a hit? How many times have I run around second-hand shops or any kind of shop trying to get a spoon and ending up with a set of twelve while Rosie sweats and shakes in the van? Her bag's open now and she has everything she needs. She's laying it out with clinical precision on the toilet cistern.

'Well?' asks Rosie.

I look round at the dingy, damp toilet. I need some heroin and smoking half a bag isn't going to sort me out.

I say: 'Oh, fuck it.' If I'm ever going to find out what's so great about injecting drugs, this grey, miserable northern day is the time.

'I'll do it for you,' she says. She takes off her belt and wraps it tightly round my arm for a tourniquet. This is personal. It's intimate. But her hands are shaking. They are almost out of control.

'I've got to have my hit first,' she says at last. She ties the tourniquet round her wrist until her hand's bright red and she dabs between her fingers for a vein, tapping the needle in, then pulling it out. Tap pull, tap pull. She manages to draw some blood but the needle's out and now she's panicking to get it back in before the blood congeals. Finally, she succeeds. She pulls off the tourniquet and, eyes closed, sinks back as the heroin spreads through her body. Her nose and eyes were running with dribble, but now, within seconds, she is dry again. Heroin has restored her.

'Come on, then,' I say. I watch impatiently as she prepares my hit. She takes the spoon and drops the heroin in, brown and powdery like brick dust. She adds some grains of citric, just a few granules to break down the gear, and then some water. She holds the lighter under the spoon. She's cooking it. When it bubbles it's sterile.

I extract the filter from a cigarette, not all of it, only a few millimetres so it feels like a cotton swab between my fingers. I drop the filter on top; she puts the needle on it and draws the drug through the filter. When she's doing it for herself she can manage all this with one hand but for me she uses two.

She finds a vein in the tattoo on my arm. The quick prick of the needle. I wait for the hit. I feel it first in the back of my neck, then in all the nerves in my body. I'm on fire, I'm shaking, I'm going into spasm. Fucking, fucking hell. Something mad's got hold of my body and is bashing me all around the ladies' public toilets. There's a pneumatic drill in my veins. I want a piece of leather in my mouth to stop my teeth from biting off my tongue. I'm exploding. What's happened? This isn't how injecting's supposed to be. It must be Rosie's fault! She's trying to kill me.

Angry then furious and then livid, I grab her round the throat. I see her face. Her eyes are wide with terror, even her freckles are pale.

'Sorry, sorry,' she says, 'I must have got some dirt in . . . Oh fuck, it's a dirty hit, shit, shit . . .'

I raise an arm to attack her. But she's already leaving.

'I'll get you some more, it's the only way . . .'

I follow her to the van. I feel as though I'm going to die. My whole body is still shaking with spasms as she drives to another dealer's. My teeth are clenched. She goes in and I sit in the car holding my body, waiting. I think: this dirty hit is a warning. It means I should never try injecting again. I know that, after an experience like this, nine out of ten would go no further. But I'm already an addict. And I know that Rosie's right, the only way to stop this misery is another hit, a clean one this time.

Rosie emerges with a bag and we go to the seafront and park by the public toilets. There is no one around on this cold winter's day. The wind blows Rosie's hair in all directions until we enter the damp stillness of the toilets and it suddenly hangs motionless. I am still shaking. My teeth are chattering.

She prepares another hit and this time, after I feel the prick of the needle, something wonderful happens on this rainy day in the ladies' public toilets on Morecambe seafront, so wonderful that I know it will change my life and there will be no going back.

Crack is loud and glimmering and exciting and it is Jodie. Heroin is a warm embrace. It is a fire, a comfortable armchair, a thick rug and a lot of love and it is Rosie. Heroin relieves all physical and emotional pain. Take heroin and everything will be all right. When Rosie puts the needle into my arm she is injecting pure liquid velvet into my vein and when she takes off the tourniquet and the velvet spreads all through my body I can feel the warmth wrapping itself round every nerve, stroking each vein lovingly. I've smoked it a lot but the experience is intensified a thousand times with the needle. Now I understand why people do this. Now my curiosity is satisfied. They do it because this is beautiful. Rosie is beautiful. Life is beautiful. Even fucking Morecambe is beautiful.

At first, I gouch. That is, I fall straight into a sleepy, warm oblivion. I've seen Rosie do it: her head falls onto her chest, her pupils turn into tiny pins, she dribbles. It's disgusting, it's self-indulgent and now I know how it feels. Fucking fantastic.

When I wake up, I still feel good. I continue to feel good for the rest of the day and much of the night. My sense of well-being just doesn't go away. The best parts of my day are enhanced and the bad bits fly past. In fact, everything is so good that I know I have to stop injecting and stop right now. Heroin has filled the hole in my soul. It is the missing piece of my jigsaw. I should never inject again and I should stop smoking. It's going to be hard, but I know that if I don't stop now then I am in great danger.

It's Saturday. On Sunday, Rosie needs another bag and she gets me one.

No. I told myself yesterday I wouldn't touch it again. Ever.

I have the bag.

Now I am definitely going to stop.

On Monday I have another bag.

Okay, that's it. Injecting has been interesting but it's all over for me now.

On Tuesday I'm sick. My nose keeps running. I can't stop yawning or sneezing. I throw up. My bones burn. I am miserable with a deep, creeping misery. Life is awful and it passes too slowly. The world's in monotone. Everything's grey. The fucking clock is moving backwards instead of forwards. Nothing goes right. It rains hard all day. I throw up again and my bones burn until my body is covered in arcs of pain. The rattle is stronger after injecting because injecting gets all the drug into your body. And the better the hit, the worse the rattle.

But if I'm going to stop, I know that now is the time and I must go through this.

Rosie has a hit. I can't bear to watch her. Sweat pours off me. The fire has entered my bone marrow. I want to stick a knitting needle into my bones and gouge out everything in there that is burning. I shake. I shiver. I can't talk, I can't eat and I can't keep still and I can't evade the agony.

Rosie offers me a bag. It costs £10. For just £10 I can end my misery. And for £10 I do.

It's incredible. I know all about heroin and I've still fallen down the hole. I've already seen that most addicts have a honeymoon period that entices them into addiction so that they don't want to give up until it's too late. I smoked my way through that period and I wanted to give it up then, too. Now I want to stop injecting. But I already know that I can't.

I admit to myself that heroin was already a necessity in my life and that I already had a problem even before I injected. But now it is very necessary, more necessary than food, as necessary as water. Without it, I can't get up in the morning, I can't talk, I can't function, I can't live. I have to take it if I don't want to feel terrible. It's not that heroin gives me so much pleasure any more. I turn to other drugs for that. It simply alleviates the symptoms caused by its absence. A hit restores me to how I was before I needed it.

So now Rosie and I bang up together but it doesn't bring us any closer. Instead, we just argue more over who gets the bag and who pays for it and how we divide it up. I do love her, though. It's just that my love for Rosie and my love for heroin sometimes get confused.

Chapter 24

My old mate Daniel writes to me. We haven't spoken for a while because our lives have taken different courses. He'd buy drugs off me sometimes in Birmingham but he really isn't into the same music. He's always meaning to get to a DIY free party but somehow he never makes it. Probably he wouldn't understand if he did. Now he's back in jail for another violent robbery and he's not going to change. But our friendship is still deep. It's only five years since we were incarcerated in a cell together and that bond of brotherhood holds true.

Dan's letter looks innocent enough but we used to be tight and I still know all the codes: he's telling me to get down to Birmingham fast.

'Don't go,' says Rosie. 'I don't like it. There's something funny going on.'

'You don't understand,' I tell her. 'You don't understand about me and Daniel because you've got a close family. Where me and Dan come from, you make your own family. We've been through a lot together and we'd do anything for each other. Anything.'

'You told me,' says Rosie, 'that you don't have much in common any more.'

Did I happen to mention to her that Dan can't appreciate a sunset? That he's got no creativity or imagination? Well, despite all that, he's my brother. My real brother, Shane, left for America about a year ago to run a sound system in Atlanta. But I was always closer to Dan than Shane and now Dan's hinting that he needs my help.

Amid more protests, I drive straight down to Birmingham. Dan and about four or five other inmates are waiting for me. These other men are obviously big-time gangsters. They're looking for a reliable drugs runner now they're inside. And Daniel has told them I'm their man.

I try to stay cool when I'm around the gangsters. Dan's cool too. But actually we can barely contain our excitement as they describe the job.

'We're in with them now!' whispers Daniel as I'm leaving. Those big baby eyes are blazing in his white face. You can almost see him calculating, planning, thinking. The blue vein on the side of his head is pulsating because it's directly connected to his busy brain.

'We're made, mate, we're going to become millionaire drug dealers.' And he starts laughing. I know that laugh. It's that nervous, excited giggle I used to hear when we robbed people.

The gangsters turn out to be only one step away from the supply source in Eastern Europe and they have a big business to organise from inside the prison. As a runner, my job is to meet ordinary-looking people like roofers and plumbers at roadsides who show up in their cars with industrial quantities of drugs. I load them into the camper van. There's supposed to be bunk beds rolled up in a camper van but I just have Es rolled up. I mean, thousands of Es. I have to carry them from Birmingham to dealers all over the East and West Midlands.

This is very lucrative but dangerous work. It's exciting. It's terrifying. Not only am I being paid to move the drugs around but I make a tidy profit for myself by upping the price by as much as 50p on each pill. That's £500 for me on every thousand. Or I lose a few pills on each delivery and store them in a drain in Kidderminster near Dan's house. I soon accumulate a nice private stock of Es, and when I sell them I'll give half the money to Dan.

Rosie comes with me on my runs and the two of us look like carefree students instead of dealers whose van is loaded to the gunnels with ecstasy. Rosie doesn't find this exciting. She is beside herself with tension. Her hair starts to fall out. Deep down, I'm scared too. But I'm not going to admit it.

'These guys will break your legs if they decide you're not useful any more,' she tells me as we drive around with the drugs rattling behind us. 'At the very least.'

I shrug. Doesn't she understand that I'm one of the big boys now?

'And if the police stop us, you'll get life for this lot.'

'They won't.'

'Daniel won't care.'

'He's my friend.'

'Will he be visiting you in jail for the next twenty years, then? Is that what friendship is?'

'You don't understand our friendship. It's a question of honour.' Honour? Now I really sound like the gangster I want to be. But it's true that Daniel and I would go to hell holding hands.

'I understand one thing. He's not going to be the one with a life sentence.'

I am, of course, an addict. But my habit's so under control that I manage to keep it secret, even to some extent from Rosie. A habit like mine makes life difficult: I have to get the drugs in secret, hide them, find private places to shoot up. Now I'm injecting not just heroin but coke and crack too. Once you start, you'll inject anything. Smoking and sniffing and swallowing will not do any more. You can't stand to see half the drug disappear into the atmosphere at the end of a crack pipe. You want everything straight into the veins for the purity of the hit it gives you.

I'm so desperate to escape the whining Rosie and have a peaceful, safe hit that one weekday morning, when no one's around, I visit a prostitute in Birmingham. I'm not talking about the cheap girls who sit in the windows of Balsall Heath: I've come a long way since that adolescent stuff. I mean a classy girl. She's beautiful and Chinese and when I tell her I'm a drug dealer she doesn't believe me. I show her that I am carrying 500 Es around and suddenly she's all over me. Dealing is so good for the ego. The prostitute and I spend the morning together. I inject crack and heroin in the privacy of her beautiful penthouse. It feels good. I don't like to use alone and using has become a lonely activity these days.

But Rosie has her secret too and eventually a dealer tells me. He hints that Rosie's always sneaking in and asking for heroin when I'm busy delivering drugs. I am furious and very worried. Everyone will know I have a junkie girlfriend. And that will make them wonder if maybe I'm a junkie too and nobody trusts a junkie; certainly he cannot be a drugs runner.

When I learn what Rosie's been doing, I drag her off by the hair and am violent and abusive in front of everyone. It's vital that I'm separated from her habit in their eyes. Plus, I am really livid. For the first time in my life I have a good job with easy money and all the drugs I could want. And Rosie's jeopardising that.

I barricade her in the camper van and won't let her out.

'You've ruined my fucking life,' I snarl.

She cries and the more hysterical she gets the nastier I become. She beats her hands against the van sides, sobbing wildly, and I feel nothing but disgust. I see that picture again, the one I hate, the one that appears in my head when I don't want it to. My mum, writhing and screaming on the floor at the farmhouse and the look of distaste on my father's face as he stands over her, still as a rock. Mum was mad. Dad was mad. So how has this happened? How is it possible that I've turned into Dad? And Rosie, the love of my life, has somehow turned into Mum? Are we mad too? Was Rosie like this when we met or did I do it to her?

I hope I've done enough to allay the fears of the dealers I'm working with and convince them that I'm not an addict and I'm trustworthy and, whatever my girlfriend uses, I'm no kind of a junkie myself. But people are whispering about me. I can feel it. Everyone's paranoia is growing and there was already enough paranoia because the money involved is big, the police are a constant fear, and the gangsters are dangerous too.

I know that the buzz about me has reached Dan and the gangsters, masterminding their operation from jail, because something strange happens. I talk to Neil on my mobile and a few minutes later he calls me back.

'Some guy phoned me the moment we'd finished speaking. He was asking about you.'

'Asking what?'

'About the things we'd just been saying. He must have heard us somehow.'

So, they've got my phone tapped. The big boys are checking out my every transaction. I scent trouble.

'What sort of guy do you think he was?' I ask Neil.

'The sort who means business.'

'Oh my fucking God!' says Rosie when I tell her. 'We've got to get out of this.' Her eyes are wide with anxiety. She pulls back her hair in a gesture of desperation and it comes out in her hands.

I know that she's right. The gangsters are turning against me. Dan's turning against me. It's time to cut and run.

I sell my half of the Es I stole for Dan and me and we get in the van and head north. My foot is flat on the gas. A few hours later, the phone rings. The voice is scared.

'I had to give away all those fucking Es you sold me!' says the dealer we've just left. 'A bunch of heavies surrounded the house. They poured petrol through the letterbox and said they'd torch the place if I didn't hand them back. Said they weren't yours to sell.'

By now we are far up the M6 and we didn't leave a moment too soon. All Rosie's predictions have been proved right. My brother Dan has turned against me. He's gone with the gangsters.

There is a silence in the van. It lasts for miles. And then, when we're beginning to feel safe again because we're getting near Kendal, we start to fight. We say terrible things to each other, the way we always do when we row. I pull off the motorway and stop the van in the middle of nowhere so I can concentrate on shouting. Rosie starts to cry. I shout louder.

'What's the matter with you?' I scream at her, exasperated. 'All you ever do these days is cry.'

'I'm . . .' Sob. 'I'm . . .' Huge sob. 'I'm . . .' Get on with it. '. . . pregnant.'

Oh, the silence now. We're in a silent van in a silent lane on some silent moor far from anywhere in Silenceshire.

Pregnant.

That means she's going to have a baby.

For perhaps a minute the monumental nature of this news over-whelms me. A baby. You have to feed it, clothe it, take care of it twenty-four hours a day and then it grows bigger and bigger and its needs change but they still have to be met. The baby becomes a child, a teenager, and you have to love it and look after it and teach it how to live. You can't be selfish, juvenile and single if you have a baby. That's how my dad was and it wasn't good enough.

The knowledge, the sense of responsibility, the enormity of it all, is fleeting. 'Aren't you pleased?' sobs Rosie.

'Yeah. Of course I am,' I say, putting an arm round her. 'A baby. Yeah, I'm pleased.'

'You do want it. Don't you?'

'Yeah. It's . . . it's great news.'

Rosie's wanted a baby for a long time. She's been telling me that but I couldn't see past my own needs and my own habit. The words didn't mean anything much but now I understand that, for her, a baby is a solution. We travel constantly, our need for heroin, like a will-o'-the-wisp, keeping us in constant motion, always arguing, and now Rosie wants stability. She believes a baby might give her that.

I feel full of doubts and worries. I start the van again. Its motor fills the silence as we head back to Kendal and our old flat. Mum's still living in the Lakes and so are my two sisters. Bethany's going her own way, she's learning to party while Kelly's knee-deep in small children. I see them sometimes. We learned to live separately in the same house when Dad dominated our lives: now we live separately in the same town, and none of us, except Kelly, has anything to do with Dad. When he visits Kelly from Durham, Bethany avoids him. If he's in town, she doesn't want to leave her house.

'What's the problem?' I ask, my eyes focusing on Bethany for maybe the first time in years. She's very pretty and one glance tells you that she's sweet-natured and open-hearted. Daddy's girl. I used to be so jealous of their special, private relationship, the horses, the jokes, the way his big hands were gentle around her. And now she won't even risk seeing him on the street.

Bethany can't meet my eye and I can see that she doesn't want to talk about it. I don't probe further. I'm too preoccupied by what is about to enter my own life.

As Rosie's belly grows, I am often seized by fear at the responsibility that awaits us. I get a part-time job on a rich man's country estate and we try to ease up on our heroin use for the baby's sake but now that I don't have to keep my habit hidden, like something in a drawer or at the back of a cupboard, it expands. It expands to fill the flat, it fills my life, it swells until I know that I'm not managing it any more. It's managing me.

When Rosie is eight months pregnant and round as an apple, she tries to restrict her intake to smoking. She uses methadone to help her. I try to give up heroin completely and the withdrawal symptoms are terrible. We rattle together, our eyes and noses streaming, our heads aching. We burn, we vomit, we shiver, we shake, we cry. We find each other intolerable and each other's rattles intolerable too. For day after day our bodies feel close to disintegration. Until the day we give in. The effect of the first hit is instantaneous. My weeping body is suddenly dry, I am young again and my body is whole, all the thoughts and ideas inside my head are whirring once more because someone just switched on the power.

Now I've had a hit, I stop worrying how we'll cope with a baby and a heroin habit and start to feel excited. That inner core of loneliness that I never want to think about or confront, which I've felt ever since I was a little boy and which heroin has done so much to fill – if I build a family around it, then maybe that loneliness will go away. Having a baby will be a wonderful experience.

In April 1996 the baby is born by Caesarean section after a long, emotional night. I am standing by Rosie's head with my mask and gown on, the staff hold up a sheet, and suddenly they are dangling a shrieking little replica of humanity upside down in front of me.

This is my son. I can't believe it. I am filled by a mixture of emotions I can hardly bear. Deep, deep love, deeper than anything I've felt before, so deep it scares me. I am allowed to hold him and he looks up into my eyes and for a minute he's quiet. His weight is slight, his body presses against mine trustingly. He doesn't judge me or think I'm bad. And for a moment, anything's possible. He's start-ing his life. Maybe he means I'll restart mine, too. I am joyful. I am euphoric.

We're going to call him Jack and in the hospital I form a bond with my little son, a bond of love that is stronger than any bond I've known before. The only thing that has ever really mattered to me is drugs. Now there's Jack.

They take us into a room and Rosie falls asleep almost at once and Jack wraps his tiny fingers round mine. Gradually my joy is diluted by fear. Jack's so helpless and we're responsible for him. How am I going to look after him when I'm such a kid myself, as self-centred as any baby? Do I know how to love him? I remember that stone of crack, swirling round and then disappearing down the toilet pan. It was something I loved dearly and I flushed it away. Remembering it frightens me now.

I sit in the hospital ward talking to our baby, just talking as though he can really understand me. Although he has been born an addict, the life that stretches ahead of him is full of possibilities. I tell him that everything has gone wrong for me but I'm going to try to be a real father to him, not like my dad. I'm going to take care of him and make sure that all the things that have happened to me won't happen to him. I've already managed to get a proper job and next I'll stop taking drugs and then I won't have to supplement my income by buying and selling them any more. And we'll be a real family.

I leave them at the hospital and go home to the flat and start to clean it. I feel tearful. I am the little boy who has suddenly had to become a grown-up. But it is necessary. Because now I am a father.

I really try to keep my promises to Jack. For the first six months of his life I am always fighting the withdrawal symptoms from heroin. But each time I give in and the cruel mistress exacts her revenge and takes me back on a deeper level of addiction. I'm stuck in a cycle I can't escape from and all the time there is the noise of a baby crying.

I am selfish. I don't turn down my music when Jack's trying to sleep. I lie in bed when I should be taking him outside. I shoot up when I should be helping to feed him. I take him places where needles are lying around. Rosie's always leaving me and going back to her mum's with him. But I love Jack more than I can express. When I feel his tiny body curl against mine, when I touch his soft, soft head, when he looks into my eyes with a love and trust I can't betray, then I make a decision.

In one last bid to change my life, I show my old portfolio of pictures to a renowned photography course in Blackpool and they accept me as a student. I'm going to become a photographer. When we fail to find affordable accommodation in Blackpool, I think of moving to Newcastle-upon-Tyne. The university there has another good photography course and accommodation's cheap in that big city. I show my portfolio to the university's art department and they agree to a transfer. So I'm moving to Newcastle where I was born and both my parents before me. Everything in my life's been blurred by drugs and my need to get them but I can perceive, through the haze, something solid. A course, leading to a job, leading to an income . . . I'm going to stop dealing and using and start living. With my family around me.

My big sister, Kelly, steps in. She and I never mention Dad: all I know is that he lives in Durham with his new family. But now Kelly tells me that he based himself in Newcastle immediately after the divorce and he and his partner still own a small flat there where they're prepared to let us stay.

Rosie and Jack and I pile into the camper van. We drive over the Pennines to our fresh start. Amazing high, bleak scenery, blindingly cold winds, snow falling, Jack crying in the back while we sniff cocaine off the dashboard: it doesn't feel like the journey to a new life.

I am nervous and excited because I am going to see Dad. I love him and love him deeply because he's my dad and, despite everything that happened between us, I'm looking forward to seeing him. I'm twenty-four and I haven't seen him since I was sixteen.

He's come up from Durham and he's waiting at the flat.

He looks just the same. A cowboy, and at least three times bigger than he actually is, like the Marlboro Country advertisements on a roadside billboard. One glance at him and I am a nervous wreck. I want to reach out to this father of mine, the way Jack holds his little arms out to me. I want to but I can't. There's a long childhood of rejection stretching between us. I see those steely blue eyes, that hard face, the tattoos across his hands, and I recoil. I'm six years old and I'm terrified. He looks me up and down and for a moment I see what he sees. Pupils like tiny pinholes, watery eyes, runny nose, twitching, scratching. All the hallmarks of an addict. Dad knows. He knows all about me. He looks down at Jack, who is in Rosie's arms.

'All right, sonna?' he asks Jack. Jack stares back. I don't want Dad to touch him.

His partner arrives. She bustles around making tea. She's nice. Doesn't she know what he's really like? We drink our tea and the conversation does not flow smoothly. When everyone gets up to go, Dad and I find ourselves alone together in the kitchen for a moment. He gives me that keen, icy look and I quail before him like a small boy.

He says: 'You can't blame me. You can't blame me for the way you've turned out.'

Then he leaves with his partner.

Chapter 25

Soon the heroin Rosie and I have brought with us is all used up. We start to rattle.

'We knew it would be hell, but if you can just support me now,' I tell Rosie, 'then after this degree everything could be different.'

I need her help. I need her behind me every step of the way or I won't be able to come through this. And Rosie, of course, can't give me that support. She's in her own world of addiction and craziness in which taking care of Jack requires a superhuman effort. And she does take care of him and she is superhuman. As for me, I can't cope with him at all. I simply love him. But whatever a child needs beyond that, I can't give it. I can't give it to myself, let alone someone else.

Rosie and I argue. Jack watches. His small, round face looks from one to the other and then he starts to cry, but even this doesn't stop us. Our fights are crazy, violent affairs, a mixture of love, anger and resentment. They are, in fact, unbearable. And one day, Rosie can't bear them. She takes Jack and goes. She's left before but this time her absence has a new finality and the loss is infinite because she has taken Jack.

My resistance to heroin crumbles. Within days I'm using again. But scoring isn't so easy in Newcastle. The heroin trail seems to peter out before it gets to the north-east. Not for the first time, I lead a double life. By day I am at college, enjoying my photography course and mixing with nice middle-class students. By night, I am hanging around the worst housing estates in the worst areas of the north-east, looking for heroin.

I spend whole evenings sitting in tower-block flats with other addicts waiting for the dealer to come back. The dealer's wife looks fed up. She's trying to do her ironing and there are twenty addicts crammed into a too small, too hot room. But the dealer can't afford to have us all hanging around in the street outside, attracting attention. So we're on the floor, on the sofa, on chairs, and we're all suffering because when you know that your hit's going to happen, the symptoms always get worse. We're aching and burning and our noses are dribbling. Some addicts have kids running around in nappies who want to go home. People are crying, rocking, scratching. Ever since I've been addicted to heroin, my life has turned into a waiting game. Waiting, waiting, waiting for my drug. Wishing time away while I wish my drug would come. I sit in the Newcastle council flat and I can only think of one thing, and that's the length of time I've been waiting, waiting. We're all desperate, all twenty of us, even the children. I hate them all. I keep thinking: ten more minutes, I'll wait ten more. And then ten more. Until I've been waiting for hours. And I hate the dealers because they've got powder power. They're gouched out somewhere and they're keeping all these sick people waiting for what they want because they're selfish bastards and they've already got it; they're probably asleep while we're aching, rattling, dribbling. I know, because as a dealer I've done it myself. As a buyer, I'm thinking: where are they, why don't they come back and give it to me? The pinholes in my arms all grow into little mouths and every single one of those mouths is saying: feed me. Fucking feed me. I want to stick my fingers in the holes and stop the itchy scratchy. But I just keep on waiting. You're always fucking waiting, waiting, waiting for heroin.

Then, when at last it comes, I buy enough for today and tomorrow. But I know that I won't be able to stop myself taking it tonight and then I'll be back here or in some other godforsaken place later. The shortage of heroin in Newcastle drives me away each weekend. Often I go down to Nottingham. I know where to score here. My weekends with my friends are relaxed, or there's a wild party. I get close to Ange, an artist who does set designs for parties. Heroin's my mistress now so sex isn't as interesting as it used to be, but I get as close to Ange as an addict can. She introduces me to her friend Sean. He's a dark-haired, dark-eyed gay student who's doing a sociology degree. He takes an interest in my photos.

When DIY announce they're going on a tour of America, he immediately tells the DJs Digs and Whoosh: 'I have an idea and it's brilliant! You need an official tour photographer.'

They look interested.

'Mr Mark Johnson's your man!' Sean announces. He has a very particular way of speaking.

It happens that a few magazines have already asked for photo-diaries of the tour.

'How long will you be in the States?' I ask. They shrug. They don't know how long or even where they'll go because their approach is anarchic.

I say: 'My brother runs a sound system. He's based in Atlanta . . .'

Everyone thinks that's a good starting point. Before long I'm involved in the tour and before much longer I'm going. As official photographer. That means leaving university and abandoning my course. I'm sorry for that but I can't miss the tour and, anyway, America will be a sort of photography course. I'll see my brother Shane for the first time in a few years. And I'll start a new life because it'll be much easier to kick heroin in a new environment with a group of friends who are doing the same thing than it was in the loneliness of Newcastle.

For me the America tour lasts seven months, until the summer of 1997. It is mayhem. I take every drug available, including two new ones, crystal meth and DMT, which both blow my mind. But I don't take heroin. I certainly would if I could get my hands on it but I can't read the heroin landscape over here. It's almost impossible to score and when I try I end up robbed at gunpoint. So, instead, I drink to excess, do crack, cocaine, anything at all that will relieve me of my monstrous desire for one thing: heroin. A few friends are experiencing similar withdrawal symptoms. I take copious amounts of drugs while the music drives us from Atlanta to San Francisco. Clean-cut young Americans love our crazy English behaviour, our music and our scene. Ironically, deep house came from the States but didn't explode until it reached England. Now we've brought it back and we're regurgitating it for them. The Americans are just discovering some of the drugs, the free parties, the scene that we discovered years back and they are having their summer of love. Ours ended a long time ago. And as for being tour photographer, well, I soon swap my camera for some cocaine.

One night, in a club, I can't stop taking cocaine. Whenever the music ends and my world goes silent, I turn from a wild party animal to a frightened kid, stalked by old fears and desperate needs. There is still music and the lights are still low and there's still some cocaine around, but I've run out of money. I want that cocaine. I can't leave the table. So when a dealer offers me more cocaine in exchange for a sexual encounter, I accept. I must have that drug. The bass throbs inside my brain. I can see the black hair at the top of his head but not his face. I don't need to. I know it's Trevor from Kidderminster. For a brief moment I smell the sweet, mucky smell of farm animals, remember the grey of the breezeblocks round the cow stalls, and the club music gives way to the silence of the vast, empty cattle market. And I mustn't tell. Trevor will deny it and no one will ever believe me. Little poof.

Afterwards, I am humiliated. I'm not gay so why did I let him do that thing? Do I care? Should I care? I've taken so many drugs I don't know who I am any more and I have no norms. I am lost. I am ashamed. I catch the next plane to London, back to the arms of my lover and great comforter: heroin.

At the prospect of imminent arrival in a country where heroin is widely available, I start to rattle unbearably. Nursing a terrible hangover, I sit on the plane shaking and my symptoms have the intensity of a forest fire although it is almost eight months since I first started this terrible attempt at withdrawal. But my body knows, my soul knows, every molecule and corpuscle and blood cell knows that at the end of the flight there will be heroin. Haunted by memories of what I did and didn't do, I am plastered to my seat, sweating and dribbling, as I wait, wait, wait for the plane to land. I'm always fucking waiting for my drug but this is one of the worst waits ever.

I get through the airport and Rosie is there. She has gear in the front seat and Jack in the back and I don't even see him, I only see the gear. Within a short time there is a needle in my arm. Relief, warmth, relaxation, the drug welcomes me back to its kingdom. The horror and self-disgust that has been sitting in the seat right next to me on the plane evaporates. I'm a human being again and everything's going to be all right.

Only now can I hug my Jack and stare at him. He's not eighteen months yet but he's less baby and more boy. Blond hair and blue eyes, even I can see that he looks like me. He's that little kid I used to be. He stares at me wisely and without recognition. My beautiful son.

We go to back to Kendal. We always go back to Kendal. The grey streets and the grey rain haven't changed and our relationship hasn't changed either. It's as volatile and angry as it used to be. Rosie can't stand my chaotic, crazy drug-fuelled behaviour. She goes. She takes Jack to her parents. I find a small, squalid bedsit over a hairdresser's.

I now accept that I can't live without heroin. I need it. In addition, crack is back in my life as it was my heroin substitute all the time I was in America. Almost immediately, I am back to dealing and using and not less than before. A lot more.

If I have to wait for my drug, I rattle monstrously. Heroin is my love, she is my mistress. When I am away from her for too long she says: are you leaving me? Don't leave me! And she makes me suffer so much that I always go back for the relief she brings. She restores me, she makes me whole, she returns me to normality. Only she can make me function. She gives me nothing more, no pleasure, just relief from the misery of her absence. If I'm looking for pleasure I use crack with heroin, if I want to achieve that euphoric dream-like state called gouching, then I take Valium or Mogadon with heroin because my mistress is not generous. She wants me back but she gives me nothing.

I pick up my record collection from my sister's and try to make the bedsit feel like home. There's a single bed. And a television.

Rosie sometimes lets Jack stay with me and tonight we've both fallen asleep in the bed. I'm in a heroin stupor. The television is on. I half wake up in the night and there's an urgent voice announcing the death of Princess Diana. I fall asleep again. I must have dreamed it. But in the morning there are many serious faces confirming her death. People are crying. Jack's nappy is falling off him it is so full, but I don't have the energy to change it because I hurt all over. I must score in order to function but I don't have the energy to get up. More people cry. Through the window I can see that the world is a grey, wet, depressing place.

Jack snuggles up to me and I push him away. He starts to run around, breaking the bedsit up, and I am powerless to do anything but shout. The noise reverberates inside my head making it hurt still more.

'Quiet!' I yell. I close my eyes. There is silence. I open one eye. Jack is looking at me. I close it. I am aware that he is climbing up onto the bed. I feel his small hands puncturing the sheets. Then slowly, slowly, he crawls over my body. His fingers are cautious. He distributes his weight carefully. As though I'm a volcano that might erupt, he puts his arms round me. Surreptitiously. So I won't notice.

It's too much. I can't stand it. I can't suffer this attention, his hands clutching at me, wanting things, wanting attention, demanding love, wanting, asking, needing. It hurts too much. It hurts because I can't give him anything. My own needs are too great. My own needs consume me.

I pull him off. He looks up at me and he's not even bewildered: it's what he expected. It's what dads do in our family.

I drag us outside so I can score. When I've got the gear I park in a lay-by. There's a truck at the far end; otherwise it's empty. A few feet away cars rock ours as they pass, ignoring us.

Jack's hungry and he's crying. I have a bag of sweets. I keep him strapped into his car seat at the front and I climb into the back. My hands are shaking so much that I can barely get the fucking sweets open. I rip at the bag with my teeth like an animal, then I throw one to him and he stares at it and stops crying at once. That's his hit sorted out. He's busy with the wrapper while I deal with my own bag. I've got good veins. My veins are the envy of my friends. I've been banging up into the same tattoo in my arm for two years now and I don't even need to use a tourniquet. There's none of Rosie's tap tap tap with the needle for me.

I'm just heating the spoon when I glance up and see Jack's small face. He's straining round in his car seat to watch me. I drop the lighter and throw him another sweet and he grabs it and stops trying to see what Daddy's up to. Before I stick the needle in I throw him another to ensure me a couple more minutes of calm. As he reaches for it I catch sight of his face. White, tired, unhealthy. The kid whose parents can see no further than the end of their own needles. A massive hole opens up inside me of desolation and shame. There's only one way to close it. Thank God for that needle.

Rosie can see that my life consists only of using. She looks with disdain at the squalid bedsit.

'What's that?' she asks, hearing someone whistling again and again on the street outside. She pulls aside the black bin-liner at the window. Lit by the garish white of the hairdresser's halogen bulbs below is the dribbling face of a heroin addict, turned up to my bedsit, his eyes dull with need. Kendal's no longer the drug-free backwater it was. Lots of our generation are addicts and they know where to come for their fix.

'Customers whistle. Instead of a doorbell,' I explain.

She becomes more and more reluctant to leave Jack with me and usually won't let him stay for longer than it takes her to score. But after a lot of negotiation she finally drops him off again for the day. I assure her everything will be fine. I'm lying. Actually, I'm feeling sick, very sick. But I should be okay when I've had a hit. I tell her I'll be taking Jack to the park but I rush off to score in Morecambe with him. I come back with half a gram.

Jack's bored. He's been sitting in a car and now he's back in my small room and he's running riot. It's exhausting just watching him. He wants this, he wants that. He plays with something for a minute and then runs off. He cries. He makes his nappy dirty. He roars around like a maniac and won't listen to rational argument or respond to shouting. I can't cope with this two-year-old. I love him down to the soft blond hairs on his head, but I love him most when he's asleep, his face round with innocence, his body still. I can't cope when he's like this.

I go into the kitchen and cook up the entire half-gram of heroin. All of it. As the relief floods through me I hear Jack yelling about something and when his yelling gets a bit louder I open my eyes. I'm on the floor. How did I get here? There is an immense noise in the room. The needle's still in my arm but the sky outside is dark. It must be evening. Christ, oh Christ, I must have gone over. How long have I been here?

In the same moment that I realise I've been lying here all day locked in the bedsit with Jack but oblivious to him, I become aware that the noise in my ears is many voices. There is screaming, shouting, crying. Hammering and banging, too. I drag myself upright. Jack is leaning against the door, hysterical, his nappy falling off. I pick him up and he's wet all over from piss and tears. I unlock the door. Here's Rosie, angry and sheet-white, her screaming mouth expanding to fill her face. She flies at me and tries to punch me, emitting high-pitched noises, grabbing Jack. Behind her, a crowd of neighbours stare at me. They are silent.

'What was Daddy doing?' Rosie demands. I hope that the neighbours can't understand the words that somehow filter through Jack's wet-mouthed sobs. He's saying: 'Daddy was asleep on the floor.'

I am deeply ashamed. For weeks I use on the memory. I can't argue with Rosie now when I'm denied contact with Jack. Even at Christmas.

On Christmas morning I get up at half past six. It's cold and dark and that's how I feel inside. I'm an iron man, made of cold metal, walking through the black morning, hollow and clanging. The streets are empty. No one sees the iron man.

I go to Rosie's parents' house. The lights are already on downstairs. I hope I'm not too late. I prowl around in the garden and position myself outside a gap in the curtains. I can't see much. I press my nose to the glass. It is very cold and I can't breathe because my breath turns to mist and obscures my view.

A tree. Tinsel. Tiny, shiny lights in many colours. I step to the right and to the left and then, with my face at right-angles and my cheek squeezed against the pane so I can see with one eye only, I catch sight of Jack in his pyjamas. There's Rosie, too. She looks up and I step back rapidly but she hasn't seen me. She's handing Jack presents one by one and he's tearing off the paper and scrunching it up. He's fascinated by the paper alone, by the act of opening. Rosie gently steers him to the contents. He's getting too excited to look at the presents. He's jumping around. His small, skinny body is frenetic and I smile and it makes my teeth cold. If I was in there with him I'd pick him up and hug his little legs and arms tightly for a moment so he can remember how it is to be still and not wriggle.

I hear his voice, high-pitched, and I see Rosie trying to shush him. He's too young to understand about Christmas, probably too young to understand much about presents but all the same I want to see him open mine. It's a Spiderman suit.

They move out of view. My metal body is very cold, so cold I can't feel it. I can't feel anything. I wait. I listen. I watch for the sudden appearance of Spiderman. Then there is more light and it's coming from upstairs. Rosie's parents are getting up. A change in the consistency of the air around me tells me it is almost dawn. I have to go or they'll find me. I look one last time into the warm room. I can't see Rosie. I can't see my Spiderman. He doesn't know how much I love him and he doesn't know I'm here.

Chapter 26

The Lake District is full of forests. Some are ancient, broad-leaved woodlands teeming with busy wildlife. Some are more modern coniferous forests with straight trunks in long rows, the interior barely penetrated by light or animal life. I love these tree places and I'm going to be spending a lot more time in them. I've got a job. Thanks to some old schoolfriends, I have been taken on by a forestry company as a trainee tree surgeon.

I am determined to give up heroin so I can become a good tree surgeon. As a last resort, I visit Kendal's own drugs counsellor who gives me a book to help me. *What to do if you're a heroin addict.* It's full of little cartoon figures easing the rattle by having tea and chocolate or hot baths. The cartoon figures don't look like I'm feeling. They look happy. I try to imagine I'm one of them. I run a hot bath. It doesn't help.

The drugs counsellor sends me to the doctor who gives me a prescription for methadone. It's supposed to help you withdraw but my previous attempts at enduring the rattle have taught me that withdrawal from methadone is worse than withdrawal from heroin. However, I take it. My other cushion, as ever, is alcohol.

I love my new job. Ever since I gathered conkers as a kid in Kidderminster, ever since I visited the Allbuts' house by the woods, I've cared about trees. I love the stillness of the forest, the variations in its shades of light and dark, the strange beauty of its vertical landscape. And now trees are going to help me get better.

When you climb a big tree, you're moving into another world. It's a micro-environment, full of wildlife, supporting its own little fields of ferns and insects and chattering birds. The trunk is huge and rough-skinned and it's so solid that it supports you while you enter its world. I tie the ropes, clip on the karabiners.

Once I'm off the ground, all my focus is on where I'm moving to next, on the next level up. Where my hands are going, where my feet are going, where the rope's going and whether I can lasso the next branch successfully. Climbing is about movement and that's all I think about, no matter how hungover I am or how hard I'm rattling. I learn that you always move for a reason and you never move without economy. No scrambling, no rushing. I love it. I just have to get high. It's what my life's about.

And when I'm up there, at over a hundred feet, even though I'm scared, I stop and lean on a branch and look out from the world of the tree. For the first time, I know something everyone else has always known. The Lake District is beautiful. It has taken me years to appreciate the place because it meant misery and imprisonment for me as a kid and then it was a place I came back to whenever I was crazy. Now, admiring it from inside a tree, it takes my breath away.

I look across the canopy of the woods and there are other trees and in them are maybe thirty other men. You can see the white of their helmets or hear their chainsaws and I remember that I'm an arborist too, a qualifying arborist, and that makes me feel good. Today we're doing National Grid clearance. The electricity is 400,000 volts and it's been switched off while we take down the overhanging branches but we still have to be very careful to rope the branches down without touching the lines. National Grid work is a licence to butcher a tree and I disapprove but it's the only way I'm going to get my qualifications. I carry out the work with as much kindness to the tree as I can. I'm in a crew of lads who all feel the same way.

I try hard on my training courses and I study in the evenings. I'm lucky enough to be schooled by some of the best tree surgeons in the country. This job gives me my first ever sense of self-worth because I know I'm good at it. There's only one problem. I can't live without heroin. Not even with methadone. Not even with alcohol. I wake up in the morning with black eyes and I know I've been fighting but I was so drunk I can't remember who with or why. A chasm opens up inside me and I ask myself who I am. A drunk whose mum doesn't visit him, who sleeps with women but has no girlfriend, who fights with strangers for no reason, who isn't fit to see his own son. The chasm opens into a massive, dark, gaping abyss and it's too much. The physical anguish of a rattle I can probably cope with. The mental anguish defeats me. There is only one solution and as soon as my first pay cheque comes through it's feasible again: I put a needle in my arm.

So now I have to accept that I'm a junkie and destined to remain one. I must learn to live with my habit. Some people manage their habit for years. Their friends and neighbours don't know they're addicts. They quietly shoot up and their life has a sort of equilibrium and if I can do this then I'll be able to see Jack and become a real father to him, keep my job, become fully qualified and maybe even get a girlfriend. Everything will be normal and heroin will simply fill in all those lonely gaps.

As usual after a period of withdrawal, I go back onto gear at a deeper level. My needs are now substantial. I don't have one job: I have three. I work in the woods all day. Then I rush over to Lancaster to score and inject, still in my working clothes. I have to deal a bit as my pay cheque doesn't go this far. Then I have to look after myself. That is, study, eat, get my prescription drugs, wash, attempt to socialise, go to bed. And all the time, although I'm married to heroin again, I'm still having a passionate affair with crack.

I can't always manage. There are days when I don't have any heroin and I'm rattling so badly I have to score to get to work. I often ring in sick and my colleagues frequently have to cover for me. But if I can get myself into the woods then the big trees do something miraculous to me and I climb. Because I'm off work so much, when I'm there I have to be the fastest, keenest, bravest tree surgeon.

I can see the boss thinking: He may look like a dead body, but at least he's keen.

There are still DIY parties at the weekends. They don't have the wild originality of those early parties but anything new and different is doomed to be commercialised or to dissolve in its own momentum. The party scene in general is dissolving.

So now I'm working to use and using to work. I am moody, withdrawn and off sick too often but I'm still a good arborist. I'm always promising myself and others that I'm going to come off drugs and change. My sister Kelly and her current partner help me. They see that I can barely care for myself, beyond getting and taking my drugs, so I stay with them and Kelly makes sure I have a meal in the evening, and her partner, Paul, a jolly butcher, makes my sandwiches for me in the mornings. But they have a hopeless, helpless addict in the house. Soon I am stealing her car to score. When she finds out about my betrayal, there is a moment of white-faced disbelief and then she crumples. She shouts and cries at the same time. I can cope with her shouting. It's her disappointment that hurts me. I leave. I've used up all her kindness.

I can't afford my own place any more as my wages are going entirely on drugs. The other lads have three-bedroomed houses, nice cars and great holidays. I have to steal my lunch from the local shops.

I don't want to be this way. I hated myself for stealing from Kelly but I couldn't stop myself. Drugs have stripped away my flesh. Anything that's good and everything I've ever learned about how to behave is being lost, along with my humanity. What's left behind is hard and primitive and cares only for its own survival.

I need somewhere to go and when a lad comes back from Ireland saying there's a job for a qualified climber doing high voltage line work I know this is the answer to all my problems. Ireland is a beautiful country. Its landscape is fine, its people warm, its history lyrical. In Ireland, I'm going to start a new life. In Ireland, I'll get clean.

I have my last hit in the toilets of Manchester Airport and flush away the works. Then I set off for my new life. I arrive at dusk and am met by my boss and driven to an outdoor-pursuits centre in

County Wicklow where we are housed. The place is stunning. I try to lose myself in its green valleys and lakes because I know that tomorrow, when I've had the last of my methadone, I'll be too sick to appreciate anything.

I rattle, miserably and almost uncontrollably, for a whole week. I tell my colleagues I have a bad cold. I drink heavily with them. And on the seventh day we are paid.

By now I am almost senseless with need. In the middle of the night, when the boss is asleep, I take the company van and drive it into Dublin. I know where I'm heading for. The worst, most shitty areas. That's always where I have to go for my drug.

I find some ugly places and ask directions from dubious people and soon my search takes me to high-rise housing estates that are even more desolate than any of the desolate places I have been so far. But the place is surreal. Up an alley in the middle of the night is a small kid trotting by on a huge shire horse.

Since the IRA is capable of torching your house if they catch you dealing, scoring is an even more furtive activity here than in England. Around the tower blocks is waste ground where horses are tethered. Inside there is a smell of nappies and vomit and piss.

A kid aged about seven shoots by on a bike with no saddle. He asks me what I want. He is arrogant because he despises me for needing heroin and frightened because he'll have his legs broken by the IRA if he's caught. He disappears and I wait in that desolate landscape of big horses and broken fridges and mud. Eventually the kid reappears with the gear. I shoot up behind a tree. As I leave I see other addicts hanging around in the shadows, chasing small kids on bikes.

From now on I am to be found at night in Ballymun, Clondalkin, Fatima Mansions, Tallaght, Finglas, parts of which are Ireland's roll-call of urban deprivation. Whenever I am paid, I come here straight away and whatever I can get I use almost immediately. The quality's shit and the price is four times higher than in England and it's so impossible to get clean needles that I end up pretending to a chemist that I'm a diabetic and then using the same one over and over again even when it's blunt. Returning to base, I falsify the van's mileage. In the morning, the boss looks at my exhausted face. And he knows.

I can't go on like this. It's impossible to get enough drugs in Ireland to feed my habit. I'm a climber now and I can scale the tallest trees and prune them or section-fell them and my skills are in demand anywhere. I don't have to suffer here. I go back to Kendal to pick up my own climbing gear. Rosie and I take Jack for a walk in the park, the same park where we met that day, a million years and many grams of heroin ago.

I'd forgotten how beautiful my son was. He's small and sweet-faced and he looks up at me with the same unquestioning love and trust that I saw when he was a baby, when I first held him and felt a renewal of hope, the joy of possibility.

Jack doesn't play. He walks between us gravely, giving each of us one of his small, warm hands. A kid is supposed to hold his father's massive hand and it should mean safety and love but when I showed my father that innocent love, he rejected it. Now I hold Jack tight. Drugs have almost replaced him in my life but I love him and I want to show it. I don't want him to feel rejected. He tries to wriggle his hand away from mine.

Rosie's really serious about getting off gear. She's waiting for a place at some kind of rehab centre down in the West Country where she can take Jack. She gives me a phone number and says she'll be gone in a week. I remember my own useless spell in rehab, back in Birmingham. I wish her luck.

Then I head off to a job in London. I need two things to be readily available: trees to work on and drugs to score. London has both. And clean needles are free at any chemist's.

I get a job with a company based in east London and they even offer accommodation. It's a caravan in the scrapyard where they keep their trucks and equipment. At night, I am alone in the yard with a group of moth-eaten wolfhounds.

One of my first jobs is to take down the diseased plane trees at 11 Downing Street. Then we work around St Paul's Cathedral. As usual, when work is finished, I head straight off to score. My life is focused on drugs, not work. I need heroin before I can get up.

There are days when I struggle to find the strength to lift a chainsaw.

One afternoon the boss calls me over.

'Listen, Mark, I want to talk to you . . .'

I know what he's going to say. I wait.

'Mark . . . I'm going to have to let you go.'

I nod. I am shocked but not surprised.

'I'm sorry. I'm very sorry, mate.'

I start to argue. I don't want to let him down. If I try a bit harder . . . but he holds up a big, callused hand. 'Look, the other lads just do not want to work with you. They're tired of carrying you. So get yourself sorted out, Mark, put on some weight, get well, build yourself up a bit . . . but until then, I can't use you any more.'

Chapter 27

I am humiliated. I don't want to be here when the other lads get in and learn I've been sacked. I walk away from the caravan with my stuff in it, away from the scrapyard and the skinny wolfhounds and I head for the Jubilee Line. There's only one thing to do in the circumstances: score.

As the train rumbles towards Waterloo, I know I'm not going back to the caravan. I'm not going back anywhere because there's nowhere to go. I run through all the options in my mind. I remember all the people who have shown me kindness or offered accommodation. Their doors are all closed now. I've abused their trust. I've taken all they can give me and more. I've been on this railway all my life and this is the end of the line.

We arrive at Waterloo.

I don't have anywhere to sleep tonight or the next night or the night after that or any night. The money in my pocket's going to be spent on heroin and crack. People who don't have anywhere to go are homeless. I'll have to sleep on the streets. I'm homeless. I am sick with fear. I'm homeless.

I get onto the Northern Line.

I'm a junkie. I used to think I wasn't a junkie because I didn't inject, then I thought I wasn't a junkie because I could manage my habit and live a normal life, then I thought I wasn't a junkie because

I didn't live on the streets and now I know I must be a junkie. I'm sick. I'm homeless.

I look at the other passengers. They're all thinking thoughts about their busy lives and my life's empty now, it's empty of everything but drugs. In their briefcases and handbags are keys. Keys to flats, keys to houses. They're going home, they're going to work, they're going to meetings. They've all got somewhere to go.

The train arrives at Tottenham Court Road. The doors slide open. I walk through them quickly, merging with the crowds, as though I'm like them, as though I'm one of them. Although I'm not. I'm alone, no one cares about me, I have no home, no roof. My body aches, my legs are leaden, my bone marrow is thick, gelatinous globules of pain, my nose runs, my head hurts. I am scared and I badly need to score, badly, badly, I need to score badly now.

I get outside onto the street and that old buzz is still there, the buzz I felt with Jill Allbut all those years ago. My memory of that trip to London actually halts me for a moment, halts me right there on the pavement and almost overpowers me with sadness. Jill brought me to London and was kind to me and I felt safe. And now there is no kindness and no safety and it is many years since I have felt the warmth of their affection.

I remember how I was so excited by London, by the constant movement on the streets and the size of the statues and the buildings. Later, in Kendal, I used to sit in the long grass by the river smoking and skiving with my mate Ian and I'd tell him how I'd go to London. That was a millennium ago. And now, a thousand years later, I'm here and I feel the buzz of the great city still. But this was never how I meant to arrive. This was never who I meant to be.

The realisation that I'm here, now, and I've got nowhere to go tonight, that I'll be sleeping on the streets, jolts me back into movement. I feel fear's iciness. It drives me on, looking, looking to score.

I see a small, hunchbacked man shuffling along the side of the pavement. I know him: it's Steve. Relief. Anticipation. Steve will have gear. I've scored off him before on my trips into the West End.

You can tell he's been on the streets a long time. He's about my age but his clothes are ragged and oily and the toes of his shoes are curled up. His face is dirty and I don't know him well but right now he feels like my dearest friend in the world.

He looks at me and no greetings are exchanged.

I say: 'Bring me in.' If he brings me in now, he can share with me later. But he shakes his head.

'Haven't got none,' he tells me.

'I need gear now. I can pay for it.'

He looks interested. He's an addict. He knows that if someone can pay for themselves, the chances are they can pay for him too.

'Let's look for that Italian,' he says. 'Luca. He can always get it.'

Luca is an Italian junkie I've seen once before. So now we're looking for Luca. Oxford Street, Dean Street, Old Compton Street, Frith Street. I'm rattling. I remind myself that there's a bit of money in my pocket so I know I won't be rattling long, but it's that waiting thing again. Waiting, looking, waiting for my hit. How many hundreds of years have I spent just waiting? I'm starting to shake now. I remember that I've got nowhere to go tonight and the sick, empty, lost feeling opens up fissures in my soul and the rattle slips down inside these chasms like poison and it penetrates my bones, my heart. My heart. It's rattling.

I'm getting desperate. Frith Street, Manette Street, Charing Cross Road, Sutton Row. Finally we see Luca in Soho Square and he gets on his mobile phone and arranges to meet someone who has heroin and crack. He takes my money but Steve gets a shifty, streetwise look in his eye and tells me not to trust Luca because we don't know him well. So we follow him up and down the busy streets of Soho at a distance, very slowly because Steve shuffles along in his hunchbacked way. We look only at the greasy-haired, dirty figure of Luca. A lot of other people pass us but we don't see anyone else. We're waiting. We're fixated. Then, finally, we see the transaction take place and Luca makes his way back to Soho Square and so do we and he hands over the gear.

An irony. Central London is the easiest place to find drugs and the hardest place to find anywhere you can take them. I look wildly around the bushes in the square but Steve leads me away. We walk differently now. There's a spring in our step. We make jokes. We're on our way to a hit.

Carlisle Street, Wardour Street, Brewer Street, Glasshouse Street. And then we're at the toilets in Piccadilly Circus underground, Shaftesbury Avenue exit. Down the stairs, through the door and into the underworld. Businessmen, gays, doors open, doors closed, men flitting in and out with their faces turned down. Only one person stands still.

'That's Dave,' says Steve.

Dave's at the basins and a dog waits patiently at his feet. Dave has his top off and a can of Special Brew in his hand. He's supposed to be washing but actually he's gouching after a hit. His eyes are closed and he's wailing. I understand that wailing. It's not that he's in great physical pain: he's just had a hit. But the hit has failed to quench some deep mental anguish.

Steve and I make straight for a cubicle with a coke can we've picked up in the street and some citric. We have to use his works because I don't have any. I don't care about sharing a needle. We need a bit of water too but now our hit's so close we're not going to traipse over to Burger King. Steve flushes the toilet then scoops some water out of the pan. I've never done that before.

I sit on the cistern and Steve sits on the toilet. If anyone looks underneath the door, it will seem there's only one person in here. We have to get out as soon as we can because Steve says the Africans who supervise the place will bang on the door if we stay in too long.

We have a snowball: crack and heroin. I try to breathe through my eyes and my ears and close myself up so that I can get the big whoosh. You can almost see where the crack is in my body because as it passes all my hairs stand on end. It's moving up to my head and here it comes, the crack high. It's a spinning top, a bucking bronco, a rocket to the moon. It explodes into my head and it doesn't make love to my brain, it fucks my brain. Oh, it is so good. Oh, it is better than anything else anywhere.

Then, within a few minutes it is ending and the warm fuzziness of the heroin takes over, brings relief from my re-emerging pain, eases the come-down.

But we're still pranged. Feeling the crack terror, the irrational panic, our hearts pumping, looking everywhere, we leave the cubicle. There's Dave and his dog in front of the mirror. They haven't moved. They're a still-life amid all this frantic motion.

We go up the steps into the Piccadilly madness of all those people and footsteps and it's too much for two guys trying to manage the mad bustle inside their heads, the voices muttering, muttering between our ears, the footsteps hurrying in the corridors of our brains. We can't stand it. After a hit we need some peace. We turn up an alleyway and keep on walking.

Glasshouse Street, Golden Square, Beak Street, Lexington Street, Broadwick Street, Berwick Street, Rupert Street, Coventry Street, Leicester Square, Cranbourn Street.

There's a Catholic church here. I go up the marble steps and try the door. It's locked. But Steve has already turned right where there's a hatch. He's a regular and he knows. He asks the woman behind the hatch if his friend can have a cup of tea and a sandwich as well. She must be a volunteer. She looks like some of the ladies who go to my mum's church. She's grey-haired and she doesn't smile or speak to me or even look kind but she's businesslike and I'm grateful for that. She hands me tea in a polystyrene mug and a sandwich wrapped up tightly in clingfilm.

We go back down the steps and I give Steve my sandwich. I know that even when I'm not pranged I won't be able to eat it; I'm too scared and sad. He sticks it in his pocket. We walk about and time passes, a minute, an hour, three hours, it all feels the same. I need another hit and there's no waiting this time because I bought a few extra bags from Luca.

After the hit we walk further and then, at a corner, without any warning or goodbye, Steve peels off. Suddenly, he's gone. I'm by myself. Night is falling. I panic. My loneliness feels bigger than I am. I remember that I have a son and I don't see him any more, and that it's a good thing he can't see me now. I fight tears.

I wander. I am scared. This is a hostile environment. You've got to be off your head to live here. And you've got to have nothing or they'd find you, the voices, the footsteps, and they'd strip you down and take it all.

Wardour Street, Broadwick Street, Poland Street, Oxford Street, Wardour Street, Brewer Street, Beak Street, Broadwick Street, Berwick Street, Brewer Street, Glasshouse Street.

At Piccadilly I climb down the stairs and there's Dave again. He's begging in the tube station with a cup held out, his dog's head on his lap and his own head bowed as though praying. He's stopped wailing. I talk to him a bit.

We both need a hit so I use up the last of my cash on a couple of bags for us. He says that when I need one and he's begged a bit of money, he'll bring me in, too.

By now it's dark. I'm shy when I tell him it's my first night. He's kind. There is a transparency about these street people and I see his kindness as clearly as I see any part of his body, like his fingers or his nose. We sit together at the bottom of a flight of steps at the back of Piccadilly station and talk. First, I do all the talking. I can't help it. I just have to. It all comes out. My family, my dad, my habit, Jack, how I've tried to get clean so many times and then how I trained for a job and tried to manage my habit but nothing's ever worked. I can't get off the gear. And I've used up all the goodwill anyone ever had for me. So there's nowhere else to go tonight.

Dave is sympathetic: he strokes Boots the dog and tells me about himself. I know there are people living on the streets from all over Britain and all over the world, but Dave actually comes from central London. I can hear it in his accent. Real London, quite gentle, the sort of accent I've only heard in old movies. I watch him while he speaks. Thick black hair, crew-cut, thick eyelashes, a few home-made tattoos. He tells me about the terrible abuse he suffered at home. His father used to whip him like a dog. He holds Boots closer as he talks. At one time we both had normal lives. But this is not normal now, we are not normal. I want to cry, the kind of howl Dave was doing earlier, to express my misery.

When they close the gates on the stairs for the night we set off together. Dave carries a load of baggage: a sleeping bag, a carrier bag or two, the dog . . . you can tell he's been on the streets a long time. But it's my first night and I have nothing. A gloom has settled over London, broken by the dazzling bright lights of Piccadilly. The colour of the lights is unnatural. It doesn't occur in nature. The lights are flashing out some message that is for other people, not for us. The streets are still busy but the people are mostly younger now, Londoners clubbing and partying, foreigners watching them, watching each other. No one sees us. They know what we are.

I stay close to Dave. I am relieved I have found someone kind to be with on this broken-hearted night. He walks as slowly as an old man, although from his life story I've already worked out that he's not yet thirty. His dog, a quiet and smooth-haired mongrel, walks at his pace.

Dave guides us to a cinema doorway in the Haymarket. We need some cardboard and that's something I can do, so I go off at my own fast speed and prowl around until I find some outside a shop. We put it on the pavement and lie down with Boots the dog between us and Dave's blanket over us. Although it's summer, we are cold. It begins to rain but because Dave is kind he lies on the outside, so he's the one who gets wet. I should be able to sleep as I stay dry, but there is a howling draught from under the door behind me.

We don't talk. I close my eyes. Boots is already dreaming dog dreams, doing little twitches. I feel the cardboard beneath me, and beneath that the hard pavement. I shiver under Dave's blanket and am glad of heroin that numbs all feelings. I don't want to know about my feelings. I don't want to care.

I wake up at about nine o'clock, cold, stiff, damp and very miserable. When I open my eyes I can see the drizzle. I remember that I've just spent my first night on the streets. And I'm rattling. Feet are walking past. I have a worm's eye view of London. Heels and trainers and knees and coat hems and briefcases and handbags. No faces.

Dave's still asleep. Aching, I drag myself up onto my feet and head for the bank. I pass golden statues of plunging horses. I know I have a bit of money left. I was hoping it would be £100 but it's only £50. I withdraw it and score almost immediately from a bloke who tells me I can find him in Soho most mornings until ten-ish. So there's no waiting this time. I make my way back to Dave and by now it's pissing with rain. People are standing under bus shelters staring out at me. I wake Dave up with a bag.

Dave and Boots take up their begging post by the toilets at Piccadilly. He says he has his regulars and they take care of him.

'I'll warn you now,' he says. 'Bank holidays are the worst. Sundays are bad, Bank holidays are fucking shit.'

Probably he means begging. But I don't want to beg. I don't want to give people the chance to reject me simply by walking past me on the street. Plus I couldn't earn enough money from begging to support my habit, which is now so immense it feels bigger than Soho, bigger than London. I need all the crack I can get: ideally, I'd inject at every opportunity, certainly more than once an hour if possible. As for heroin, there's no upper limit but I can't survive on much less than two grams a day. A .2g bag can cost up to £10 although I can usually blag the dealer a few quid down. Even with blagging, my habit costs at least £300 a day and often a lot more, and there's only one way to make that sort of money: stealing.

As soon as my money's gone I'm in constant circulation, endlessly vigilant, looking for stealing opportunities like unguarded handbags or tourists so busy with their camera that they forget their wallets. I'm always looking to score. And I'm always looking for friends. Everyone on the streets is my friend now, and no one is. I notice how we assemble randomly in shabby groups or chase each other around blocks.

'Bring me in, bruv.'

'Sort me out, bruv.'

'What you got?'

'All right, bruv?'

We flock in a park with the birds and then, like pigeons, without warning, we suddenly disappear in different directions. Or we walk in twos or threes or more, people joining us without greetings and peeling off without farewells. When we're together I feel warmed by great friendship and fellow feeling. Then suddenly I find myself alone, pranged, panicking.

Since I'm new, I don't say much. I listen to the others. All the talk is survival talk and I have a lot to learn. Different places to score. Which day the Oxford Street coffee shops throw out their stale biscuits. How the Broadwick Street toilets are presided over by a big black woman called Momma who is more likely than most to give you time for a hit before she bangs on the door. Where to steal sushi. How to get at the supermarkets' discarded food. Where to sleep, where to go for a hit. How to fool store detectives. I listen intently, a diligent student because information is life.

There's almost no kindness on the streets; this is a jungle and we all have to survive. But most people show me their softer side because I'm new. I find it hard, very hard, to make enough money for all the drugs I need and I'm sick a lot of the time. I'm sick and miserable one morning when I meet up with a lad who's a bit older than me on Shaftesbury Avenue and I'm drawn to him. Ginge is big and chaotic and quick-witted, and he reminds me of me. We go for a hit together in one of the weird concrete toilets that are situated on street corners like bunkers. We pay our 20p and the concrete door slides open to admit us to the tomb.

A baby-changing ledge folds down for a shelf and we put all our surgical instruments on it: our spoon and citric and coke can and the works. When Ginge has his hit he pulls his pants down to the middle of his thigh, flicks the top off a huge scab on his groin and sticks a gigantic syringe and fat needle straight through the hole into his main artery. And people are always telling me that I have good veins. I watch this operation with fascination as I sort myself out.

We're talking afterwards, coming down carefully, when without warning, the automatic door slides open. Passers-by are treated to the sight of two junkies and their paraphernalia and one of them has been caught with his trousers down. We blink out at the daylight and the people stare into our dark underworld.

'Oh shit,' says Ginge. 'I forgot there was a fucking fifteen-minute time limit in here.'

'Warning. This lavatory will disinfect,' announces a soul-less voice that has never needed a hit in its life. 'The disinfection procedure is carried out through the interior of the cabin. Warning. Please vacate the cabin immediately.'

'Better move fast or we'll be fucking drenched,' says Ginge. 'Come on.'

I follow. He isn't exactly going to show me the ropes – no one's going to do that in this jungle – but he's going to take me along with him.

On Shaftesbury Avenue, Ginge disappears. I am plunged into a dark, lonely world when I realise he isn't by my side. Then I catch sight of him in a phone box, anxiously searching the coin return for forgotten change. These disappearances are frequent. By the time we've traipsed around Soho I know that he's incapable of passing a telephone box.

We cut down a little alley towards Charing Cross Road and we're in a red-light district. There are girls hanging out of some of the upstairs windows. They show no interest in us. Downstairs a few pimps stand about, pressing cards and numbers and pictures on people. They don't reach for their cards when we pass. We go in through a peeling door and I wait on the ramshackle stairs while Ginge nips up and knocks. I hear the door open.

'Need anything?' he asks. There is the sound of distant chatter. Women's voices call to each other. Soon Ginge comes bounding down again reciting a list. Nivea hand cream, small red towel, nail varnish remover . . .

Leicester Square, Rupert Street, Raymond's Revue Bar, up the alley and round a corner to a rabbit warren of brothels. At night this place probably has some allure, with its dark shadows and bright, bright lights, but in the daytime it's all the colour of dirt. Even the pictures of the girls look dirty, their flesh grey. We're in another world, a labyrinth of passages, staircases, doorways, dim red lights. A few men rush past us on the stairs. A couple more are already drunk, bouncing off walls as they lurch about in the narrow passages.

We work our way along the doorways, knocking wherever there's a red light or a card pinned up boasting a fleshy model. When the door opens, the women inside don't look much like the models on the cards. Some are alone, others are in groups, sitting waiting for clients, drinking or brushing their hair or reading magazines. The girls come in all shapes and sizes and colours. Some of them are very

young, frightened Eastern European girls, too scared of their pimps
to spend any money. A few are beautiful. Others are old, with runny
red lipstick and tits like dried prunes poking through their 1970s see-
through nighties. At each door we get a snapshot of their lives. The
tasteless red wallpaper, the twenty-four-hour girl-talk, the fear, the
boredom, the longing to be somewhere else.

When we have a list of things to steal which is almost too long for
us to remember – cosmetics, towels, toys for their kids, underwear,
hairspray – we hit the Oxford Street shops to steal to order.

I was an accomplished thief as a kid and shoplifting turns out to be
one of those skills, like riding a bike, that you don't forget. Ginge is
good, but he's been around a long time and he's known to every
shop and every policeman. He wears a black leather-look puffa
jacket with the insides ripped out so he can fill it with stolen goods.
His trousers are black, his trainers are filthy, he is pale and spotty and
unwashed and as soon as he walks into shops any store detective is
going to be on full alert. He knows that, so we keep moving, working our way through shops at a fast pace.

We take the goods back to the unsmiling girls who pay us pathet-
ically little for our trouble. We might only get fifteen quid for
stealing ten items. It seems to me that this is a lot of work, and
knackering work, for not much money, but it's Ginge's speciality and
he's known to all the girls round here. The worst of it is, when we
hand over the stuff to really pretty prostitutes there's a strange, keen
kind of hurt. They hardly look at us. We are invisible to beautiful
women.

After our hit in the concrete toilet turned into such a public
event, Ginge leads me somewhere he promises is better. Brewer
Street, Old Compton Street, Greek Street, Sutton Row. On the
way he puts his head round the door of a second-hand record shop
up an alley.

'Hi Simon!' he calls to the guy behind the counter.

'Got anything for me today?' asks Simon.

'Maybe later. This is Mark,' says Ginge and I grin at Simon. Then
we're on our way again.

'Simon buys DVDs,' says Ginge. 'He'll take anything.'

We turn into a side road. He leads me to the back of a building. There are offices and shops at the front but here on the dirty dark side are no windows, just some stairs hidden behind waste bins. The stairs lead to a ledge. The ledge is probably a fire escape route but it might as well have been designed specially for junkies. Under cover, half dark, with a good view of who's coming but overlooked by no one except the occasional surprised passenger at the top of a double-decker, it's a junkie paradise. The West End's swirling all round us but this is an oasis of calm. About ten other junkies and assorted pigeons are using the place right now amid the litter of drug paraphernalia: spit, needles, cans, bottles of water.

'Watch out for them,' says Ginge, indicating a couple of junkies further down the ledge. They're so still they could be dead, except they're watching us. 'Twins. They're dangerous, a pair of lunatics.'

Parked nearby is the needles exchange van. Thousands of people pass it every day in different streets and probably hardly notice this small, nondescript vehicle. You have to be a junkie to recognise the clean needles symbol pasted on it discreetly. I go to the window and the man inside hands me some needles, a hand wipe and a sin bin, where I'm supposed to put the used needles.

'Do you know how important it is to use needles safely?' he asks as he hands it over.

'Oh yeah,' I assure him. I know how important it is and I try to use clean needles but when I've got the gear and I don't have a needle then I'll do anything. I've taken a dirty one out of a sin bin before now and God only knows who used it before me. And I've shared with Ginge today, who almost certainly has the virus. Not that I care. Dying is not something I think about or understand. Living is only about hits for me now. I'm like a fairground machine. Put in some money and it's all lights and colour and music. The money runs out and it stops.

Chapter 28

By the standards of street sleeping, my first night with Dave and Boots and a blanket was quite comfortable. Now the nights are colder and lonelier and it seems I go days at a time with almost no sleep. I'm so pranged on crack that I just keep walking around. I have started looking in dustbins. It gives me something to do with my paranoia and it makes me appear so much like a tramp that no one bothers me, not the public, not the police. It's like wearing camouflage or being invisible. I walk carefully, with one foot in the gutter and one on the kerb. This distracts me from my paranoia and the cruel voices that taunt me inside my head. Idiot. Junkie. Failure.

Whenever I pass a dustbin, I stop and search. I find a handbag. It has been stolen and the thief took all the money out but there is a bankcard still inside it. I take the card. I find some half-eaten cookies in a paper bag in another dustbin and I realise I'm hungry and I eat what's left of them and then carry on walking. More slowly now, because my shoes have started to rub my feet.

I go back to the same doorway where Dave and I slept that first night and I get some cardboard again but it barely cushions me from the stone pavement and Dave isn't there and nor is Boots. I recognise the draught that howls from under the door.

In the morning I can hardly get up. I know I weigh less than ever but my body feels heavy like lead. I am a machine. Great pistons push and pull each foot up and down, up and down, up and down. Giving a rhythm to my pain brings a sort of comfort. The mighty pistons govern my slow progress along the street. My head throbs, everything aches, my feet feel skinless. I am sick, I am sick. I look up. I am passing the golden, plunging horses. I have to get some money somehow. I have to score. I am filled by an immense weariness.

Then, in my pocket, I feel the stolen bankcard. My pace quickens and a little of my energy returns, enough for me to stagger to the NatWest bank and tell the prim-faced woman at the counter how I found the card. She nods without smiling. She looks at me through thick glasses. The glass that separates her from the public is thick too so it seems she is far away from me.

The cashier takes the card and consults her computer terminal for the card's history. Tap tap tap on the keys, the hint of a dance beat under her fingers. I look around. Inside. I am inside, under a roof. Most of the roofs I know these days are over busy shops or cold stone doorways or public toilets. But the bank is warm and hushed and even when people talk there is the sense of the thick walls around us and thick carpet beneath our feet. It is metres away from the streets I live on, and many worlds away.

I become aware of a man looking at me. He's standing at the next counter, waiting for his cashier to beat out some bass on her keyboard but he's looking at me. In fact, he was listening openly when I told my story and handed over the card. He's a small, turbaned Sikh and right now, he does something very surprising. He smiles at me.

My cashier returns and, wordlessly, her lips still tight, hands over my reward. It's £20. I nod and slip it in my pocket and turn to go. I haven't got to the door when the Sikh stops me.

'Excuse me,' he says, his voice soft, his tone pure kindness. 'But I couldn't help overhearing your story. I'd like to tell you how impressed I am that you handed over that bankcard.'

Evidently he didn't see the cashier pay me my £20 reward. Evidently he doesn't realise that I can't do anything with a stolen bankcard, or I would certainly have used it. Apparently he has no idea that I survive almost entirely on criminal activity. He's naive. And his naivety is my opportunity.

'I'm homeless,' I explain. 'I did have a job but I got sacked in a round of redundancies and no one could help me, not my friends or my family, and I'm only on the streets until I can get myself sorted out . . .'

He nods sympathetically while I give him my blag, lots of it.

'It's amazing that your honesty remains in these circumstances. I'd like to help you.'

My nose twitches and not just because I need a hit.

He gets out a card. 'This is my name and number. Call me and I'll do my best to help you find a job.'

'Thank you, thank you,' I say. 'I really want to change. I can't go on much longer on the streets, it's killing me, but I have to eat and clean myself up in order to present myself for work because no one's going to want me looking like this . . .'

His face creases with kindness and he reaches into his wallet and presses a £20 note into my hand. I thank him and we both step into the outside world, its air, its movement and dust and smells. My habitat.

'Good luck,' says the Sikh and we melt into the passing crowds.

A little bit of me is sorry to fleece him but I'm an addict and for years now I've been fleecing anyone who's shown me an ounce of kindness, including my own family. He's restored my faith in humanity, at least for this morning, but his kindness has opened up a few fissures and I don't want to look down them into the vacancies beneath. I must keep my mind, as well as my body, constantly dosed with drugs, or panic, emptiness and isolation overtake me and that's when I must, must, must have a hit and stop the terror.

The heroin soothes away my physical pains and eases my anguish. The crack euphoria floods my mind. Afterwards, when I've come down from the wildness of the paranoia it induces, I meet up with Ben. He's very tall and gangly and he is filthy. There are levels of filth on the street and Ben's level is high. His hair is greasy, his skin spotty, his neck ringed by dirt. And his feet are hanging out of his shoes, when it's quite easy to steal a new pair. So he must be a beggar. No one's going to give money to a clean beggar.

He's thoughtful and soft spoken, even well spoken, a refugee from the middle classes. Ben's the sort of man you can confide in but he doesn't share his story with me and I don't ask. Since that first night with Dave, I haven't asked anyone anything. I know that nobody chooses to be here. We're outcasts, we all know that; we all must share histories of abuse or mental illness or anguish of some kind, and we have to accept each other because no one else will. No questions necessary, no probing appropriate.

I get talking to Ben. How hard it is to sleep, how cruel the mornings are.

He nods. He understands. I want to latch onto this man, grab him and hold onto him but you can't do that on the streets. You can't do it ever. You're living with your own isolation.

Ben says: 'It's worse in the beginning. It takes a while to learn how to live.'

He takes me down the Mall where the cars move with a sort of reverence and no one hoots. At the end we pass Buckingham Palace. We pause at the railings. A flag flies overhead. A black car slides out through the gates, which may or may not contain the queen. Tourists cluster. Policemen watch us. Briefly I feel united with the other people here. The queen is separated by her great wealth from all of our lives and we are all onlookers together. Then we move on.

Ben leads me to an old, white, smooth-faced building behind Victoria station where rich people must have lived a hundred years ago. It's called the Passageway and we're allowed to push four hard dining chairs together and sleep on them until two o'clock in the afternoon. There are about ten smelly men already doing this and I fall asleep to the sound of snoring. When we're woken up and chucked out at two, I can barely walk. My feet are raw slabs of meat, my body burns, my head aches. I need a hit and I'm in no fit state to raise the money. This threat to my survival terrifies me.

Ben says: 'Come on, mate.'

I lean on him as we shamble to Victoria station and down onto the tube. In the ticket hall passengers scurry in all directions like ants. Standing still feels like a criminal offence. Ben gets behind a passenger in the hubbub and slips through the ticket machines behind her.

She doesn't even realise she's just got two through for the price of one. Ben's movement is rapid and graceful like a raindrop falling.

Ben turns and looks back, waiting for me. I'm nervous. I stand in the short line as paying punters stick in their tickets and the arms open for them. When the woman in front of me moves through the machines, I copy Ben and move forward too, skimming right behind her but not quite touching her. I'm not graceful like Ben was but my body slips through the barrier as though I am invisible. I hear the arms close shut behind me. So I am invisible. I am a ghost on the tube.

On the southbound platform, Ben stoops to pick up a cup from under a seat and when a tube train comes in he jumps aboard.

'Now, watch me,' he says.

He walks through the first carriage and, once the train is moving, enters the second carriage through the connecting door. The punters are miserable as soon as they see us. They look away rapidly. They read their newspapers, they study the floor, they stare at the darkness out of the windows.

Ben closes the door behind us and runs a hand through his greasy blond hair. He says in a loud voice: 'I'm homeless. I need something to eat and a bed for the night. I'd like to ask you please to help me out.'

He walks up to a small, round bloke who'd rather read his newspaper and stands there until the man grudgingly puts his hand in his pocket and fishes for his loose change. After that, Ben walks down through the carriage and people on all sides put money into the cup. He's big, he's intimidating, he looks like a desperado and no one's going to argue.

At the next stop we hop off the train.

'See how easy?' says Ben. 'The bloke in the suit: if he hadn't put his hand in his pocket, no one would have given anything. Get the first one and the rest follow.'

He reaches down into a rubbish bin and hands me a cup, shaking out the coffee dregs. The train departs, leaving a whoosh of underground air on our faces like a brief warm embrace. My feet hurt so much that I steady myself against the platform wall.

Ben says: 'I'll start further down the train and we'll meet.'

I don't want to beg but I can't think of any other way right now of getting my hands on the money I need.

The train stops. I get on and forget for a moment how sick I feel because I'm a different sort of sick now, sick with fear. I go to the connecting door. I slip through it into the next carriage as the train starts and I shut the door behind me. I clear my throat. A lot of people look up. They try to turn away but I don't let them. There must be fifty people, maybe even a hundred. It feels as though I'm about to address the entire Royal Albert Hall.

I speak to them all: 'I'm homeless.'

Hearing my own voice say it, announce my shame to the world, takes my breath away. I give a short gasp before I go on. 'I'm homeless and I've got nothing to eat and nowhere to go. I need some food and a bed. Please, can you help me?'

I stand and look at them, the way Ben did. It's hard. I'd rather look at the ground but that isn't going to get the coins into the cup. The degradation. The shame of asking for, demanding, money. I have sickened myself but now I have to go through with it.

There's a silence. You could cut the atmosphere with a knife. I stare out a group of girls who are sitting nearest to me. They're about eighteen and I'm making them nervous. There's already a lot of paranoia on the tube: nobody talks, nobody meets anyone else's eye, nobody's sure where to look. Now I'm playing on the fear passengers feel when someone actually engages with them.

The girls slowly open their handbags and coins, £1, 50p, 20p, drop into the cup. I hate myself. My shame feels like physical pain. But all of a sudden everyone's hands are moving and they're all reaching into wallets and purses. I've got them. I work my way down the carriage muttering thank-yous and the cup's soon making the pleasant, thick clinking noise of coin on coin. I go through a connecting door and there's Ben. He's worked his way up the train towards me. His carriage is as silent as the one I've just left.

The tube slows. As soon as it arrives at a station we're out onto the platform.

'Easy, see,' says Ben.

'Fucking hell. I mean, fucking hell,' I keep repeating. My feet still hurt and my nose is running but I can live with it because I've got a cup full of money. A sign tells us we're in Brixton. We cross over and leap on a northbound train as the doors close, in case we've been caught on camera. We get out at Oxford Circus and walk to Tottenham Court Road. When I count the money in my mug, it comes to £18. I should be able to blag a dealer down to £18 for a bag of each.

Ben takes me for a hit on the ramp of an underground car park. There are a lot of junkies here, gouching and out of it, with their blood and cans and works, sitting a few feet away from the cars going down the ramp. They glide right by, unseeing, creating small disturbances in the air around my face.

'Did you see that?' I ask Ben.

'What?'

'Jeremy Beadle just drove past.'

This makes us laugh for some reason. Jeremy Beadle in his big shiny car just drove past. We sit and laugh and I realise this is the first time I've laughed on the streets or even smiled, and I've never seen anyone else laugh either.

Ben's mate, John, shows up. He's tall and straw-haired and he has a guitar on a string over his shoulder.

'I know you,' he says, and I stare at him. His jagged face suddenly matches up with a face I used to know.

I grope my way towards another world and another time, a greener world. The time of Rosie. A travellers' site, where I used to sell drugs, where she'd retreat after a row and I'd come and find her. A site in Somerset.

'Frome!' I say. Fields and trees and Rosie, sitting in the back of the camper van, tapping around her fingers with a needle while outside are voices.

John grins a crooked grin. It's the John I used to sell to.

'I remember that camper van of yours,' he says. Oh, that camper van. Lovingly restored for thousands of pounds, finally sold when I got back from America for a quarter-ounce of heroin.

The three of us sit and talk on the ramp while cars bearing

businessmen and celebrities slide past us. It's strange to have a shared past with someone here. Back then, we were both dealing and we were both addicted but our addiction was more manageable. I wasn't even injecting, I was smoking. They were sweet days. We talk about people and places and events from that other world and this makes me feel more substantial: I'm a person with a past and not just a ghost.

I see Ginge often. He's here, he's there, he's everywhere, stealing, scoring, using, darting in and out of every telephone box in west London. I've already understood the chaotic nature of his life. Sometimes he has more than enough heroin, sometimes he's got nothing, sometimes he does crazy things to get more, sometimes he runs out of steam and collapses sick. He burns a lot of energy to get his drugs. I am probably more like Ginge than anyone else I've met here. I'm not like Ben because I'm not a beggar. And I'm certainly not like Dave, who has managed to stabilise his life, as far as a junkie can. Dave always begs in the same place in Piccadilly Circus tube station, he can rely on his regulars to put money in his cup and keep him and Boots alive, he eats meals and moves slowly. He paces himself. For an addict on the streets, he's in reasonably good health. And he's endlessly kind-hearted. I sometimes see him being kind to other people the way he was to me. There's a kid called Katie who can't be more than seventeen, a heroin and crack addict. She's skinny and she has scruffy blonde hair and when I knocked around the streets with her for a day or two I could see the big, leery, noisy woman with missing teeth she's going to become. But now she looks young and vulnerable. She's abused on the streets, just like she was abused at home. I've sometimes seen good, kind Dave taking care of her.

On a busy, late Saturday night Ginge is circulating in Soho as usual and I hook up with him. He suggests that we tax a rent boy, that's always a good route to easy money as they're fairies and they don't fight. We find one working near Piccadilly, a chubby lad of about eighteen with a desperate look about him. He's grubby but he's wearing good clothes. We push him up against the railings and start being nasty.

'Come on, you've made enough tonight . . .'

'No I ain't made a penny!' he assures us, eyes wide.

'You fucking have. Get your hands down your trousers.'

'I ain't made nothing tonight.'

'You're talking shit. Give us some, come on.'

We pull him into a dark car park. People see us dragging him and threatening him but no one stops us. It's as though we're all painted red, we street people. When we look through crowds, we don't see the normal people. We only see the other people painted red: junkies and dealers and criminals and dossers. And when normal people look through a crowd, they only see each other, not the red people.

'Now get your hand up your arse and get it out,' we tell him.

The rent boy's scared and he squats to pull out from his arse a little plastic container that might just be from a Kinder Surprise chocolate egg. Now this isn't what the makers intended it for. But inside is indeed a Surprise: some cocaine, plus about £60 in notes. We take it all.

'Fucking bastard wankers,' he roars after us tearfully. We ignore him. We're busy dividing up the money.

I don't eat much. I'm not interested in food. I certainly don't go sniffing around soup kitchens. I'm usually too pranged when the kitchens are out and about and they're for a different kind of home-lessness, the kind that sleeps in doorways on main streets and demands attention and doesn't want to be invisible. I'll have a cup of tea from a church or occasionally I'll steal some sushi from Sainsbury's. One night of the week Starbucks puts out sacks of their old biscuits. Every evening Pret a Manger disposes of unsold salads. You can eat like a king here on other people's waste. But my diet is mostly Snickers bars. I discover that, as long as I have crack and gear, I can survive on nothing more than a few Snickers a week.

Days pass. I remember how it was so important to gain acceptance in jail. Acceptance is an understanding that you're here and you're staying here. I try to gain acceptance now. But there's one big dif-ference between the streets and jail. I knew I was coming out of prison at the end of my sentence. And I don't know where this will end. I try not to think about that.

I'm walking down Beak Street past one of the second-hand record shops when I halt. I've remembered something that happened in my first week on the streets. I was with Ginge and he put his head round a door near here and said hi to someone called Simon who buys DVDs. I turn. I pace the streets until I find the shop. I put my head around the door.

'Simon?' I ask.

'Yeah?'

I go inside and check that Simon still wants DVDs. He nods.

'Seven quid each.'

I discuss what might interest him as though I'm a responsible sales rep wearing a tie and taking orders, but it's obvious that Simon doesn't really care what I get.

Seven quid each! Why didn't I try this before? I head straight off to a shop selling DVDs and indiscriminately pick them off the shelves. I use a razor on the security tag, slip them into my pockets and get out of the shop fast. It is almost ridiculously easy. The shop value of each DVD is £20 to £30 and when I get to Simon's I find there are ten in my bag. Without questions or even checking what they are, Simon hands over £70. I am rich. I have just earned more in ten minutes than I could in a day of turning in bankcards or begging on the tube or stealing nail varnish for prostitutes.

So this is the way ahead for me. Now my path is clear. The West End is a Mecca for DVD theft: there are six superstores within a short sprint. A quick survey of a variety of little Soho outlets, from record stores to sex shops, reveals that I can offload as many DVDs as I can steal.

Now my life changes. I have a job, like Ben on the tube and Dave at Piccadilly. I steal DVDs for a living. I set about it in a professional, systematic way. Unlike the beggars, I can't let myself get too dirty and untidy. I have to steal or borrow clothes that will make me look at worst like a scruffy tourist. I can't let my hair get too long and greasy and from the neck up I have to be clean. I have to circulate round the big stores in different clothes and at different times so that no store detective gets to know my face. I'm even prepared to buy a false moustache, but a few weeks later I find something much more useful than facial hair.

I am having a hit behind a chemist's near the Tottenham Court Road end of Oxford Street when I notice that a delivery is arriving at the back of one of the music megastores. When I've come down and am feeling comforted by the heroin and not too toxic from the crack any more, I go and take a look at the delivery. There's no one around to stop me. I put my hand in a box and pull out some black T-shirts. One of them has the shop's logo but stamped across it is the magic word: SECURITY. These are the T-shirts the store detectives wear.

I grab a handful and get away fast. And now I develop a technique using my new T-shirts. I drag myself into the shop early in the morning when the assistants are careless and there aren't many customers around. Off comes my jacket to reveal the word SECURITY. Then I kneel down and sweep stuff into my bag. I don't pick and choose. I don't lift in ones and twos. I run my arm along a shelf and tens of DVDs drop into my bag. Probably no one even looks at me: if they do they think I'm a member of the security crew. To save razor-blading, I've lined my bag with silver foil, which fools the alarm as I'm walking out. And then it's straight off to Soho to cash in. I can earn about £400 a day like this. It pays me to hang around outside another music megastore waiting for their SECURITY T-shirts to arrive too.

And suddenly I can afford the drugs I need. The mornings are still appalling as I wake up sick and frozen, drag myself from doorways, force those pistons to work, half crawl through the rain to steal some DVDs so I can score and get my first hit. But I'm managing now. I begin to delude myself that I am managing well. I even tell myself that life is better this way. Survival is a straightforward objective and it simplifies everything. I have to get drugs and take them. All the other stuff: managing relationships, finding housing, paying rent, waiting for wages, leading a social life, getting transport, it's all gone away. Drugs have left my life free of complication. All I have to do is get money so I can get drugs, get citric, get a spoon and water from McDonald's and get the stuff inside myself. Simple. Except that each day my feet hurt a little more, each day the come-down is worse, the rattle's worse, the chasm of isolation and humiliation and panic grows inside me and needs more and more drugs to fill it.

It turns out that Dave was right about Sundays. I soon learn to hate them. There's Saturday with its buying frenzy and its night-time clubbers. Then there's Sunday when the streets are quiet, the people are different, some of the small shops are closed and the big ones shut at four, and none of my usual means of fundraising works. We all feel desperation on Sundays. Someone organised like Dave probably saves up a bit so he can score on Sunday but chaotic addicts like me have to take whatever we've got now so when Sunday comes round we have nothing. Then, thank God, it's Monday and people are busy and shops are open and there are many footsteps again. But one Monday, the rhythm's broken. It's like a Sunday, only much, much worse.

It must be a bank holiday. I'm desolate. I can't get any money anyhow. I must have a hit. I beg other addicts to bring me in. I'm always bringing them in and they owe me a favour, but no one ever remembers. In fact, everyone thinks I owe them a hit. So we're all walking around all day believing other people are indebted to us.

By afternoon I can't go on. I'm very sick. The rattle is unbearable. My drug use has escalated ever since I struck gold with the stolen DVDs and now going without is terrible. I've been swept up by a drugs tsunami and on bank holiday Monday it's dumped me high and dry on an empty island. I can't sleep, I can't lie down, I can't think, I can't stand up, I don't know what to do with my mind or my body, so I curl up in a ball near Eros, which is eerily traffic-free today, and start to whimper. A pair of feet in ill-fitting shoes shuffles past me, then stops and turns back. I look up. It's Steve, my first friend here on the streets.

'What's up?' he asks. But he knows what's up and I'm too sick to answer. He looks relaxed, as though he's just had a hit.

'Bank holiday rattle?'

'Bring me in,' I whisper.

He shakes his head. No gear. But he hauls me to my feet. Steve's source of income is begging and that's probably what we're going to do now. I am too desperate to decline, too sick to protest.

He drags me up to Tottenham Court Road. Progress is slow. I'm
complaining all the way, wailing and crying with pain. Near Centre
Point, Steve digs an old McDonald's cup out of a bin and tells me to
sit down on the pavement. I won't hold up the cup. That's too beg-
garly. So I put it down near me. Steve goes about twenty metres
away. I know that to beg successfully I should catch people's eye. But
I can't. I know I should speak to them. I try.

'Er . . . got a bit of change to spare?' I mutter without looking at
anyone's face. They must be able to hear my shame. Every single pair
of feet that passes me is a rejection and it hurts. It cuts into me. The
worst thing of all is that, if I glance upwards from a nice pair of heels,
I see pretty girls, the sort of girls I would have gone out with once.
Now they make a wide circle round me because they're scared,
because they're disgusted.

Occasionally someone gives me money. I try to thank them but I
can't.

I glance over at Steve. He hasn't moved since the last time I
looked at him. So that hit wasn't gear. A couple of beggars on the
other side of the street don't move either. They're all pharmaceutical junkies. They inject methadone ampoules. People buy methadone
amps from the crooked doctors who flourish in the West End. The
pharmaceutical junkies who take it can sit begging for hours
without moving a muscle.

But I can't. I can't sit still any longer. I've been demeaned and
degraded for hours and hours. I am rattling so much my body is on
fire. And I have made precisely £8, which is only enough for a single
bag if I blag the dealer. I throw away the McDonald's cup and walk
away past Steve. He doesn't see me. He's happy with his meth amp.
He's there but he's not there.

I go into the tube station. Oh, my feet. Pain. My bones. Pain. My
head. Pain. My heart. Pain, pain, pain. It's late afternoon now. There
are tickets lying all over the floor: whoever usually sweeps them
away is enjoying the bank holiday with their family while litter
mounts up at the station. I stoop down and small rivers of fire flare
up in every joint, making me cry out in protest. I pick up all the
tickets I can. Most of them are spent but a few of them are day

returns or the kind of tickets that enable you to roam zones freely. Passengers have either dropped them by mistake or because they have no further use for them.

I go straight to the ticket office and intercept people in the queue. I offer valid tickets at discount prices and it doesn't take me long to get rid of them. Suddenly, I'm elated. I almost have enough for a bag of gear and a bag of crack. I run down to Leicester Square. Tickets, tickets, everywhere. I pull the same trick. I don't care that I'm caught on the security cameras, I don't care about anything. I'm going to get my hit and tomorrow bank holiday will be over.

Chapter 29

I am learning to judge people, to develop a sixth sense which tells me who is trustworthy, who has a mental illness that goes beyond drug addiction, who is dangerous. The dangerous people are the reason I don't go to hostels, they're the reason I stay independent and isolated. I don't like the dangerous twins Ginge pointed out when I first came to the streets. They're called Keith and Malc and they prey on other street people. I've seen them playing head games with an innocent young Irish lad who'd never tried crack before, stirring his paranoia into a volcano until he became violent and dangerous like they are. I've seen them threatening other street people, stealing their gear. I'll take a hit when the twins are around but I won't sleep near them.

Other people come and go all the time. You get to know them and think they're your brother and then they disappear. Rumours circulate that they've died. Then suddenly they're back again because they were only in jail. Reports of Ginge's death have been greatly exaggerated: he's come back from beyond the grave at least three times. But often people really have gone for good. Apart from overdoses, Hepatitis C and HIV, people die from street violence and untreated secondary illnesses. You either die here or you go to hospital or you go to jail. No one ever goes home. This is home.

I bump into tall, gangly, straw-haired John from Frome one day by a bus stop, his guitar bumping along over his shoulder as usual. He's wearing at least three coats. John comes and goes in the West End. Probably he just goes down to his traveller mates in Somerset but maybe he goes to jail. Anyway, here he is now at the bus stop, not waiting for a bus but looking to score.

'I've only got nine pounds,' he says in his West Country burr. 'Bring me in, will you?'

He needs enough for crack and heroin. It happens that after some successful thieving I have £60 in my pocket so I agree to go halves with him. We look for a dealer.

Rathbone Street. Percy Street. Tottenham Court Road. Adeline Place. Great Russell Street. Hanway Place. Oxford Street. Great Chapel Street.

The dealer we find has four bags of crack. He's carrying them in a safe place: his mouth. They're double-wrapped in clingfilm so they'll reappear whole at the end of his system if the police approach and he ever has to swallow them. He spits them out for us and then says he'll be back when he's reloaded. I know him and trust him but John is incredulous that I've let a dealer walk off with our money. He's agitated. He tells everyone who passes that I've given his money away. This is humiliating and it's not true but he drags me to a telephone box in Charing Cross Road by the art college. I routinely search the coin return for change, a small homage to my mate Ginge, then I call the dealer. I phone him once, I phone him twice and that's more than enough but John insists that I phone him again and by the end of all this everyone's irritated.

We traipse back to Soho where Luca saunters past, offering Valium. This is something it's always good for crackheads to buy. I have five and stick them in my pocket for hideous future comedowns. John buys five too, then he runs after Luca and buys still more. I don't know how many he gets altogether but I have a horrible feeling he's taking them all.

When the dealer comes back I try to make John apologise for not trusting me and for humiliating me in front of all the passing street people. He does mumble something that might be 'Sorry!' but it could be anything because after the Valium he's only semiconscious. I throw his bags of crack and heroin at him but he falteringly begs me to help so I take pity and we stagger to the underground car park ramp beyond Tottenham Court Road. Not only do I have to half-carry John and his infuriating guitar on a string, but I have to take his bag too.

I am grumpy because I don't see why I should bear the consequences of John's greed and stupidity.

'These selfish fucking bastards who can't keep off the Valium,' I moan, 'they've got no consideration. None at all.'

It really is stupid to take Valium when you've got some crack waiting for you. Any fool knows that you take the upper before the downer. And he shouldn't take the gear next. He needs an upper in-between. I've seen any number of idiots go over that way.

When we get to the ramp, John flops down and his bag spills out all over the road. Irritably, I gather up its contents – a notebook and bits of paper and some photos and a bottle of water and some citric. I give him a bag of crack and cook up the heroin separately. Now I really have done all the work. I'm feeling martyred. He's wasting my valuable time and he's slowing me down. I'm busy, I'm sleek, I'm always on the move and I want to get on with my hit instead of taking care of a cretin.

I tell him: 'John, you have to do the crack first to wake you up. Got it? After all that Valium it's DANGEROUS to take the gear until you've had the crack.'

Well, talk to yourself.

'The CRACK first, then the GEAR. OKAY?'

But he should know that, for fuck's sake.

I go up the ramp and bang up my own drugs. Whoosh. The space rocket reaches the moon in one second and within ten it's dodging through the solar system where space is infinite, there are no boundaries, no beginning and no end. I'm orbiting the sun when I start the come-down. I close my eyes.

I stay on the ledge for another twenty minutes, listening to some of the junkie conversation around me. Today a couple of intellectual types are discussing nuclear physics. They sound like brilliant, educated, privileged people. What are they doing here on the ramp with their citric and their needles?

Then it's time for a busy guy like me to get back into action, prowling around, looking for money-making opportunities.

I head down the ramp. I don't want to look over at John but I can't avoid it. He's just where I left him. In fact, he hasn't moved. And he isn't moving now. His lips are blue. Has he gone over? The crack syringe is lying there, untouched. Oh fuck fuck fuck. Despite all my warnings, he took the heroin first.

My first thought is to pick up the crack for my own personal use. Then I walk straight on. I don't stop, I don't look at him, I don't roll him over to check that he's breathing, I look straight ahead and I walk. Away.

Tottenham Court Road, Oxford Street, Poland Street. Beak Street. Warwick Street. Glasshouse Street. Piccadilly Circus.

I hook up with Ben. I don't mention John. We pad off together down Regent Street into Pall Mall. We pause beside a huge red-brick wall. Behind it is something so spectacular that it takes my mind off John, his blue lips, the untouched syringe.

'Plane trees,' I tell Ben. 'Fucking old plane trees. I've never seen them so big.'

'That's Clarence House,' he says. 'The Queen Mother lives there.'

We look at the trees, the wall, the high, guarded gates. We stare into that other world then we move back into our own.

For a few days, a few weeks, I look out for John. I don't see him. I ask people. Casually.

'Er, seen John around? With the guitar? John?'

'No.'

'No, bruv.'

'Nope. Probably in the West Country.'

I hope he's back in Frome in that green world of fields and travellers. He's certainly gone from the West End. Maybe forever. I try to forget about his white face, his blue lips. But sometimes, late at night when I'm walking, one foot in the gutter, looking in bins, trying to keep the lid on my paranoia, I remember. The ten thousand voices have something to say about it. Bastard. You killed him. Prepared his hit, knew he wasn't well enough to take the right one, left him to it; you're an evil, murdering bastard.

Now I've been on the streets for a while, I really believe I'm learning how to live here. My activity is frantic: stealing, shoplifting, taxing, dealing a little. And it is followed by complete collapse. But I'm earning enough to support my habit. My feet hurt so much that it's better for me never to take my shoes and socks off. And my body is thin and scabby. But I'm surviving. I'm successful.

'You need a doctor, mate,' says Dave, the only kind voice on the street. He still tries to take care of me. When he and Ginge are together it's like having nice parents.

'I'm fine, I'm doing all right.'

'Yeah, but you're too thin. And your feet. Those scabs . . .'

'No fucking time, mate.'

I don't have time for anything. Probably I could collect some dole if I could just get myself up to Russell Square and stand in a line for hours, but now I have my own patch I don't want to leave it. My survival skills are specific to a square mile or so of the West End, where I now know every street, every shop and every opportunity. I've got a £300, maybe a £400-a-day habit and I'm too busy earning it to spend time walking out of my area for a bit of dole money which is less than I can make stealing in half an hour.

My DVD racket enables me to reach new heights of chaos and drug use. One morning I wake up star-shaped on Oxford Street. I don't remember getting there. Probably I reached exhaustion point and couldn't go any further. Someone's put a sandwich and a coffee and three quid down next to me. Thank you very much, mate. The shoppers and businessmen who've been stepping over my body all morning think I'm a lazy layabout. They don't realise I've collapsed because I'm working harder than they've ever worked in their lives, and probably earning more too. After all, I'm on £100,000 per annum, no, nearer £200,000. But that doesn't include a pension or sick pay, of course.

I'm sitting on a bench talking to Luca when something enormous crawls out from under his woolly hat, through his matted hair and down his face. It's half a fingernail in size.

I pick the squirming insect off him and crush it in my fingers. Blood pours from it.

'Well that's my blood,' says Luca in the lilting Italian accent that sometimes strangely reminds me of the Catholic youth club back in Kidderminster.

'What is it, then?' I ask, wiping the blood onto my jeans since Luca has the virus. Although it's a bit late for me to start worrying about AIDS.

He looks at me in surprise. 'Don't you know what it is?'

'Flea?'

'Body louse. We've all got them. You've got them too.'

And now I see he's right. There are tiny bites all over me and, if I take the trouble to look hard enough, tiny insects too. They don't itch or bother me except now that I know I'm co-existing with body lice I feel ashamed.

'I bet I got them swapping clothes in the Broadwick Street toilets.' The Broadwick Street toilets are a sociable place where I sometimes go for a wash. If other people are washing too, we'll exchange clothes to help fool store detectives.

Luca shrugs.

'You don't need to go to Broadwick Street. You can get fucking lice just sitting next to me right now. You tell the police you got them and they won't come near. No one will.'

'Like body armour?'

'Yeah, armour no one can see.'

All this time I've had a suit of armour and I didn't even know it. I live in fear of the police. They haunt my come-downs and feed my paranoia. If I get caught with the amount of heroin and crack I carry around then a jail sentence is inevitable. I have hiding places all over my body. Up my arse, in the foreskin of my penis, in my mouth, down my throat so that if the worst comes to the worst I can swallow it. But, since heroin use halts shitting, the only way to get that little clingfilm package out soon is by rattling myself into normal bodily functions. Otherwise I might have to wait weeks for it to reappear.

Soon afterwards, the police decide to move me along from my sleeping place in a doorway. They wave their batons in my face and ask my name and date of birth and when I've supplied this information I tell them something they don't want to hear.

'I've got body lice.'

Simultaneously, they take a step back.

'AB-D, AB-D,' they say over their radios. That means airborne disease. And from the police reaction I know Luca's right that lice are highly infectious. What police officer wants to take them home to his kids? It's beyond the call of duty. The police move me along but they don't search me.

The weather gets colder. I'm only warm enough when I've got some heroin inside me. And at least I can wear thicker coats, which make shoplifting easier. The stores do Hallowe'en and then out comes all the Christmas stuff. I've always hated Christmas. I hated the way my mum didn't believe in it because she was a Jehovah's Witness but did Christmas because Dad made her. I hate the way everyone contributes to the build-up and then nothing really happens on the day but disappointment. I ought to be glad I won't have any Christmas this year. But as the shops start with the lights and the tinsel and the nodding effigies of Snow White in their windows, I begin to feel desolate.

I want to talk to Rosie. I want to see Jack. I've lost my identity. My family might give it back. Christmas is a time for families and I want mine. I don't want to be on the streets. I don't want to be this way. I don't want them to know what I've become. Every time I think about them I feel a depth of isolation and sadness that is unbearable, that's too much to carry around with me. Where is my family? Where is my son? The Lakes? In the West Country down in that rehab place Rosie was trying?

Usually, when a mate hands me a stolen mobile and tells me to call anyone, anywhere, I stare at it and then hand it back because there's no one I can call. Phones mean misery for me because they remind me of my isolation. But this time, when Ben hands one over, I reach for a piece of paper I always keep with me. It's so creased it's barely legible and drug dealers' numbers have been scrawled all around it but in the middle is the last number Rosie gave me. So I dial it.

Someone answers. I ask to speak to Rosie. There's a pause. Then, incredibly, they say they'll get her.

I'm standing on a corner of Regent Street. The Christmas lights are on, the shop windows are bright, the bustle on the streets has increased exponentially lately and it's Saturday, so Hamleys is full of families. And I'm going to talk to Rosie. Maybe Jack too.

When I hear her voice I feel a weird melting sensation round my heart.

'It's Mark,' I say. I want to cry.

There is a pause. The silence is filled with surprise, maybe even with emotion. When she speaks, her voice is guarded: 'How're you doing?'

'I'm fine, just fine,' I lie. I want my voice to sound firm and cheerful but it's small. It's wavering. 'I'm in London, actually. Doing a bit of work here.'

'Good.'

'How's Jack?'

'He's really well.'

'Rosie, where are you?' Oh-oh. That sounded too much like a wail. I cough. 'I mean, are you still in rehab?'

'Yes, Mark, and I'm very happy. I'm clean!' Her voice is strong. Happy, even. 'It's because I've finally understood something important. I've understood that Jesus loves me. And He's changed my life.'

Fucking hell. I decide to ignore the bit about Jesus. 'So you're clean! Completely, totally, one hundred per cent . . . ?'

'I mean,' she's quick, too quick. 'I've got a methadone script. Just a small one. But I'm off gear. And I like it here. I understand what God's will is now, how He's looking after us. And . . . the baby's due soon.'

What's she talking about? What did she say? I can see crowds and hear buses and this woman in some other world's talking in my ear about a baby. Or did she?

'I said, the baby's due around Christmastime.'

The baby. Is due. Around Christmas.

'Mark? Are you there?'

'What baby?' I ask. What kind of a question is that? Is she having a baby? Has she told me she's having a baby? Would I forget a thing like that?

'I got pregnant back in the spring. When you came over from Ireland to pick up your climbing gear . . . remember?'

No.

'Remember?'

I remember walking in the park. We must have had sex back at her parents' house. It probably wasn't very good sex, I was so wasted. It certainly wasn't memorable.

Rosie says: 'Well, anyway, I got pregnant and the baby's due soon.'

Let's get this straight.

'You're having a baby? And it's mine?'

'Yes, Mark,' she says patiently.

'Why didn't you tell me before?'

'We haven't spoken for a long time, not properly.'

So this is speaking properly.

'I've had a lot to work out. I've had to understand how Jesus can help me. And, Mark, He'll help you too if you let Him.'

This is too much news. I love my son Jack and I have been the world's worst father and now there's going to be another child and Rosie is clean, or almost. Oh, and Jesus is going to help me.

'Are you okay, Mark?'

'I'm coming down to see you now.'

'You can't. This is rehab. You can't just walk in, they won't let you.'

'I'm allowed to see my son.'

'No, you're not.'

'Why can't I come into rehab too? I want to be clean.'

'This rehab is for women only.'

'Don't they take fathers? If the mothers are in rehab and the kids are with them?'

'They take men but at a different place, not in Devon.'

'Can I get clean too?'

'Do you want to get clean?'

I have that weird, melting feeling again. It spreads all through my body like heroin but it doesn't start from my arm or my groin, it starts in my heart. 'Of course I fucking want to get clean! Do you think anyone wants to live like this?'

'Like what?'

I am careful. 'You know. I mean, using. Using all the time.'

She gives me a number. She tells me who I should talk to. 'Phone if you really want to see us and get clean.'

'I fucking do!'

'Jesus loves you, Mark. Let Him into your life. But don't phone unless you mean it.'

I mean it. Jesus loves me and, unlike Jehovah who has been watching me and plotting the end of the world all these years, Jesus is going to sort things out for Mark. I phone a cold-voiced woman and demand to be admitted immediately to the rehabilitation pro-gramme. She tells me that she doesn't have any spaces. I talk about Rosie and how important it is that we are together and that we both get clean because she's having another baby.

'I know,' she says. So everyone knows but me.

'Can I come down to Devon?' I ask.

'The women's unit is in Devon. The men are in Somerset and we don't have any spaces.'

Devon. Somerset. Aren't they right next to each other?

'How far away is she from the men's unit?' I demand.

'Look, if you were resident you could see them on Sundays,' she tells me. 'I don't know when they'll have a place, though.'

I want a place. I need a place. I must have a place on that pro-gramme. An old vision I put aside long ago has suddenly returned: I am going to be the father of my family, clean and stable. Rosie, the mother, will be clean and stable. We will have two children and they will be clean and stable, too. And Jesus will love us all.

'Okay. I'll come next week,' I tell her.

I can hear her shaking his head.

'Just give me your number and I'll contact you when there's a pos-sibility.'

This is difficult. I give her my sister Bethany's number.

'I'll be down next week,' I tell her.

'There won't be a place next week.'

'Okay, two weeks, the baby's due soon.'

'I doubt there'll be a place. It could be months. You'll have to wait until I call you.'

'But I want to see Rosie and Jack . . . she's having a baby . . .'

'That won't be possible,' she informs me. And she puts the phone down.

I shake with anger. I stalk the streets. I phone the woman back three times and the third time I shout at her. I steal from Liberty's openly, brazenly, angrily, and no one stops me. I score. I have a hit. And I'm still livid. Who is this person to say I can't see Rosie? Who are these rehab people Jesus loves so much? Then, later, when I'm crumpled in a doorway, I start to cry. Does it matter who the rehab people are if they can cure you? I didn't think a cure was possible but Rosie sounded so firm and strong and clear and clean, like she hasn't sounded ever. She's doing so much better than me. She looks back on her life and I was her rock bottom. Jodie's clean and leading a godly life up in the Lakes now; I was her rock bottom too. They all get clean when I get out of their lives. I want me out of my life too. I want to be clean. I cry and cry. It's that anguished gear wail, the one Dave was doing when I first met him. And Dave is here.

'It'll be all right,' he says kindly. 'But you need a doctor.'

'No I don't.'

'I'm worried about you, mate. You need someone to look at those feet.'

And, for the first time, I agree with him. How can I go to Rosie's rehab with feet in this state? They might guess where I've been living. Rosie might guess. Jack might guess. He's three now, could he understand about his dad being on the streets? And what about my body lice? If I arrive with an airborne disease they'll turn me away for sure. Jesus loves but probably he doesn't love body lice. I might give them to Jack. To the baby.

'They'll do your body lice too,' says Dave. 'So let me take you to the clinic.'

Chapter 30

On Monday we steal some clean clothes and pad along at Dave's snail's pace to a clinic in Great Chapel Street where the nurse treats my feet. She soaks them and rubs on substances from bottles and finally my socks come away from my scabs. When at last, for the first time in months, my feet are bare, she turns them over gently in her hands, not as though I'm repulsive but as though she doesn't want to hurt me. It is strange to have someone touch me in this soft, kind way, someone dressed in white, clean and sweet and peaceful. She's like someone from another world. Maybe she's an angel.

'Shower now,' she says. 'Here's some anti-lice cream. Rub the cream all over your body, wait ten minutes, wash it off and then do it all again.'

I nod. I go into the shower room. I stare in the mirror. There's a naked man staring back at me. I don't recognise him. He's so skinny that his ribs show, all his bones show, his hips are stark. His skin is transparent, veins are visible on his chest, veins everywhere are horribly swollen, especially on his arms. His fingers are swollen. His arms are tattooed but this does not hide the deep, dark track marks, the scarring. His face is white but the rest of his body is a dirty grey and the skin round his eyes has blackened as though he doesn't sleep for weeks at a time. He has the tiny bites of body lice all over him.

His feet are covered in scabs. He looks sad and angry. God, how can that man be me?

I wash as the nurse has instructed me. The water cascades over this body of mine, the skin and bones, and its touch is warm and generous. I can't hear anything but the patter of water.

In my new, clean, lice-free clothes, I sit in the warm surgery as the nurse dresses the scabs on my feet.

'I'm going into rehab,' I tell her. 'I'll be joining the mother of my son down in the West Country. She's already clean and I'll be going into rehab as soon as they've got a place.'

The nurse pauses and looks at me. She seems genuinely pleased. 'That's good,' she says.

Over the next days and weeks I phone the rehab centre and I phone Rosie and, when it's nearly Christmas, a woman answers and tells me that Rosie's had the baby.

'It's a boy,' she says. 'He's to be called Freddie.'

He's my son. I should help decide what he's called. But I don't say this. I'm too overwhelmed by guilt and shame because I'm not with my family: I'm on the streets.

'Of course,' the voice says briskly, 'he's on medication. For the methadone withdrawal. The hospital's sorting it out. Otherwise the baby seems well enough.'

'When can I see them?' I ask.

'When the men's centre can find a place for you,' she tells me in a voice that indicates she knows all about me. She puts the phone down. Apparently it hasn't occurred to her to congratulate me.

I am gutted by this call. I have a new son and no one will tell me where he is or when I can see him. I have a family and they live in another world, far away. I am on these busy Christmas streets alone and unloved. I need a hit.

The mania that precedes Christmas has reached its height here in the West End. In a few days it will be Christmas Day and then it will all stop. Christmas is going to be a thousand times worse than ever before. It will be the bank holiday to end bank holidays. It will be freezing cold, the shops will close and they will stay closed for a long time. The offices will be shut until January. There will be fewer people, less traffic, almost no opportunities to steal except perhaps at New Year when the big millennium celebrations might offer me the odd chance to roll a drunk or steal a handbag. And there will be coppers, lots of them, in plain clothes, on every corner.

I go to a phone box and call my little sister, Bethany.

'It's Mark.'

'Hi, Mark!' She's the only person in the world who ever sounds pleased to hear from me. 'What are you doing for Christmas?' she asks.

'Er . . .'

'Are you in London?'

'Yeah.'

'Are you all right?'

'Rosie's had a baby,' I blurt out. And I tell her about it. 'I'm waiting for a place in rehab too.' I hear my own voice. Small, desperate.

'You'd better get yourself on the next train up here,' says Bethany quietly. And my heart jumps. I thought I'd used up all my goodwill from everyone. But Bethany's still there for me.

I'm going to start again. I'm getting off the streets. I'm going into a normal house with normal people and soon I'll be in rehab, then I'll get back with Rosie and not one but two children, and this time we'll be different and it will all be normal.

Of course, there are a few problems and the first of these is transport. It's difficult to go anywhere in my state of need. That's why I've stuck so rigidly to my patch of central London: because moving far from my drugs supply creates hideous problems.

I pick up one of the free magazines that litter the tube stations and buy a car from an ad at the back. My new Mini Metro costs £50. It consists mostly of rust. It has no MOT or tax, I have no insurance or driver's licence, and I don't care. I have a busy time shoplifting so that I can take a few gifts for Bethany's kids with me. That is a normal sort of thing to do. It is important to be normal.

I drive up to Warwick. When it rains, the Mini Metro skids all over the road. I don't even have to look at the tyres to know that they're bald. I can't stop because I have to get up there fast, between hits. Then, just before arriving, I have a hit so I don't walk in rattling.

I get to Bethany's with a small bag that is virtually empty except for the stolen Christmas presents. Bethany greets me warmly and her two little kids run around treating me like their long-lost playmate. Even Bethany's partner, Darren, is friendly. They live in a small block of flats surrounded by other small blocks of flats. It's not upmarket but it immediately fails my junkie's property-evaluation test: one glance tells me I won't be able to score here.

Bethany walks inside hugging me. She's small and very pretty and a bit overweight. When we've closed the door, she looks at me hard. She is silent. Then she turns away and leads me in.

'Well,' she says over her shoulder. Her voice is wavering. Is she crying? 'You've lost a bit of weight but I expect you'll put it on over Christmas. Everyone does.'

Bethany isn't a Jehovah's Witness any more and she doesn't take their anti-Christmas stance. She's got small kids and a Christmas tree and she's full-on festive. Darren stays friendly but whenever he's in the room I catch him staring at me. I put the kids' presents under the Christmas tree and try to play games with them. But I know that I'm clinging onto normality by my fingernails and if I try too hard then I'll certainly slip down the cliff face.

A meal's ready and we all sit down in seats and high chairs, and the sight of real food with bright vegetables on a plate shocks me because it's so long since I've seen it. I try to eat but I'm not used to big roast dinners.

'Don't you like it?' asks Bethany anxiously.

'It's delicious. Really lovely,' I assure her. 'I don't eat much these days.' And I tell a load of bullshit about how climbing all those big trees in London really takes it out of me and often I'm too tired to eat afterwards. Once I start lying, it's easy. I turn the clock back six months and tell them I live in the caravan and then I talk about the London plane trees and how I've worked at St Paul's Cathedral and 11 Downing Street.

'You must be doing well, or they wouldn't let you loose on those trees,' says Bethany enthusiastically. Too enthusiastically. She knows I'm lying, she's heard it all before. Darren says nothing. He eats and watches me.

After lunch I need a hit and I go to the bathroom and stay there a long time. I don't take crack, only heroin. After all, I have to act normal. And this is my last bag so I'll need to score. When I come out, I tell Bethany I'm just going to catch up with some old mates and I head straight for the M42 in my rusty Mini Metro looking for drugs.

I go to Birmingham, to the old places where I used to score with Jodie. I feel as though my life has been one crazy circle of drugs. Here I am in the park again where Jodie used to pick up clients. But it's changed. Different places, different people. Next time I'll stay on the M42 and try Wolverhampton.

Christmas is a blur of drugs and tinsel. I keep dashing up the motorway to shitty crack houses and then back to my nice sister trying to be normal. But it's obvious to Bethany and Darren that I'm not normal. They have a wild animal in their house. And they know it.

Mostly I manage to wait until they've gone to bed before I have a hit but occasionally Darren catches me hiding under the table. I'm not sure if he sees the needle in my arm. Every morning they find me asleep on the sofa in my clothes, because by now I'm incapable of getting under covers like a normal person. I overhear whispered conversations, Darren begging Bethany to tell me to go, but I'm not living in a world of reality any more and I don't know what's actually happening and what's paranoia. When Bethany borrows my coat to dash off to the nursery school, she puts her hand in the pocket and I think she gives me a hurt, sad look. Am I imagining it? Later I find I've left a needle in the pocket.

I make a bit of money over this period selling some Es and coke to Darren's younger relatives. I even earn some legitimate money: an uncle of Darren's asks me to do a few hours' tree surgery. I'd forgotten how it feels to wear a harness, to climb higher than the houses, to touch the rough bark and understand the force of long, slow steady years of growth under my fingers. For a while I forget everything else as I enter the tree's world. I should do more of this. I still love it.

I spend every day on the phone trying to extract a payment from the forestry company I worked for last year. They agree they still owe me something and, in the meantime, Bethany gives me money. So I survive. Just. And then, after Christmas, Rosie's rehab centre rings. They have a space for me.

'We'll expect you tomorrow,' says a brusque voice in a tone that suggests they're not looking forward to meeting me. But I don't care. I am jubilant. Now I know for sure that there is a god.

Mum comes over from Oxford where she has a live-in job with a wealthy family. I sense there have been many anxious conversations about me between Mum and Bethany over Christmas and now here she is, small and round and the same as ever. I have a hit before she comes. I want to seem as normal as possible. But from the way she looks at me, I know that normal isn't her first impression.

'Mark, I don't know you,' she tells me. She looks over at Bethany who is suddenly red-faced and close to tears. 'I don't feel I know you at all. You left home when you were sixteen and I haven't really known you since then.'

I throw myself on her mercy. I have lied to her and stolen from her and behaved badly, but now I have a chance. I tell her about rehab. I just need £50 to get down to Bristol because they've said I can't take the car so I need money for the train.

Mum's look is unyielding. She's heard it all before. I always need another £50. It seems to her that my whole life I've been just £50 short. She sighs.

'No, Mark. We haven't seen each other for a long time and you've begun by asking me for money.'

I try to explain again why I need it. I don't know how to show her that this time, for once in my life, I'm being totally honest. I get down on my knees. I beg her. I plead with her. I start to cry. Bethany starts to cry. The kids start to cry. Mum begins to look scared because I'm so pathetic. But I don't stop. I really need this £50 for rehab. I'm desperate. You're my mother. Please give me the money that will change my life.

She caves in, perhaps from embarrassment. The next day I am gone. I'm glad I won't be going back to trouble sweet, sad Bethany again, not until I'm better anyway. My conscience, something usually as flat and lifeless as yesterday's roadkill, is pricked by the trouble I've brought her. On the train I try to recall the events of the Christmas season. I can't. Were the children there all the time? What are their names? Did I have any real conversations with anyone? What did Darren say to me? All I can remember clearly is the feel of that big tree beneath me as I climbed it for Darren's uncle. The thick rope in my hands. That magical moment when I emerged through the crown and the tree remained like a strong tower under my feet while above me it was suddenly diluted and there was light all around and a view that stretched for miles. Yes, I remember that, otherwise I barely noticed anyone or anything outside of my need for drugs and more drugs. The rest of the world has become a blur somewhere round the edges of my needs.

Thank God it is the end of a year, the end of a century and the end of a millennium, and Mark Johnson is going to change.

Chapter 31

I start my new life rattling at Bristol station. I am met by a small, fat, bald guy in a farm truck who drives us out of the city, past the motorway and through a labyrinth of country roads that get smaller and narrower and bumpier until I don't know if I've got a heroin rattle or just a road rattle.

Finally we arrive in the middle of nowhere and, guess what, there's the motorway again, snaking along nearby. I am instantly filled by unhappy memories and bad premonitions. Last time I was isolated in a beautiful green wilderness that everyone else admired from their car windows at 70 m.p.h., my life was filled with utter hopelessness. Then I remember Rosie and Jack and new baby Freddie and how I'm going to change my life. I get out of the truck and go into the house.

It's an old stone farmhouse with about five bedrooms and a small bakery attached. The bald man runs the centre with his big, fat, rosy-cheeked wife and, more interestingly, his attractive, blonde, teenage daughter. I wait to hear their strategy for changing my life. I wait to hear exactly how they're going to get me through my rattle, because it's bad and I know it's going to get worse. I've done so much rattling now that I am a walking encyclopedia on the subject of rattling and I know that I'm going to need a lot of help to get through this one, the psychological horror of it apart from the physical miseries. I've never actually heard of a serious addict getting clean but I have one shining, dazzling example: Rosie. She's on methadone but she's almost clean and if she can do it, I can. And the kids are my big incentive.

But by the end of the first day, disillusion is setting in. By the end of the second day, disillusion has turned to torture. The fat man and his apple-cheeked wife don't have a rehabilitation strategy which works for someone like me. They don't know how to help me. I need some kind of emotional support, although I've no idea what, and all they're offering is prayers. Prayers are what I don't need because my rattle is following a familiar pattern. The chasms are opening up and what's crawling out all over me is fear and self-loathing. Yes, here come the voices again. I call them the Committee and they're telling me that I am evil, I am a criminal, I am abusive, I am exploitative. Without heroin to protect me, the Committee takes a critical review of my life and concludes that the defendant has been wholly bad. And, along with the extremes of physical pain inflicted on me by the rattle, this is too much.

The fat man would like me to do some work in the bakery but I can't do anything. I can't even think straight. The other blokes watch me silently. One becomes a mate. He's called Hilary, a name he's been teased for all his life and now is no exception. Hilary is suffering too and, since he's been around in Christian rehab a while longer than me, he's already learned the ropes.

'They can't expect you to stop with everything like this. Do it gradually,' he says.

'Where am I going to get some gear out here, for fuck's sake?'

'Not gear. But there's drink. At the off-licence.'

'And how do we get to the off-licence?'

'Easy, we talk Sally into helping us.'

Sally is the gorgeous blonde daughter. The reason she's not short and fat and apple-cheeked like her parents is that she's adopted, a thoroughbred brought up by donkeys. And what donkeys they are. No way would I have filled my house with desperate male addicts who are coming off heroin and rediscovering their libido, not if I had a daughter who looked like Sally.

Hilary and I set about persuading the lovely Sally to obtain a big bottle of vodka for us. And she does. We also get our hands on some Valium and temazepam. This is easy: a new lad arrives from Wales and we meet him at the gate before Apple Cheeks can get there, offering to stash his supply of prescription detox drugs in a safe hiding place. But of course we take them ourselves.

That night, dinner is a quiet affair. We've had the vodka, we've had the prescription drugs, the Welsh lad has guessed what's happened. When he realised, the sadness in his eyes made me feel bad. But now he's keeping a livid and brooding silence while Gareth, the pastor who reigns supreme over the whole Christian outfit, has arrived in his huge 4x4 to eat with us. And Hilary and I have our noses in our mashed potatoes.

'Whatever can be the matter?' asks Mrs Apple Cheeks. 'I've never known the boys so quiet.'

The pastor looks as if he can guess what's the matter. However, he brings good news. There's to be a special church service tomorrow, a pre-millennial service, in Devon where the women live. I dimly perceive, through my haze of drugs, that tomorrow, in church, I'll be seeing Rosie and Jack and the new baby. Thank God I kept back a few Welsh Valium to get me through that one.

I arrive at the church feeling about a hundred years old, my body splintering into columns of pain every time I try to get the mighty pistons working. I throw back some Valium when I think no one's looking although it feels as though people are looking at me all the time. Is this paranoia or am I really the object of some interest?

The man in charge of the Devon site stares at me when he thinks I'm not looking. The local members of the congregation, mostly long-nosed, middle-aged women, remind me of my mum's friend Maureen. Their husbands look awkward: they've been spruced up for the service. Gareth, the 4x4-driving pastor, is here. Mr and Mrs Apple Cheeks and Sally are here. And then the women arrive.

I'm sitting at the back with Hilary and I see Rosie before she sees me. She walks in with Jack behind her and a small bundle in her arms. Suddenly everyone else is faded and old and monochrome while Rosie, tall and lean with long, thick hair, her face strong, her clothes flowing, is in glorious Technicolor. She catches my eye and something like a smile appears, then she quickly looks away and turns towards her seat with the other women. Jack is following close behind her. Three now, almost four, he walks tall, his face solemn. He's looking round for me and somehow the focus of my attention draws his eyes to mine and for a moment there is a meeting. His pace falters. I want more than anything for him to run to me. My son. My own boy, taller now, leaner now, with some hint about him already of the adult he will become one day. I smile, widely, so widely my face feels as though it's splitting. I'm using muscles I haven't used for months, maybe years. I'm looking at my kid and I'm smiling.

Jack doesn't come to me. He does not return my smile. He stares for a second and his stare, searching, wise, scares me. What have they told him about me? Then he swings down the aisle behind Rosie and takes a seat next to her. My eyes follow him. I am aware that half the church is looking at me. They know. They all know everything. I hate it.

The service begins. There are tambourines. There are guitars. There is a small band and singers and one of them is Sally. The pastor starts off quietly enough but soon he is waving his arms around and shouting and the congregation is doing the same. This lot make the Jehovah's Witnesses look like Trappist monks. There is more singing and arms everywhere are shooting into the air. I watch Rosie. She has carefully put that small bundle of life down next to her and her arms are up there too, her hands are reaching up towards the Lord and she's swaying along with the music. It's a long way from the raves we used to go to. Jack turns back frequently to observe me. I always smile at him but he never smiles back. Is he checking whether my hands are up there? They aren't.

The pastor runs down the rows and people gabble away at him in foreign languages or no languages at all. A few worshippers faint, sometimes groups gather round one person and yell godly words, and I get my head between my knees, my body aching and shaking, religious fervour swirling all round me, and I think: how have I ended up with these fucking maniacs? And why is Rosie one of them?

The service goes on forever and by the time it stops I am almost unconscious with rattle pain, physical and mental. Hilary sticks his arm under mine to hold me up. Only the knowledge that now I can really see Rosie and Jack and the baby helps me out of the church behind everyone else. Hilary and I stand around outside smoking and then we troop into a hall. It is filled with big, round tables and along one wall are serving hatches. Rosie is sitting at one of the tables. She is surrounded by church women. I feel shy. I walk over to her and immediately the women around her fall silent. They glare at me. So they know how evil and abusive I am.

'Hi, Rosie,' I say.

'Hi, Mark.'

Jack stands firm at her side. He doesn't respond when I talk to him and he remains stiff when I hug him. He must have been told he has a very bad daddy.

'How're you?' I ask Rosie.

'I'm doing all right. Ever since I learned to trust in Jesus, everything's been all right for me.'

There is a collective nod from the hawk-eyed women round the table. I look at the tiny baby in Rosie's arms and I want to melt. I take his little hand and he wraps his fingers round mine.

'Freddie,' I say softly. 'Hello, Freddie.'

I want to hold him and Rosie senses this and the coven gives a sharp intake of breath as she hands him over. Freddie opens his big eyes and looks at me. My methadone baby. I hold him still and he blinks. I get that new baby joy again. The joy of possibilities, of new starts, of another, different life.

I rock him gently and his eyes close. I start to walk about with him and there's tension round the table, as though the old girls want to grab him back. I remember something that happened a thousand years ago. How the midwife and Mum and maybe everyone in the family nearly shot over and grabbed Bethany back when she was a newborn and I took her in my arms. Everyone knew how evil I was even then, but I meant Bethany no harm and did her no harm and, as for Freddie, I love him, pure and simple.

Freddie falls asleep and eventually I hand him back to Rosie. I pull up a chair and we talk a bit about the birth, which didn't this time end in a Caesarean, but we are watched by a hundred eyes and our every word is monitored by many ears. I am uncomfortable. Someone brings Rosie her lunch from one of the hatches. Everyone at her table starts to eat. I don't have any lunch. I don't want any. Rosie tells me to get some but I'm too embarrassed to eat it with her. I don't like eating in public; it was hard enough at Bethany's and it's hard at the farmhouse. After all, I've been eating scraps out of bins for months now.

Hilary signals that he's got me some food and I sit down a way off and try to eat. Then, when people look as though they're finishing, I shuffle over to my family again and shyly hand over the presents I've brought. They're a bit battered by now but Jack's face lights up. For the first time, he smiles at me. The old women watch in silence as he unwraps his pirate ship. I think he likes it. He starts to play with it. He's getting less icy with me now but he won't let me join in. Then, when I see some of the other kids are playing football outside, he agrees to go out with me. And so, amid a group of strangers' children, watched by a row of suspicious faces, I play football with my son, my bones aching, my head throbbing, pain pulsating through my body and my soul. This is terrible. This reunion has been embarrassing beyond words.

Jack doesn't talk to me much. Sometimes he looks at me, hard, when he thinks I don't notice. I want to take him in my arms the way I wish my dad had taken me. But Jack's too wary.

When we go back in to Rosie, there is more stumbling, public conversation. She's helping me but not much. Jack watches me in a way that is both knowing and adult. He is already a young man, he's like other people, in control of his life and even his mum's, and he knows his dad's sick and sick people need help. He is still only three, for fuck's sake, and he's grown up. I want to cry. I want to wail like the little boy he should be.

In the afternoon there is another bloody service and it's as bad as the first, perhaps even more frenzied. I spend most of it with my head between my legs. I get the last of my Valium inside me. Afterwards we don't go straight back. They inform me that there's to be a meeting for me with Rosie's pastor. I think this might mean that at last I'm going to be given some time alone with my family but no, Jack isn't there. The baby's had a feed and falls asleep. Rosie's sitting across a table from Anthony, her pastor. Anthony's wife is there, too, observing from one side. I am led into the room and it feels like the headmaster's office.

Anthony starts speaking.

'We're here to discuss your plans for yourself and your family. Rosie has become a Christian and now that you're in rehabilitation we'd like to encourage you to aspire to similar values. You have Rosie and two sons to support so finding yourself a job should be your first priority . . .'

The Committee has stepped outside my head and is lined up in front of me. At first I am meek and mutter things about being a tree surgeon and wanting to become a family again and then, when my body reaches a pinnacle of pain, a furious devil jumps out of me.

I leap to my feet.

'Who the fuck are you?' I roar. 'Who do you think you are? What is this control you have over Rosie and why are you trying to control me?'

He stutters his replies but I can't stop now. I am outside my own body, standing aside from my pain. I am a separate being composed entirely of anger.

'And, I mean, what's going on between you and her?' I demand. 'Do you fancy her, is that what it's all about? Are you fucking her, is that why you think you can control her every move? That's it, right? You fancy her! You're fucking her!'

Anthony the pastor is red-faced. The pastor's wife is red-faced. Rosie is almost crawling under the table with embarrassment. The pastor's wife would like to pick up the table and hit me with it.

Anthony remonstrates with me.

'You are fucking shit,' I inform him, I inform all of them. 'You think you can run people's lives by fucking with their heads, but you can't, you're shit, you're shit, and I don't give a fuck about you or your rehab because you're all nuts.'

Rosie's head is in her hands now. I dart out of the room and try to calm myself down outside with a cigarette. When I return every-one's still in their seats and Mr Apple Cheeks is there too.

'Whatever's wrong?' he asks, all dimples. I feel anger take me over once more.

'Fuck off!' I yell dangerously and Mr Apple Cheeks leaps up and tries to rugby-tackle me. I jump to one side and he starts to chase me around the table.

'Fuck you, fuck you,' I cry as he hurls his sweating body after me. Probably it would be comic if it wasn't so horrible.

Suddenly, I stop and turn. 'I'll belt you if you come any closer,' I inform him and one glance at my face says I'm serious. So I've just proved that I'm an evil, violent, abusive monster. And rehab's over for me. I was there less than a week. I have been sick throughout and all the hopes I've been pinning on this last resort have now evapor-ated. So there's nothing left for me. There's nowhere to go. There are no more chances.

I am dumped in Bristol where I make a social security claim and find that the money owed by the forestry company is now in my bank account. I catch a bus to Birmingham. I am desolate. I have no future. I have even obliterated my past.

By the time evening comes, there is a needle in my arm. The chasms in my soul, which have turned into canyons, close at once.

It is time for the new millennium to start and everyone else on earth thinks this is worthy of celebration. I spend the night in a house in Birmingham that is empty of everything except heroin addicts and their works. I find a bathroom, lock it, open the window and watch the fireworks, standing alone in the bath, and I take so much crack that there's blood everywhere. All the time another addict is bang-ing on the door because he wants my gear. 'I know you're in there, I know what you're doing,' he whines over and over again.

The year 2000 holds no hope for me. I am hopeless. I am useless. I am evil. I am beyond redemption. There is nowhere for me to go, nothing for me to do. January the 1st dawns and I consider all my options. There's Warwick, but Bethany probably can't take any more of me. However, I did enjoy that bit of tree work for Darren's uncle;

maybe I could ring the tree surgeon in London I used to work for and tell him that I've been in rehab and I'm fit now and ask for my old job back. I'll have to change. I'll have to manage my habit, and that won't be easy with all those drugs only a tube ride away. Alternatively, I could go to Nottingham where I have many DIY mates, although I'll never learn to manage my habit in that crazy, chaotic environment. But deep in my heart I know that my drug use now exceeds anything that is acceptable to any of my friends, even in Nottingham. Some of them are married with families and don't want me shooting up in the bathroom.

I'll go back to London. I'll ask for my old job back. I'll manage my habit.

I return to Bethany's for the Mini Metro. When I ring the doorbell, she is shocked to see me.

'Oh, Mark!' she says. She thought I was in a peaceful West Country community getting rehabilitated.

'Oh Mark!' And in her eyes I see it all. Her disappointment. Her disillusion.

'It didn't work, Bethany. Those Christians were awful. I wasn't allowed to see Rosie and the kids alone and they turned out to be a bunch of nutters . . .'

She invites me in and gives me something to eat. But, her voice sad, she says: 'Mark, you can't stay here. For your sake. And ever since I found that needle in your coat pocket, I've known it's not safe for the children either. Oh, Mark, I can't stand being around you and watching what you're doing to yourself.'

It seems to me that even my little sister is telling me to fuck off because I'm such a loser. That's how I hear her words.

'I don't want to stay here anyway,' I announce, all bravado. 'I'm going down to London. Got my job to go to.'

And I take the car keys and get in the rust box and somehow it judders and spits its way down to London. It probably couldn't have got much further anyhow. I park it outside a beautiful house in Knightsbridge and throw the keys over the garden wall and walk away.

I find a phone booth and call my last employer, in Canning Town.

'Yeah, the caravan's still here with your stuff in,' he says.

'I'm better now,' I lie. 'I got clean after some rehab down near Bristol. I'm fit for work. I want to work. Do you need me?'

He sighs. 'As a matter of fact, I do need a climber. I'll pay by the day.'

I catch a train back to Canning Town. The man looks me up and down doubtfully.

'Are you sure you're clean?' he asks.

'Yes. Oh yes,' I lie.

'Right, you start tomorrow morning.' He still doesn't sound too sure.

The caravan is disgusting. My climbing gear's still here. When I open drawers, I find needles. When I look in cupboards, I find needles. There isn't much else.

I spend two days rattling hard, controlling my habit with alcohol and anything else I can get my hands on. I am trying not to take any gear because I'm going to manage my heroin use from now on. I am going to manage it and get normal so I can see my children in a normal way. But to normalise myself for work, I need other drugs. I buy a plastic bottle of methadone, green sticky stuff, which I hide in the axle of the caravan. It is vital for my wellbeing. Without it I'll be rattling too much to think, too much to work. It is the elixir of life. During the night, I hear something outside the caravan. I am scared but finally I open the door. I reach down to check that the vital bottle is still there. I have to feel the reassuring moulded plastic between my fingers. I must feel it or I will die. But I don't. It has gone.

I leap out of the caravan and run across the scrapyard and the dogs start barking and jumping about. I run straight into their kennel and there, among the long, thin limbs of mottled wolfhounds, is the plastic bottle, gouged open by canine teeth, its sticky contents all over their straw bed. My world is finished. Normality is impossible. My life has drained away in a dog kennel. Oh, you fucking bastard dogs.

The boss arrives the next morning to find me incapable. I am too ill to work, and anyone can see it. He knows he can't employ me any more. I know it too. For the second time I leave that scrapyard with a feeling of hopelessness and despair. Once again I catch the Jubilee Line to Waterloo. Once again I am going to the West End to score because there is nowhere else for me. I have tried every solution and nothing, nothing, can relieve me of my habit. The streets of the West End are all that is left. So this is where the railway was leading all along.

I walk back into my life here and everything's just the same. The places, the people, the dealers. No one greets me and only the body lice are pleased to see me. Apart from Dave and Ginge, no one's even noticed that I haven't been around for a couple of weeks.

Chapter 32

It takes a few days to get back into my street habits. My shoplifting skills need honing. I come close to getting caught. In the corner of my eye I see a sales assistant take a staff member aside for a muttered conversation and that staff member looks at me directly and then gets on the phone. A net is about to close on me. Carefully, swiftly, I put back all the DVDs that are in my bag. As I leave the shop they try to arrest me and are surprised to find I have nothing. But their suspicions remain.

'You do a great job of looking like a Swedish tourist,' says the store detective. 'And you're good at what you do. But we think you've been doing it for a while. We know you now, so don't come back here.'

I'd like to thank them for the Swedish tourist compliment but instead I go straight to the Broadwick Street toilets, swap clothes with someone, and fifteen minutes later successfully steal ten DVDs from them.

Although DVD theft is my main source of income, I have lots of other ideas and after a short time back in the West End I start to feel confident. I was a fish out of water through those mad Christmas weeks away. This is my home and this is where I flourish. I'm probably the only person on the streets who makes so much and lives so well. There are a lot of gangsters in the West End and I'm proud to feel I'm like them.

The Highway Code: Street Survival on a Snickers a Week and a Lot of Drugs

Remember, these are criminal activities and could land you in jail

1. Go to internet cafés with a mate. The mate has an internet problem he needs a girl to sort out and while she's helping him, hook her handbag out from under the desk.

2. Buy drugs. Take most of them but sell some.

3. Steal drugs. Take most of them but sell some.

4. When your face is getting familiar to store detectives, find yourself someone who's new to the streets and send him into the shop. Stand outside waiting for the DVDs. Sell them and give him about 10 per cent of your takings.

5. Act as a runner for dealers.

6. Smash and grab in shops on days when you're desperate to score. If you run in, take what you want and head out fast, you'll probably get away with it. And if you don't, then you can look forward to a stay in a nice, warm cell with legal drugs supplied. So you can't lose.

7. Sniff out plain-clothes coppers so you can indicate their presence to big drug dealers.

8. When the Groucho Club closes, offer to show all those media types the way to another all-night drinking club they may find interesting and get paid commission there by the doorman. Make sure you tell your sob-story on the way and the media type might just fish £20 out of his wallet.

9. Hunger gnawing at you? Craving chicken, avocado and bacon on ciabatta with a hint of mayonnaise? Stand

outside a fancy sandwich bar sniffing and scratching and they'll soon give you a coffee and a delicious sandwich just to go away.

10. The disabled toilets at University College Hospital will provide you with a warm place to bed down on a cold winter's night. Of course, the floor's not exactly a feather bed and, beware, the cleaners arrive early.

11. Rats are not your furry friends: they are pests who can come between you and a good kip. If you sleep behind waste bins you'll certainly get them running over you all night. Building sites are even worse. Think about this before you snuggle up in a cubby-hole.

12. Steal mobile phones. You'll find a ready resale market. If they actually ring at the time, persuade the buyer it's just your mate calling.

13. Pick-pocketing skills not up to scratch? Don't waste time and take risks by practising. Just find a skilful pick-pocket and be a good team member. Use your wits to point out all the best opportunities and then help by distracting the victim so your mate can do his work.

14. Hang around by a hole in the wall at night. When a punter gets out his bankcard, form an orderly queue behind him. Then, at that vital moment when the pin number's in and the money's coming out, crash into the punter and get your hands on his money before he can.

15. Drunkenness has reached epidemic proportions on our streets. Show those late-night drinkers the error of their ways by rolling them as they stagger out of the clubs. Do it by covering them with a blanket and it can actually look as though you're helping them instead of lifting their wallet.

16. Always be ready. Always be alert. There are many opportunities to make money by cheating, stealing and lying on London's streets. You just have to be ready for them.

Of course, I have my darker moments. The come-down from crack is getting worse and I'm taking so much that I eat almost nothing. In fact, I now weigh less than eight stone and that's thin, very thin, because I'm six foot tall. Dave tells me I'm looking emaciated.

'Go see a doctor, mate,' he says.

'What for? I'm fine.'

Sometimes I do crack all night. That's when I start walking round and round on my own, in my special way, with one foot on the kerb, one in the gutter, slowly, slowly, my head down so everyone will think I'm a tramp and they won't intrude on my paranoia or catch my eye or even notice me. I forget that I don't have to pretend. I really am a tramp.

I have nothing of my own now except for the things I find when I'm looking in bins. I like to look in bins because it gives a kind of rhythm to my walks, a structure in the chaos. Bin coming up, look in it. Bin coming up, look in it. And it gives me a motive to keep moving forward.

I find things that other people don't want. They become my things. I start a Collection of Found Objects. They're mine, but there's something of other people left on them, which gives me a weird kind of contact with normality and normal people. There's a brown plastic art box with lots of little trays that lift up when you open the lid. Some large needles, not the sort I use but sewing needles, which glint in sunlight. A notebook with a strong silver-coloured metallic cover, lots of stickers inside, small empty pages and a blank diary section. There's half a spoon, its broken handle an elaborate Celtic knot. Some small paints. Paintbrushes. I love my Collection. I hide it in special secret places under bridges and down drains and behind stones. It is precious.

I am having a hit on the ledge at the end of Tottenham Court Road when one of the dangerous twins, Keith or Malc, storms up to me and steals my bag as I'm about to bang up. No one's ever done that before. I could fight him but his twin's standing right there. I've been bereaved. I've lost my drugs, so mourning's more in order than fighting.

'Take it then, mate,' I say bravely.

The twin laughs and swears at me. I wait. I watch him. Then, just as he's about to bang up with it himself, I pounce. I run along the ledge and ram into him so that the works, the needle, the drugs are all splattered everywhere. That way, neither of us gets it.

'You fucking, fucking . . .'

The other twin is reaching for his knife and I don't hear anything else because I'm running away so fast. Malc and Keith remind me of the psychotic brothers back in Kidderminster who used to finish the bottle and then start eating the glass. I lurk around Tottenham Court Road looking for someone who'll bring me in. Finally here's big Ben, loping off for a hit after a successful evening's tube begging.

'Those fucking twins,' he says when I tell him what happened. He sorts me out. I stay out of everyone's way in the doorway of a grey, modern courtyard where all the offices are small and people have their own businesses. Film editing. PR. Graphic design. Some of them are working late tonight. I watch them as they leave. I've always thought people were mugs for going off to work in the morning and then coming home at night but I can see from their faces that their jobs bring them a sort of satisfaction.

One night I find a brand new king-sized duvet in a box in a skip. I wrap myself up in it like a worm and wake up sweating in the morning sun. That's a good night. A bad night is when I'm curled up in a doorway and a bunch of men attack me. I don't see them, I only feel them through my blanket. I feel their feet pounding against me, hear their laughter. In the morning my body is black and blue. I estimate that there were five or six of them and my sense is not that they were young lads on a drinking spree but businessmen in suits, glad of someone helpless to hurt in secret, glad of a chance to damage without fear of reprisal.

Another night I find myself a couple of big cardboard boxes outside Hamleys, the toy shop, and set them on a huge plastic bread tray in a road that's been turned into a cul-de-sac by building work. No one will disturb me here, not even the rats that can penetrate so many of my cardboard defences and run over me while I sleep. I cut a hole and crawl into the boxes, using the sin bin provided by the needle exchange as a pillow. I congratulate myself on my deluxe bedroom. But I am awoken by mad yelling and hammering on my roof. I shoot out of the hole like a rat and find that a line of trucks is waiting for me to move and about fifty builders are standing overhead on their scaffolding giving me a rousing cheer. I hobble up the road showing them two fingers, shouting at them all to fuck off. They roar back at me. I don't listen to the words they're saying. I feel like less than nothing. Probably they've been trying to get me out for a long time but I've been oblivious and no one wanted to open the box. No one ever does. They're scared of what human cargo they might find in cardboard boxes in Soho. They laugh with relief as well as cruelty at the scrap of humanity they do find.

I spend a lot of time in toilets. Sometimes I feel very bad in toilets. I can be in a cubicle after a hit, crouched or curled like a small dog or a whipped child, cowering in terror. I'm coming down and I'm pranged and I can hear voices and footsteps and my own paranoia is palpable. I am overwhelmed by my fear of the police, of disaster, by my fear of fear. Outside the cubicle door I see shadows. The shadows flit about, terrifying me.

At Easter, I'm stealing some kids' toys for a prostitute from a tiny branch of Hamleys in the Covent Garden piazza when a young sales assistant catches me. I mean, she's the sixteen-year-old Saturday girl, she's tiny, certainly under five foot, and extremely skinny and she's straight on me when I walk out of the shop. I try to escape down the piazza and she's after me. She grabs me and legs me over so I can't move. The humiliation. I know I'm thin, even emaciated, I know that Dave keeps telling me to eat more, but being sat on by a child is just awful. I hope she gets body lice.

Out comes the manager and he calls the police. I, of course, have some gear on me but while we're waiting for the police to arrive I manage to manoeuvre myself so I can shove it up my arse.

'I've got body lice,' I announce to the two approaching coppers, so they don't come near me. They have a big discussion about whether they should walk me to Charing Cross Road police station around the corner or put me in the van and finally they decide to put me in the van. They don't do this unkindly. Strangely, although they are my greatest enemy, the police speak nicely to me.

When we arrive, there's a doctor waiting. He sees my scabs and my thin body and he is both kind and considerate. He says he'll look for some clean clothes and he gives me some de-louse cream for the shower. Best of all, he prescribes a lot of drugs because he can see that I have a very big habit. He gives me copious quantities of dihydrocodeine, a morphine that is a heroin substitute, and Valium.

I have a hot shower, a warm cell, good drugs, a blanket and a pillow. Instead of my lousy clothes I am given a white paper suit to wear. My head hits the pillow. I am safe and warm. I feel as though I've just been released from jail.

Although the police officers don't come closer to me than they have to, they speak to me sympathetically and compassionately.

'How long've you been on the streets then?' they ask.

'How're you managing?'

'All right, mate?'

They look at me with pity, they even seem to understand how low a junkie can feel. I am amazed. The figures who haunt my come-down paranoia are policemen, but now I'm here with them they're not terrifying. They're nice.

The next day, still awash with prescription drugs, still wearing my white paper suit, I am put into a police van. Since it is Easter I am driven to a special magistrate's court far from the centre of London. Where are they taking me? I don't care because I've had my dihydrocodeine. I only hope it's not beyond the end of a tube line.

The magistrate gives me a day in jail or a £100 fine and, since I've already had a day in jail and I haven't got £100, I am released immediately. I am taken downstairs and none of the court officials will go near me. They play a childish game, backing off as I walk past them:

'Don't come near me!'

'Ooooh, don't touch me!'

They're like the nasty kids in a playground. Then they throw me out. I'm wearing my white paper suit. I stand there in the street in alien clothes, my feet bare. I am lost, I am embarrassed, I am nobody. A moment later the door opens again and a black plastic bag is chucked out into the street. It contains the shoes and lousy clothes I was wearing when I was arrested. I look up and I can see them all laughing at me from behind the glass doors of the court.

Shamed and marked out by my strange paper clothes, I look around. Where can I change? This is embarrassing but I have a more pressing problem. I have heroin on me still but I need to get some works before I can have a hit.

Looking like a spaceman, I pad around this distant part of London, wherever it is, until I find a chemist's that is open. Nearby, there's an Indian shop for the citric. I go to a public toilet to change and have my hit. Then I jump a tube home. I mean, back to the West End.

For a brief period I felt like king of the West End, big like a gangster. But gradually this existence is grinding me down. I begin to feel, bit by bit, that I'm losing the daily battle for survival.

One night I go over. I have a hit in a small park near Charlotte Street and when I wake up the next day the needle's still in my arm, my lower legs are bent back under me and my body is in a straight line from my knees. I am blue with cold. My clothes are wet. I must have been in this position for many hours. It is many more hours before I am able to move at all, let alone straighten my legs or stand on them. I sob with pain. I am very sick. The heroin I took must have been from a freakishly pure batch to have given me an overdose like this. It is a cold night. I could have died. I wish I had.

At this time, I'm selling my stolen DVDs to a lad called Wilf who works in a Soho sex shop. The sex shops in this road all do a lot more business than you'd guess from their small, shabby interiors. This is gangsterland. Wilf has bosses and the bosses have bosses. One of them is a big man with a Mexican-style moustache who says, in good but accented English, that he'd like to talk to me. He makes me nervous, but when I learn what he wants I can't stop a wide smile spreading across my face. He's asking me to sell drugs for them.

My new job is fantastic. They give me crack and heroin split into .2g bags and double-wrapped in clingfilm. I carry about thirty of these in my mouth. I walk around the West End selling and when I first leave the shop I can't speak for bags. When I've spat out a few, I get a bit more verbal. I charge anything between £7 and £10 a bag depending on the market, and as soon as I'm empty I go back to Wilf to hand over the cash and reload. When I get a bit more experienced, I can fit even more in my mouth. Fifty bags and I look like a hamster.

When I've sold thirty bags, I get to keep five. That's why this is good work. And I love it. I'm often sorted out for drugs, I'm busy, I have all the kudos of being a dealer in demand and I'm in with some gangsters. Why do I get so miserable sometimes? Because now I know for sure that I'm invincible. In my mind, I'm running the West End.

Chapter 33

I'm sitting on the steps to Piccadilly Circus underground, feet scurrying past me. I've been doing crack all night and my drugs job won't start for a few hours yet but I can't wait for a hit. I'm desperate but I'm tired, too tired to go thieving to earn the next hit. No spring in my step now, just aching feet. No big-boy gangster stuff, just the reality of all those dark places opening up inside me.

The Committee in my head starts up. I'm evil. No one cares about me because I'm not worth caring about. I'm less than dirt because at least people wipe dirt off their shoes but no one can even see me. They're all rushing right past me because I'm the invisible man.

Dave's outside the toilets as usual with Boots curled up by his side, begging quietly. He's the humble sort of beggar who doesn't try to intimidate people or make them look at him and people don't only give him money, they stop and talk to him sometimes. You don't have to talk to Dave for long to see what he is, a man too sweet-natured for this bad world.

Right now there's a girl bending over him. She looks oriental. She looks rich. You can tell from the way her thick, dark hair's bobbed. You can tell from her shoes. You can tell from her clothes: Burberry scarf and a pale cream raincoat. I've seen clothes like hers in the designer shops I pass. They begin with a V. Valentino? Versace?

The next thing I know, Dave's getting up and he and the girl are walking off together, Boots as usual one step behind Dave. They're walking towards me. They pause as they pass.

'This is my mate, Mark,' says Dave politely. He tells me: 'We're off for some breakfast.'

'You come too?' the woman says. She's about twenty-five and pretty as well as rich. I don't seem to have any previous appointments, so I get to my feet.

'Where you from?' I ask.

'Japan.'

'Ah, Japan. Very nice.' Dave glances at me. The glance says: Fucking hell, Mark, what do you know about Japan? I glance back. The glance says: This woman is going to be good news. You can have her over for a lot of money, Dave.

We make our way through our world, up Rupert Street. When she sees us pause by a shop, she asks what we want.

'A couple of cans of Kestrel Superstrength would go very nicely with our breakfast,' I tell her and she takes us into the shop and buys us two cans each as if this is normal, so maybe that's really what people have for breakfast in Japan.

Up Wardour Street and along the Raymond's Revue alley. The Japanese woman is wearing little high-heeled boots and they click-clack, echoing a bit. It's raining. She does up her cream raincoat.

We stop at a greasy-spoon café and the woman flutters into a seat in her nice clothes and if she doesn't usually eat in this kind of place then she doesn't show it. We order immense breakfasts to eat with our Kestrel. She has a coffee. And all the time Dave and I are entertaining her. Even a debutante would be delighted by our wit and charm. She asks us about living on the streets and we tell her some good stories and whenever I catch Dave's eye there's a look in it that says he's blagging her for lots and lots of money.

Always restless and still needing that hit, a desire that even a full English breakfast can't satisfy, I say I have to go and buy something for me and Dave now. She reaches for her brown leather designer handbag and asks how much I need. I estimate £40. I can see there are hundreds more in her purse. She smiles at me and her smile is sweet. Her hair falls over one eye and she brushes it away. She is pretty and without guile.

I go off with the cash, telling Dave I'll be back. He knows what I've gone for. Before I've even left the café they're locked in intense conversation. So intense that when I've scored it seems to me that Dave's going to have her over for a lot more than £40. I may as well just keep the bags for my own use. When I've had my hit I forget to go back.

I get on with my busy day and I don't give Dave and the Japanese girl another thought. And then a little before midnight, I see her again. I'm trotting down Shaftesbury Avenue and she's up by the fire station in Chinatown and she's signalling wildly to me.

'Mark! Mark!'

I go over to her at once. She looks anxious. She asks if I've seen Dave.

'No, why?'

'Because he go get something for me and he don't come back,' she explains.

'Get what for you?' I ask. So she's unloaded the contents of her wallet into Dave's lap and he's off gouching somewhere. But she takes my question seriously and reaches into the brown handbag and produces a card.

'I can't say it . . .'

On one side of the card is the name of her hotel in Baker Street. I turn it over. On the back, she's copied out the words she can't pronounce. Cyanide sulphate.

I stare at her.

'Cyanide sulphate?' I say. 'Cyanide?'

The girl explains in broken English that she wants to kill herself. She's depressed and she doesn't want to go back to Japan where she's divorcing a cruel husband who hit her and abused her. She'd rather die.

'Now come on,' I say, all blag. 'It can't be that bad. Look at me, I'm on the streets and I'm still smiling.'

I flash a row of rotten teeth at her. But she's not entertained. She wants her cyanide and Dave said he'd get it.

Of course Dave's pulling a fast one but since he's disappeared I say I might be able to help.

'How much did Dave charge you?' I ask.

'Two hundred pounds.'

Two hundred pounds! Let me help you, please.

'Dave not take money. Money still here.'

So Dave didn't have her over. That means I can! I look to the heavens. Thank you, God.

We walk up towards Oxford Street together and I try to talk her out of killing herself, except I'm not trying very hard because if she really wants to die then I get £200. At the top of Charing Cross Road we turn right and huddling in doorways around the bus shelters are crowds of black dealers. They always look ridiculous. They're pretending to be people waiting for buses when anyone can tell they're just selling drugs.

I take the woman down a side street and I say: 'Those men there have got what you want.'

'How much?' she asks.

'Two hundred pounds,' I say and she reaches into her handbag and pulls out her purse and hands it over. The notes feel so good that they warm my hand.

'Now, you hold my bag,' I instruct her. 'That way you know I won't run off.' What a crazy thing to say. First, because it hasn't occurred to her that I might; she's simple and trusting. Second, because my bag contains a sin bin, a few needles and some citric, a bottle of dirty water and half a Snickers. It isn't worth £2 let alone £200. But she holds it close to her as though it came from Versace.

I score four bags of crack and four of heroin and I get a good price and then I keep the change. It isn't cyanide sulphate but taking one bag of each would certainly kill her if she's not used to these strong drugs. Just to be sure she gets what she wants for her money, I'm planning to give her two.

I lead her round to the ramp by the underground car park. It's quiet at this time of night except for junkies wailing. I give her two bags of brown and two bags of white, the citric and the works and I explain to her how to take it. She listens carefully. She asks me to explain it again. She nods. So, I've done what she asked. Now she's going back to her hotel to do it.

She looks around. 'Where you sleep tonight?'

'Somewhere near here, probably. A doorway.'

She shakes her head.

'No. I pay for hotel for you tonight.'

We get in a cab. We are silent. She looks pale and frightened. Is she really going to kill herself? I start to speak but she waves at me to be silent. Her mind's made up. When we're between Russell Square and King's Cross, I point to a cheap hotel. She gives me £60 and then we say goodbye. She watches me go in and when I turn in the foyer I see her drive away, her designer bag stuffed with drugs, to kill herself in her hotel.

There is a Russian bloke in reception. I'm worried he won't want me staying here but he barely glances at me. It's the kind of place where they rent rooms by the hour and ask no questions.

I go to my room congratulating myself on a lucrative evening's work. I have drugs, I have a bed, I have money and now I can have my hit. As usual, paranoia sets in as soon as the rush is over but this time the paranoia is different. I am almost swept away with horror at what I've done. That woman wanted to kill herself and I helped her. I might as well have shoved the needle in her arm. I might as well have killed her myself. I probably *have* killed her.

I am so shocked, scared and miserable that I want to die now. After crack, the paranoia is stronger than the guilt. It is inevitable that I will be found and arrested. I get on the floor and put my ear to the small strip of light at the bottom of the door. Is there any movement or talking? Are they coming for me? I'm listening so hard I dare not breathe. Finally I fall asleep here. Later I wake up on the floor. I walk away from the hotel and go to score.

When I bump into Ginge, I tell him the whole story. I can't get it out of my mind. Ginge listens and says nothing but I soon know he's told Dave everything because, whenever I pass anyone, they have a message for me. Dave's angry. Dave's looking for me. The next time I see Ginge I say that Dave's probably just angry because he wanted to get his hands on the girl's £200 but Ginge says no, Dave's furious because I never should have given the Japanese woman those drugs. And I know he's right and it hurts.

I don't go near Piccadilly Circus for a while. I get on with my busy life. But all the time I know I killed someone. And it wasn't an addict like John from the West Country or the countless other people I've supplied. It was a depressed young woman from a faraway country. Yes, Dave's right to be angry. But that's a glimpse of my heart that I can obscure quickly with a hit.

A couple of days later, Dave finds me. He's not alone: he's got a group of lads with him.

'I've been looking for you!' he roars and his face is red, angry, contorted. 'How could you fucking do it to her? You fucking bastard!'

'You don't know she's fucking dead!' I shout.

'I do! I do! Because she was supposed to meet me and she didn't come. Shit, Mark, she was lovely. Why did you give her the heroin and the crack and the works?'

'That's what you would have done,' I say, sulkily.

'I wouldn't! Mark, I fucking wouldn't!'

I realise I could have had her over with an empty bag. More for me and she'd still be alive. Or I could have run off with her £200 and left her holding my dirty old bag full of needles. But instead I faithfully delivered her suicide weapon.

'I want to fucking kill you!' roars Dave.

He advances towards me but I am quick. I get out my knife and hold it up to him and the lads who surround him.

'Fuck you, fuck you, I'll fucking cut you if you come any closer!'

Ordinary people are walking down this street. Without looking at us, they make wide circles around us, expressions of distaste on their faces. Because we're street addicts, swearing and brawling with each other, probably over nothing.

Dave turns and walks away. I am glad that confrontation is over. I've been avoiding it for days. But in a way it isn't over. I have to live with the knowledge that I killed the Japanese girl and I have to live on the streets without Dave and his kindness. Dave, who's always been there for me when I'm at my lowest, like a patient parent. Dave, the only person who worries about my health, tells me to go to the doctor, takes me to get my feet treated.

I am plunged into a deep depression that not even drugs can alleviate. I isolate myself, going to different back streets, sleeping in different doorways.

When I wake up in the door of a deserted shop, I'm rattling so badly that I feel I can't go on with this life of madness. I'm so, so tired. I've no energy left to run about. It seems to me that for years now my greatest fear has been sickness. I've spent my whole life trying to avoid the rattle and now I can't summon up the energy to fight it any more. I'll give in. I'll stay in one place and rattle and rattle, scratching my body lice here in the doorway, until I die.

After a while, as always, the sickness gets worse than the depression. When I am on fire, when my body is disintegrating with pain, I drag myself upright and then stumble to my feet. I try to stand up carefully, like a very old man, because if I bend my legs then my kneecaps feel as if they'll pop because there's no fat layer any more at the back of my legs.

Gradually, slowly, I start to move. My joints are rusty pistons. I set them in motion. The sluggish old machine starts to work. The scabs on my feet are a pack of wolves, tearing away at my flesh. It's a different kind of pain from the rattle, more superficial, more irritating but easier to ignore.

I bump into Gobby Gaz, a former male model, now ravaged by the virus. He has open abscesses and is rotting from the inside and he smells like it. He brings me in. We have a hit together from the top of a Coke can, sharing needles, sharing blood.

Ten minutes and I should be myself again and back in action. Busy, busy, busy, that's me after a hit has restored me. But I don't get much of a rush from the crack. The sky rocket runs out of fuel before it's reached the earth's atmosphere. There's no orbiting the sun today, just a crash landing. And the heroin hardly makes things better. My body pains haven't gone away. Neither has my depression.

The last hit I had was like a Guy Fawkes Night with damp fireworks. And the one before that wasn't much better.

I am ambushed by the possibility that drugs aren't working for me any more, not like they used to. This shocks me. It horrifies me. The drugs are leaving me! I am filled with grief.

I stand in the doorway staring up at the darkening sky. I start to cry. My whole body shakes with sobs. I'm crying like I've never cried before. Gobby watches me. Then he puts an arm round me. Passers-by either stare or look away quickly while I sob my heart out. I am twenty-nine years old and I am desperate.

It has started to rain. There's a church round the corner with a yard and in the yard is a tree I like and I go to it now. The tree is very low. It is evergreen and hidden among its needles are tiny cones. Its wide branches spread out over the paving stones, almost touching them. I lie down on my back and scramble beneath it.

There is another world in here. A world with no people, a tree world. Under these thick branches is a dryness and a strange sort of warmth. The dust from traffic and passing feet has not penetrated and the tree's needles are a fresh, dark green, the green of a faraway forest. The trunk rises up, until it is so obscured by the branches it supports that I can't see the top. Maybe there is no top. Maybe the tree world is endless. The branches, laden with clinging needles and cones, seem to hug me. They surround me. I feel safe here. The tree cares about me. It is looking after me.

When I'm strong enough I wander off to Old Compton Street, find a doorway, curl up into a ball and sleep. In the morning, waking and aching, I am aware that footsteps have passed me and then turned back. Maybe someone's going to give me money or try to speak to me or beat me up. I make myself smaller.

The feet are standing right in front of me now. A voice says: 'Mark? Mr Mark Johnson? Is that you?' It's not a junkie voice. It's a voice from Planet Normal.

Slowly I look up, uncurling myself for a clearer view. The man's face is staring right into mine and it's familiar. Big brown eyes, olive skin, buffed and polished. He's sleek and healthy. Trendy clothes. An attractive man. But who is he? He's from another time and another place. Who? Where?

'Mark, it's Sean Evans.'

Sean Evans . . .

'From Nottingham. DIY? Ange's friend?'

Ange, the artist who I got close to around the time Rosie left me
and I was trying to study photography. Ange, who designed the sets
and backdrops for DIY. Sean's her gay friend, I met him in
Nottingham. He was studying sociology and he was on the fringe of
the DIY crowd. And that same Sean Evans is walking down Old
Compton Street in London and he's seen me sleeping in a doorway.
Suddenly I'm too tired even to feel embarrassed. I'm almost too tired
to speak.

I try to greet him. But I don't know how any more. I can't
remember how to smile.

'Well, Mr Johnson!' He crosses his arms. 'Now then, tell me just
what you are doing here?'

All the wild times, the long, happy nights, the crazy parties, the
great music, the good drugs, the friendships, all that youth and
beauty, the blessing of Pan, it's all led me here to a doorway in Old
Compton Street.

I say: 'I'm lost.'

Sean bristles with bossiness: 'Ahem. We're not having this. I can
help you.'

I look at him. No one can help me. Unless they're on their way
to score and they're planning to bring me in.

He tells me: 'I work here in London now. For Turning Point.'

Turning Point. Wasn't that the name of the outfit that ran the big
old house in Birmingham where I went for rehab, ha ha, about a
million years ago?

'We're in Wardour Street. I'm a drugs outreach worker. If you've
got a problem, I can help.'

He makes comical little Here to Help gestures. I'm Dorothy and
I've just met the scarecrow, the lion and the tin man all rolled into
one. It's so surreal that I am slow to digest his words. I know there
are Community Action teams on the streets who are supposed to be
looking for people like me but not one of them has ever found me.
I don't go to hostels because I'm afraid I'll be trapped and bullied
there. I don't hang around soup kitchens. I'm a loner. Because I want

to be. But other people are always disappearing from the streets with Community Action and it sometimes seems they've helped everyone but me, as though I've slipped through some net because I'm invisible.

'If you want to stop with the drugs, Mark, I can help you.'

Of course I want to stop with the drugs, with the insanity of this life. But I can't imagine what other way there is.

'You just come along with me and we'll see about this, Mr Johnson.'

But I'm not coming now. I have to think about it. I tried coming off the streets at Christmas and it was a disaster. So Sean gives me directions to Turning Point and I promise I'll be along later. It takes me a few days to decide I want to see Sean. He's someone from that other world who remembers that I wasn't always a tramp, I wasn't always invisible.

The office decor is white and clinical as though it's been designed by civil servants to make people uncomfortable. Sean, however, greets me warmly. He makes me feel I'm different from the other street people in here, special, because he knows the old Mark. We go out to a café for a cup of tea. Sean asks me if I really want to get off heroin. Of course I do. No question. He says he'll try to get me into detox.

'It never works,' I say. I know all about these detox places. You rattle your way through them and then you come straight out and use again.

'It works if you want it to. And you don't come out of detox and tell yourself you're better. People in recovery need a lot of support. So next you go into rehab.'

Rehab. Well, my last rehab experience was a joke.

'Do you really want to stop?' Sean fixes me with his big, brown eyes. 'Some people need to reach rock bottom before they're ready.'

I'm sleeping on the streets every night and living by dealing and stealing, how much lower can you go?

Then I remember all the other rock bottoms. The rock bottom of being in jail without having a clear memory of my crime. The rock bottom of sending my prostitute girlfriend out to find men so I could get more crack. The rock bottom of blowing my mind with drugs and breaking down. The rock bottom of having a son and not being able to look after him, of banging up in the back seat of the car and throwing sweets to the front seat to keep him quiet. The rock bottom of the America tour when I'd do anything for a drug that distracted me from heroin. The rock bottom of hanging around some of the worst housing estates to score. The rock bottom of only seeing my children under the supervision of a hundred sharp eyes. But none of those was really rock bottom. They were just ledges in the ocean as I sank lower and lower. Now I've reached the bottom. I'm on the streets and I'm thin and lonely and the drugs have stopped working. Yes please, Sean, I'd like to change now.

Chapter 34

Next time I stop by Turning Point, Sean says that he hasn't managed to find me a place in detox yet, but in the meantime he's putting me in a rolling hostel so I have a room and bed.

I go up to the hostel, in Endsleigh Gardens near Euston station. They show me a bare double room. I don't know who I'll be sharing it with. I go outside and a group of lads from the hostel follows me. One glance tells them I've got some gear on me. At the corner they surround me.

'Bring us in!' They're not asking, they're demanding.

I say: 'Fuck off.' I escape as quickly as I can. I could be sharing a room with one of them. So I don't go back to sleep there. I feel scared shut into buildings now and beds have become alien.

Since the hostel is near the dole office I decide to claim back benefit for the last year. They tell me to come back later to pick up part of the money. But the lads from the hostel are there too. Once again, they surround me.

'Give us some money,' they say.

I manage to slip away from them but now I'm watching all the time. I rush into the hostel to show my face each day, then I rush out again without going to my room. I don't want to meet those lads because if one of them sees me, immediately the others are there and they're not individuals any more, they're one solid mass of violence, shouting threats at me. I'm so skinny I know I'm no match for them. My visits to the hostel last about thirty seconds from now on. But, during one of them, there's a message from Sean. I'm going into detox.

Detox. The word only sinks in now. Detox means no more drugs. That's what I wanted, wasn't it? The thought of a drugless life leaves me empty and terrified. How can I live without drugs? Outside drugs, I don't have a life. To help me through the misery that lies ahead, I take as much as I can before I go in. And now there's no doubt that heroin and cocaine are losing their effect. I'm getting the rattle and the paranoia without enough of the rush. So now my drugtaking reaches fever pitch as I chase that rush. I can't, I cannot, go on like this.

Detox is at the Equinox Crisis and Assessment Centre, south of the river on Brook Drive, a long street between Elephant and Castle and Lambeth. The building is a refurbished old red-brick. Most of the other inmates are street alcoholics and I know some of them: on a Sunday, before the dealers appear, I sometimes go over to Covent Garden for some booze to calm me down while I wait for gear. Usually Special Brew, a substance I wish I could inject directly into my veins. But I might also share a bottle of sherry, vodka, Scotch, anything that's going, with the drinkers who congregate there. The drinkers are different from junkies and their lives follow different patterns. Mostly they're older, many are from Scotland or Ireland, their faces are red and their noses are bulbous. Meeting up with them again here is like meeting up with old friends.

I go through my rattle, sweating, swearing, shaking and aching as usual. I'm helped by a methadone prescription for the first ten days. Then, on day eleven, the methadone stops and I plunge into an abyss. Fear. Disillusion. Panic. Uselessness. Isolation. Terrible thoughts penetrate, which drugs usually keep at bay. My kids: they don't know me. That Japanese woman: I killed her. My family: they have nothing to do with me . . . I want heroin. I want it badly. I need it to heal the deep wounds in my soul.

On day twelve I'm at my touchiest and feeling like a monster of pain and misery, when a kid comes in off the streets and starts arguing with me over what TV channel we're going to watch in the lounge. He jumps up and grabs an ashtray and I think he's going to hit me so I bite him. On the head. He howls and runs out and tries to barricade the lounge with me in it. The staff come running. They look at me gravely. They shake their heads.

'I never!'

But the staff point to the teeth marks on his head.

They say: 'Mark, you've got to go.'

I almost cry. I don't want to go. I've been through the worst of the suffering from withdrawal and I won't be able to stay clean out there by myself. I start to argue, pointing out that the stupid fucking kid provoked the fight. They say they don't want to throw me out but rules are rules and the kid's skin has been broken so I have to go. I can see this is hurting them, too. They've all tried hard to get me through my rattle.

'You can be readmitted in twenty-eight days,' they say. They organise a bed back at the hostel in Euston. I am put in a taxi and sent away. As I stand at the door, I tell the staff: 'You're going to fucking kill me.'

A woman shakes her head. She says in that quiet, resigned voice some of them have: 'No, Mark, you're going to kill yourself.'

And now I'm outside with no drugs inside me and I'm scared. The streets are cold, violent, insane. I can't cope with them unless I'm off my head too. But at first I try to withstand the pull of the needle. After all, I've gone through the rattle, the worst is over, if I can just last twenty-eight days by myself . . .

The world is steel grey. It is sharp, like a metal object. My head hurts. Every tiny movement hurts. Even breathing is like having a sock in my mouth. Getting up hurts. Sitting down hurts. The past hurts. It hits me with a series of terrible photos of all I've said and done. It's like the biggest, worst hangover because I wasn't just drunk last night. I've been drunk my whole life.

At the hostel I am given a single room because the staff know I am scared of bullying. They are kind and don't dwell on my failure in detox. But I feel it keenly. I had a chance to change and I flunked it. I am determined to stay off gear until I can be readmitted in twenty-eight days. I talk to the hostel staff. They all understand how hard it is.

'Mark, it's going to be difficult for you out here for a month, rattling by yourself,' says Jo, a blonde staff-member. 'Go to a meeting. Alcoholics Anonymous have meetings all over the place all the time—'

I interrupt her.

'I'm not a fucking alcoholic. I'm a drug addict.'

'Well, it doesn't make much difference but there's Narcotics Anonymous and Cocaine Anonymous too if you prefer.'

She's scouring the directory now. She makes a call and then turns back to me.

'Okay, Narcotics Anonymous have a meeting up in Islington in about an hour. Have you got any money?'

I feel in my pockets. Twenty pence.

She reaches into her bag. 'Here's another £1.80: two pounds will get you there and back on the bus. This is the address. Get yourself to that meeting and it will give you the support you need to go on and it might even change your life.'

Change my life? I can't imagine that. But I nod and take the £1.80 bus fare and the address. I go out onto Euston Road. Slowly. My body doesn't want to walk or go anywhere because breathing takes up all my energy, let alone moving. There are lines of bus shelters. Buses arrive like big insects sucking up passengers and then moving on. Which bus do I need to catch? Where exactly is this place in Islington? My head is spinning, my bones are aching, I can only walk with difficulty. A hit now would sort me out. It would have some real effect, too, after twelve days of abstinence.

I look at the £1.80 the kind woman has given me from her own purse and I determine to find the right bus and get myself to the Narcotics Anonymous meeting to get help to stay clean. I stare at buses and maps. I look for someone to ask. I walk along in the gutter checking the information at the front of every stop. And then I see it. In the gutter beneath my feet. Lying there, waiting for someone to pick it up. A £20 note.

I swoop and then stand, staring at it in my hand. Twenty pounds. I waver for a few seconds. Then, putting the kind woman at the hostel right out of my mind, acknowledging that I don't have the strength to get to the meeting which will give me support, with £22 in my pocket, I head down to the West End to score. And when I have the hit I get the rush and my rattle evaporates. All the pain is gone. Instantly. The world, which has been upside down and inside out ever since I went into detox, turns the right way up again. I cry with relief.

I go straight to Wilf at the sex shop and it happens there's some drugs for me to sell right now. I stuff them into my mouth.

'Where've you been? Thought you'd died!' says everyone I meet. I think: I should be so lucky. But I can't reply because my mouth's got thirty bags of heroin and crack in it.

After selling everything, I stop by at Turning Point.

'What happened?' wails Sean tragically.

'I was so strung out and this kid threatened me and I bit him so they chucked me out.'

'Do you want to try again?'

'Yes, yes, I do.' It's easy to say that and mean it while I'm wrapped round the outside of a recent hit.

'Right, we'll have you back in after twenty-eight days, I'll organise that now,' says Sean.

I try to sleep at the hostel since they've given me my own room. But I don't spend much time there or eat there because I am back in my world of chaos.

I'm returning to the sex shop to reload with drugs after some speedy sales when I catch Wilf with his hand in the till. There's no one in the shop, no dirty macs looking at the pornographic DVDs, magazines and videos that line the ancient wooden shelves. Just Wilf, alone on the peeling carpet, stealing from his bosses.

I say: 'I know what you're doing.'

Wilf is alarmed. He's a young lad, maybe in his early twenties, and he must know that his career in the sex trade will be short: this pornography is illegal and if the police raid a shop three times then it's the assistant who gets nicked. And they generally go to jail.

I say: 'I know what you're doing. So bring me in. Or I'm going to have to blow you up to the boss.'

Wilf doesn't want his bosses to get angry with him. They're gangsters and God knows what they might do. I'm only a guy on the streets who's always been pleasant enough so he doesn't anticipate too many difficulties in agreeing to my demands.

He looks sulky but silently he gives me some of the money he's stolen. Forty pounds in £10 pound notes. So now I have another source of income. Wilf will keep on stealing and every day I'll be able to hit him for £40. I certainly know how to live on the streets of London. I, too, can be a gangster. Maybe I won't bother with detox next month.

But an ocean of money wouldn't satisfy my raging habit, which has returned like a tidal wave after twelve days of rattling. By the next day, £40 seems a puny amount to take from Wilf's private business. So I take £40 in the morning and in the afternoon I go back for more.

Wilf is unenthusiastic.

'I'm giving you enough,' he says.

'I'll blow you up.'

'Look, I'm not making that fucking much.'

But I know he is. I know he's trying to cheat me. I want more money, I must have more money. And in the jungle you'll do anything to get what you want. I wander around all day thinking of ways to rinse him and when I'm really desperate for drugs I have a really desperate idea. I appear in the sex shop with a syringe. Before his eyes, I fill it with my blood.

'I've got the virus,' I say. 'And if you don't give me some fucking money, I'll bang this into you.'

He looks at the needle. I'm speaking in a pleasant undertone so that none of the customers, old men browsing through porn featuring middle-aged women dressed as schoolgirls, suspects what I'm really saying. But Wilf knows. And Wilf is scared. He's scared of me, he's scared of my needle, he's scared of AIDS.

'Okay, okay,' he says. And he opens the till and fishes out another £40. A few hours later I come back and there's another £40. The following day I drop by four times and each time there's £40 for me, delivered by an increasingly grim-faced Wilf. So that's £160, as well as my free drugs. Life is sweet. I'm no longer stuck on my endless cycle of stealing and selling and scoring and waiting and using. I have time to hang around in Soho. And at night, fuelled by crack, I'm sleepless and alert. So alert that, in the city's before-dawn stillness, I see the runners arriving at the sex shop with tomorrow's drugs. Furtively, I follow them. I follow them through the dark streets. They walk fast. So do I. They go up Tottenham Court Road. So do I. They congregate in a park near Warren Street tube, which is so tiny that I know I'll be spotted if I try to see more. I will find out where they keep those drugs. But not now.

Chapter 35

I've been around the streets with drugs in my mouth and I have customers waiting. I get back to the sex shop to reload when I notice that the other people in there with Wilf aren't punters. I pause. I'm already in the doorway. And I can see the boss. It's the man who offered me the job selling drugs. I like to think of him as Mexican because he has a big moustache and darkish skin but he could be from anywhere. And right now the boss is looking at me.

'How're you?' I say politely. The boss does not return my greeting. Behind him, I notice the boss's boss, a businessman in a suit and boots. I've seen him before but I've never heard him speak and he's silent now. He's looking at me. Next to him is a third person I don't recognise.

I have time only to take in Wilf's triumphant smile before the Mexican attacks me. He steps forward, takes my thin body by the scruff of the neck and throws me through the glass door into the shop. I hear a crash. It sounds a thousand miles away. Glass shatters somewhere on another continent, but the echo of its myriad splinters spreads rapidly round the world. I float high above the shop and look down on a scrawny individual as he is beaten up by three big men. I hear fists, I see knuckles and the last thing of all is the sole of a boot approaching my face and, far above it, cold eyes and a wide moustache. I remember my father, his hatred as he held my head in the fire. The taste of metal, blood running down my skin. And then I am waking up. I am in a bed. There are sheets that rustle and all around is a smell I know. Disinfectant.

I open my eyes to a blinding flash. I close them again. I've been hit by the rattle. Head, joints, I'm shivering and sweating and I know from how bad I feel that it's been a long time since I had any heroin. I open my eyes again. Another flash. It belongs to an apologetic man with a camera who's just leaving.

'Police,' he explains before he disappears.

'You're in University College Hospital,' says a voice. I turn my head. A nurse leans over me.

'What happened?'

'You were beaten up and left for dead,' the nurse tells me. 'You've been unconscious for a few days. The police want to talk to you. They told me to call them as soon as you wake up.'

My eyes hurt. My arm feels as though someone cut it off. I try to look at it. I can't see it.

'Where's my arm?'

'It's still there. But it's been badly dislocated and you need an X-ray.'

I groan and try to get out of bed.

'Take it easy. You've lost a lot of blood and your cuts still look nasty and you're badly bruised all over. There are some head injuries: broken nose, lots of bruising, the bone's chipped over one eye.'

Ouch. As she lists my injuries, I feel them one by one. I don't know where my rattle stops and my injuries start. I know I have to get out of here because I need a hit. And I know where to get drugs. Hidden behind Warren Street tube. My eyes and nose and mouth all water when I think what might be waiting for me there. If I can get out of bed.

I am considering how to ask the nurse for some nice, clean hospital heroin as I fall asleep. I wake up to see a man by my bed. He isn't wearing a uniform but he's a policeman. I always know them a mile off.

He asks me questions about my assailants. I can't answer any of them without incriminating myself. I say I don't remember anything.

Then he tells me about the fight. How, when the police arrived on the scene, the shop was empty except for a woman mopping up the blood.

'There was a tidal wave of blood across the floor and around the walls. Six, seven feet high.'

'What blood?' I ask.

'Your blood. We thought we were investigating a murder scene.'

Up the walls. A tidal wave. What did they do to me?

'The pavement was covered in blood too.'

'The pavement? Did they throw me out?'

'Through the window.'

I don't remember that, I just remember being thrown in.

'We have a witness. And he's a lawyer. He was passing and he saw most of it. Left his card by your body with a note telling us to contact him.'

'Who threw me out of the window?'

'I was hoping you could tell us that.'

But I'm not telling anything.

'You do realise,' the policeman says, 'that you've been a victim of crime and may be entitled to substantial compensation.'

Now this is getting interesting.

'How much is substantial?'

'It's a guess, but anything up to, say, £10,000. So I'd like to hear all you know about these people. We're very interested in their activities.'

For £10,000 I can be creative. I tell a good story and he doesn't look convinced. He goes away saying he'll talk to me again. I lie in bed hurting and concocting good stories that make me look like an innocent victim of crime instead of a criminal victim of crime. But I know I can't stay here. My rattle's appalling, I don't like talking to policemen, hospitals are institutions, there are dealers' drugs hidden down the road from this very hospital and they've got my name on them. It's time for me to go.

I get up. My body creaks and my arm hangs but I keep myself moving by thinking of the drugs runners buzzing around like flies in that small park. I find some clothes on a chair that are too big, but that's okay because my useless left arm slips into them easily. And I limp out of the hospital. Oh, those London smells are sweet today: traffic and the odour of humans and their perfumes, and dirt and sometimes dogs.

My body is swollen and sore and stiff as I rattle down Tottenham Court Road. The first mate I see is Steve. Dirty Steve with his greasy hair and curling shoes and blackheads, sitting begging on the pavement. But to me he's a fine sight.

'Bring me in,' I say. 'C'mon, bruv, bring me in, I got beaten up.'

'Fuck, fuck, look at the state of you!' He stares at me in alarm. 'I thought you were in detox.'

But he brings me in.

It's no problem having a hit with one hand. I could do it with no hands if I had to. As soon as I'm feeling better I go loping off towards Warren Street tube. I have a feeling that all the time I was unconscious I was dreaming about this place.

The small park behind the station is not much more than a broad thoroughfare for people rushing for a coffee or a tube train. Most of the feet here are scurrying past but there are various layabouts hanging around and now I become one of them. After a while, I notice a small group of men lurking around one particular tree. It's a fine old London plane, and its bark has its own patchy beauty. But the men aren't looking at the tree. They're looking round its base. After a while more people come. There's a block of semi-derelict flats alongside the park and the men cluster against one wall.

I see them move some bricks aside. I see them lift a paving stone by the tree. I see it all but no one sees me. My heart beats fast. It thumps uncontrollably in my chest. My withered arm and black eye are forgotten. I know I am about to strike gold.

In the evening the men have gone and there's no drugs runner in sight. I saunter up to the tree. I wait for one of those rare moments when no one's passing. My teeth are almost chattering with excitement. I press my foot gently against every piece of paving round its fine trunk. When I feel a loose stone I get down onto my knees and lever it up. There's a hole beneath it. I put my hand in. It feels damp. My fingers touch something. I peer into the hole but I don't wait to see what I've got, I just take it and stuff it down the front of my trousers. I put the stone back and head off fast. I am so excited I can barely breathe. Is there a God for junkies? Right now, I am a believer.

I move off as fast as I can, walking north and south and then west and finally I go to the Euston hostel and collect my key. I barely notice the kind-faced woman who gave me the money to go to the Narcotics Anonymous meeting. She greets me but asks me no questions. She doesn't have to; my eyes are pinholes. And all the time I'm trying to act like a normal addict instead of one who's wild with excitement at the most amazing find of his life.

Up in my room I open the bag. It contains three smaller bags. And in each of these are three smaller packages, the size and shape of a tennis ball wrapped in clingfilm. And each of these balls consists of fifty smaller bags still, and these are the bags you buy on the street. Each one contains .2g of heroin or crack but mostly crack and it is beautiful, yellow stone. The street value must be around £4500.

Some people look for diamonds or gold or buried treasure all their lives. Now I know how they feel when they find it. Because today, behind Warren Street tube station, I struck gold. I get a hit together in double quick time, my hands shaking with disbelief at my good fortune. The crack's good. But straight after the rush comes the paranoia. This isn't the monkey's paw sort of paranoia, when I'm waiting for the strong arm of the law to grab me from behind. This is wild, savage, all-consuming paranoia, it is paranoia with substance. Because if anyone saw me, if anyone guesses, if anyone at all suspects who stole those drugs, I am certainly a dead man. And probably they'll hurt me a lot before they kill me.

Alone in my room with more drugs than an addict can ever dream of possessing, I cannot enjoy them for fear. I am overwhelmed by fear. I have to keep the drugs, I have to hide the drugs. I keep fifty bags and then I get the other two parcels and squeeze them as hard as I can until they're small enough to shove up my arse, the only really safe place on earth. It takes a while. They're large and it hurts.

Like any addict, once I have the thing I need most, then I have to take it. My body won't be satisfied until it's had all the drugs. And so

I begin to use. I use and I use and I use, I am a monster of greed. The voices start.

I am hanging onto the walls by my fingernails and I hear them. They are talking, they are whispering, they are right outside my door. I listen. I hardly breathe for listening. Are these real voices or have my fears now become more real than reality? Where is the line between my imagination and the truth, or isn't there a line any more? The voices are discussing how to get into the room. They're going to start by trying to break down the door. They're coming in. They're coming to get me. I drag the bed against the door and the wardrobe against the bed. I put rubbish bags over the window so no one abseiling down the building or hovering outside in a helicopter can see in.

Then, my hands shaking, my fears barely containable as outside the voices get more and more urgent, I swallow drugs, about thirty-five bags, I swallow them like pills my life depends on. I haven't finished swallowing one when I swallow the next. Finally, I stop because everything that's left out I can use tonight. If the voices don't get in. And if they do I can swallow it fast.

I spend the night banging up the rest of the crack, shooting off on my sky rocket and hearing the voices as I plummet back to earth. In terror, I wait for the splintering of wood as the door comes down. I peek outside for the men who are storming the building. I listen for the footsteps, the shouting, the helicopters. And if, sometimes, the voices stop, the silence is the scariest thing of all because then I know the enemy is regrouping, reorganising, planning their next attack. They'll be back, they'll be back to get me.

In the morning I'm very pranged, but I'm rattling too because the heroin got used up long before the crack but I carried on taking the stone because I had to because it was there. And now I need heroin. I must have heroin. And that means I have to go out of my room. I have to risk it out there. I have to face the people who are out to get me.

I'm scared to go down to my usual haunts. Scared of the men who left me for dead outside a Soho sex shop. Scared of the men, who-ever they are, whatever they look like, who will have put a price on my head because I stole their drugs. Everything's different now because the whole world's turned against me. I can't walk through the West End any more. I prowl dangerously along the edge of the street, a wild animal, rabid, afraid, ready to pounce. I pass a mate who's also at the hostel. I'm cocaine-rich but heroin-poor so it's easy to give Jay a rock in exchange for a bag. I go straight back up to my room. I have a hit. My rattle eases. I start caning the crack again. I cane it all day. I've had nothing to eat except for thirty-five pieces of crack. My stomach's churning, there's a mad beast inside it and soon I am sick again because I'm rattling, rattling, needing that heroin.

Risking my life for gear, I get myself out of the hostel and down to the park behind Warren Street tube and this time, checking that no one's about, I go to the wall in the block of flats and move the bricks around and yes, here it is. Another bag of drugs. Then suddenly there's a hand grabbing at me, pulling wildly at the clothes on my back. Without looking round, I turn into an eel and scramble under a fence by the flats. My attacker, still grabbing, shouting, kicking at me, is halted by the wire. I have time to glimpse an angry brown face. I last saw this man in the sex shop with the Mexican but I don't think about it, I don't think about anything except getting away, fast, fast, my loose arm hanging and my legs aching, the drugs bag banging around inside my trousers. I get myself back to the hostel and up to my room and yes, yes, yes, here's another four big bags, each with three tennis ball-sized packs with fifty small bags in each and, although there's again more crack than heroin, I have enough gear to see me through days and nights of uncontrolled crack use.

So crack takes me over. They know for sure who I am now. They've seen me; they'll be after me. It's not just the voices of the people who are coming to get me. It's the way they're looking under the door, talking about the police, putting ladders against the building, knocking at the windows, crawling over the roof and lowering themselves down on ropes . . . my paranoia reaches beyond psychosis, it threatens to consume me. I know this is an overdose in some deep-down, long-ignored, rational part of my mind, but I'm still injecting, two at a time, holding onto the sink to vomit, throwing up drugs, shitting drugs. I lie on the bed, shitting onto black bin bags so I can retrieve the little wrappers of drugs from my own shit. I take some of it, the rest I throw back into my mouth, fast, hurry, hurry before they come, before they get it, before they get me. Crack is in my mouth, it's in my arse, and from time to time I can feel the bags exploding in my stomach, my whole body is exploding with cocaine while I watch the shadows, watch them, wait for them, hear the voices.

My eyes are flashing light and dark, my ears are booming and crashing and as it begins to wear off I lie on the floor, unable to move, unable even to climb onto the bed. My flesh is falling off my bones. I lie here for days, perhaps three days. Crack is everywhere, all over the floor, the sink, the bed. It is the Mad Hatter's crack party in here and I'm too weak to move and the heroin rattle is biting into my soul.

Finally, somehow, impossibly, I get out of the door. I have a blinding crack headache and one eye can't see at all. I stagger down to the foyer and stand there in a pair of shorts with no top. I weigh about seven stone and my skin is see-through. There is blood running down my arms. I look wildly around me, an animal who is loose in the zoo. The staff, alarmed, eyes large, sit on the stairs as I try to convince them that people up there are looking for me, want to kill me.

They attempt to calm me but I cannot be calmed. I am mad with fear. Jay, who swapped the heroin for crack and understands the problem, walks cautiously towards me, his face pained.

'Listen, mate . . .' he begins, gently.

'Get away! Get the fuck away!' I yell, grabbing the Hoover and brandishing it like an offensive weapon. 'I can kill you with this if you come any closer, I can break your fucking head open.'

'Mark, it's the fucking crack talking . . .' he says. 'You need to stop using that shit.'

But by now I've turned and I'm running, running as fast as I can through the hostel because no one will believe that they're after me. I'm screaming at the voices, because I can't stand being scared of them any more: 'I'm here, come on! Take me! Come and get me!'

I reach the door and I stop.

I hear myself.

I sound . . . completely . . . insane.

I stand very still. I think. I see myself how the staff here must see me. They'll call the police. They'll call a psychiatric team.

I sit down. I am quiet. I breathe deeply and slowly. I feel like death itself.

Jay comes up again and, warily, sits down near me.

'It's the crack,' I say.

'Yeah. You need some gear.'

'Yeah.'

We make a rapid deal, crack in exchange for heroin, and when he gets back with the gear I hand over the crack and have a hit and feel heroin's calm spread all through my body. Dave, a staff member, appears in my room and sees me in my shorts, injecting. He's staring at my body. His face is more than shocked, it's terrified. I've lost all sight of myself now and I only know how bad I look from his expression. He's a normal man who's seen a dead body.

'You're emaciated, Mark. You're very sick. You need a hospital bed,' he says gently.

I shake my head. No psychiatric wards for me.

'I'm not talking psychiatric wards. I'm talking some medical care and rest,' says Dave. 'I'm going to start ringing around for you now.'

And I half hope he's successful. But he comes back later and reports that no one will take me.

'Not long now until you're back in detox,' he reminds me. I remember detox. It was only a couple of weeks back but since then I've been dealing, beaten up, in hospital, finding drugs and on the run. It feels like a year ago.

Now that I have so many drugs, my days start to collapse. All I have to do is exchange crack for heroin to even up my supply. I don't have to rush around dealing, stealing, begging, arguing. I thought my life was chaotic before but now real chaos sets in. I prowl around all day, pranged, frightened, angry. And all the time I'm noticing something terrible. I'm taking enough drugs to kill most people. And they're having less and less effect on me. I'm getting bad come-downs and terrible rattles without great rushes. The drugs aren't working any more. I want to cry. It's happening again. The drugs aren't working.

I've been hanging around in Camden but now I venture back into the West End to exchange some crack for heroin. I'm very careful. I'm all eyes. I know that everyone's angry with me, everyone's a threat. Dealers are angry, Wilf and his bosses are angry, even my mate Dave's angry. I stay amid thick crowds of people but for junkies everyone else is invisible and I might as well have walked naked down the street because within minutes I know who my greatest enemies are. The twins, Keith and Malc. The gangsters have sent them to look for me.

One of them sees me. He points at me, points through throngs of people directly at me. He gestures to his brother a few feet away. He's carrying a Sunblest bread bag. He pulls it back so I can see the big knife hidden inside it. That knife is for me. Bread is the stuff of life but they want to take mine. I run through the crowds. I hear footsteps behind me. I run faster. I hear them, feel their breath, and when I turn I see a great, ugly, distorted face close to mine. The twin lunges for me but I dodge him.

I might have escaped from them but I haven't got away. Because now I know there is a price on my head. I've had a total of about £10,000 of drugs. The twins will be paid generously for finishing me off and they certainly want my job dealing. The police won't bother to investigate another death of another homeless person who would anyway have died soon of AIDS.

It's a few days before I go back to the West End again and this time I stay on the big roads. Charing Cross Road, Shaftesbury Avenue, Haymarket. But there the twins are once more, as though they're patrolling the streets night and day, looking for me always. I see them from afar and they see me at the same moment. I catch the glint of a knife. They dart rapidly and suddenly like fish in a pool and I turn again, pushing my way through the crowds, running for my life.

On a third visit, Keith and Malc are here again. This time they get me from behind and one of them almost succeeds in dragging me up an alley. I punch him as hard as I can and in that moment, when he's winded and his brother is just a few feet too far away to help him, I turn and run.

For a long time now, I've been deluding myself that I'm someone in the West End. Now I understand that I am less than a particle of dust here. The place is crawling with gangsters and big dealers. They might have any number of people out for me. So I can't return to the West End. There's nothing left now but death or detox.

By the time I'm due to go back to Elephant and Castle, I've used up all the drugs I stole. The staff of the hostel have taken a special interest in me because they can see I'm not far from death. They've tried to find me a hospital bed and are shocked that they've failed. Now they're all anxious for detox to work. A taxi is waiting outside to take me there. The staff are standing at the door to wish me goodbye. And I'm ready to go except for one thing. There's a bloke who owes me heroin. I've sorted out loads of crack for him but he's been hanging on to repay me because he's been hoping I'll disappear into detox and never claim the debt. And this makes me livid. I've been waiting for those bags and now the taxi's here and I won't be able to use them before I go. That bloke has tricked me out of my bag; he's had me over. Thinks he's cleverer than me, does he? I have a razor blade and I want to cut him into small pieces with it. I glimpse him on the stairs as I head for the door.

'It was my last hit before detox, you were supposed to give me my last hit,' I shout at him, brandishing the razor. I hate him. I want to kill him.

A black woman staff member looks at me sadly. She says, very quietly: 'Mark. Your taxi's outside.'

'You fucking bastard,' I scream at the man on the stairs, 'I'm going into detox without my hit and I'll get you for this!'

The frightened little toe-rag is edging up the stairs now. I wave my razor and prepare to follow him.

In my ear is the quiet voice again. 'Mark. If you do that, it's all over. It's finished for you. So walk away. Walk away from it. Get into the taxi, go to detox.'

I hear her voice and something about its softness slips down inside me like water. But I don't make a decision. I don't even know whether I'm going to kill him or walk away until I find myself turning and heading out of the door to the taxi. I could just as easily plunge after that bastard. He's got one over on me and I can't stand it. I seethe all the way to Elephant and Castle.

The staff greet me warmly, put me on methadone and escort me straight back up to University College Hospital A&E. I am deloused, given clothes from Lost Property and then a doctor examines my withered arm.

'Were you born with it?' he asks.

I tell him it was fine until a fortnight ago.

He looks at my cuts and bruises and then hands me over to a nurse whose job it is to take off my socks. Surgically. Because the scabs on my feet and toes have grown over the socks. It takes hours of cutting and soaking to part the fabric finally from my skin and the nurse retches more than once. I understand that I am not a pretty sight. I weigh less than a big dog, my knees are broader than my thighs, my skin has a ghostly transparency and my body is covered in scars and track marks. But the nurse treats me with humanity. Her voice is gentle, her way is kind. Her touch is soft and intimate. It moves me to tears. I haven't experienced this for a very long time. Back at the detox centre with my feet dressed, in clean clothes, I rattle despite the methadone. After the incredible quantities of drugs I've consumed in the month since I was last here, the rattle is cruel, it is laughing at me. After day ten, once again, the methadone is over and I'm back to cold turkey. And I can't stand it. We're allowed out and I head straight off for some drugs. Not to the West End, that's too dangerous for me now. I run up to King's Cross. I don't dare take heroin or the detox staff will notice at once. I score some crack and then go back to Elephant and Castle. In the bare, white bathroom, submerged in the tub, I have my hit.

Whoosh. For a few minutes, I'm right out of this place. I'm out of this cold, white room in this building in this city in this country on this earth, I'm right up there orbiting the moon. And then, following straight on from the high is the rush of footsteps, the murmur of one thousand voices, snarling, whispering, talking into my ear. It's the Committee. They're saying: Evil bastard, they'll chuck you out now. Back on the streets for you, no-good scumbag. We'll get you when you're out there. Or shall we smash the window and break down the door and come right in and get you now?

I stop breathing. I hide under the water. Then I break the works up into tiny pieces and crush them far, far down the plughole so that no one will ever know. Except that I know. I'm supposed to be in detox and I'm using.

I go to Wardour Street the next day, all eyes and ears and fear. I slip inside the Turning Point building.

I say: 'Sean, I used last night. I banged up some crack and I shoved the works down the plughole.'

He looks alarmed. 'You'll be discharged! I'm sure you're aware of that.'

Yes, I'm aware that if I use then I'm out. I'm also aware that if I'm out then I'm dead. There is no way I can stay on the streets and go on living. Because if the drugs don't get me, the twins will.

'Those are the rules,' says Sean. 'And you've broken them.'

My throat constricts. It's hard to speak. 'I can't stop, Sean. I can't live right in the centre of London without using. It's impossible.'

Sean narrows his big brown eyes and looks serious.

'Are you going to tell them?' I ask.

He sighs and thinks, his face clouded, his arms crossed.

My voice is urgent now. 'Are you going to let them throw me out?'

Finally he says: 'Okay, Mark, I'm going to break the rules too. I've got another solution.'

Relief. It spreads all through my body like a blush. Sean's going to save me.

Chapter 36

We are in Bognor Regis. This is a seaside town on the south coast and one of the few places in England where I haven't sold drugs or even taken them. Sean brought me here on the train. People stared at us and one person felt so sorry for me that he bought us an ice cream. We are the odd couple, me shaking and sweating, Sean holding me up.

The walk from the station is flat but it feels like a steep hill.

'I can't get up here,' I say. I am too tired, too sick, too bruised and my left arm is wasted.

'Oh yes you can!' says Sean. 'I'll take your box for you.'

I hang onto him and he carries my small brown art box in one hand and pulls me along. There's a wall alongside the pavement and I stop to lean on it every two minutes.

'Now just come along, Mr Johnson,' Sean says in his bossy voice. 'It's not far.'

We arrive at a big old rambling house.

'This is Ravenscourt Alcohol and Drug Treatment Centre,' says Sean with a flourish as though we've arrived at Buckingham Palace. But my body's hurting so much I hardly look at the place. It's another big house but I notice that it's a bit less upmarket than the last time I was in rehab, all those years and drugs ago in Birmingham. Probably it's going to be the same. It'll be another Maison de Relax and I'll have lots of girlfriends and start to feel better but it won't work. Because nothing works for Mr Johnson. He's an evil bastard and he's too far gone.

We walk into a red foyer. There are cups scattered around the place and they all have saucers on top. Weird. But I can't be bothered to wonder why. My teeth are aching more than the rest of me. My eyes hurt because my pupils can't respond to the light. My feet hurt because the streets have almost rubbed them away. My head's spinning. I'm rattling all over. I'm jelly, I'm not anyone. I have no sense of myself at all. And I'm terrified. I just know I want to do something impossible: stop taking drugs.

We are shown down a corridor to where most of the residents are sitting, smoking, in faded armchairs in a big, glassy room. I wince at the light but manage to glance around at the faces. There are about ten people and they're all different. Some are old, fifty, even sixty, a few are younger, others are about my age. Most don't look as if they've been on the streets like me: they're too healthy and well fed. One or two people greet me. I try to respond but I'm hurting too much. Sean turns into Prince Charming and does the chat for me.

An Irishwoman called Annie who looks grumpy leads us to the room I'm going to share. It's big with a bay window and two single beds and two wardrobes. A lot of people have been through this room. It has stories to tell.

I stand awkwardly, staring at my bed, not knowing what to do. Sean looks at me.

'You can unpack your stuff,' he says.

So I'm supposed to put my clothes in the battered wardrobe. But I don't have any. I open my art box and the trays lift out on their hinges. I reach in for the contents. My Collection of Found Objects: the little silver notebook; the badges; the end of an ornate old spoon; some small tins; sewing needles; paintbrushes; and a tube of paint. My possessions. I need a safe place for them. Someone might try to steal them. They've always mattered to me but just now they matter a lot. I lay them carefully under the bed.

It's time for Sean to go. I'm scared. I want to cry. I want to hang onto him.

I go to the foyer with him and when he says goodbye I can hardly stand the sight of his retreating back. I am five years old and I don't want my parents to leave me here in Bognor by myself. Sean turns. He says: 'Mark, this is the place you're supposed to be. Now it's time for you to get on with it.' He's gone and I feel empty. Like a bereaved person. I'm alone with my pain. I go to my room to lie down.

My rattle is terrible: I need to rest, maybe take a bath. I'm supposed to have been through this early-stage rattle in detox with methadone to help me but I cheated in detox the way I always cheat everywhere and everyone, even myself. So my withdrawal symptoms are acute and there are no prescription drugs to ease this at Ravenscourt. There's nothing at all. I've already been given a paper to sign, which says that I understand I'll be discharged if I drink or take any drugs or chemicals or go to a pub or have sex.

I don't like the look of all that white sheet and duvet on my bed. I'm certainly not going to get between them. I'm not going to take my clothes off either. I won't feel safe if I do that. I won't feel right. I lie down on the bed and close my eyes. I hurt too much to sleep.

A short, tubby man comes in.

'They sent me to tell you it's group therapy.'

I groan.

His voice is gentle. He is apologetic. 'Group therapy. Starting now.'

'I'm not going,' I say. 'I'm sick.'

'You've got to.'

'I can't.'

'They'll throw you out.'

Throw me out. Where would I go? Images flash through my mind. Pavements and doorways, the twins with their knife in the Sunblest bread bag, a Coke can, upended, with congealed blood in its lip.

I sit up. I attempt to heave my body off the bed. The man watches me.

'Do I have to do this?' I gasp.

'If you want to stay here. There are rules.'

So much for the Maison de Relax. I try to be a machine but the pistons won't work, the pain overpowers them. Slowly, slowly, I stand up. The man leads me to a room where the seats are arranged in a semi-circle. On them are the same people I saw earlier but now they're not smoking and they look restless, uncomfortable, as though they'd like to light up.

The counsellor in charge of the group is called Alan. He is at least fifty, slim, with black hair. He greets me. You can tell that in the past he's had one too many nights out. He has that lean old speed-freak look but there's a sort of calm about him which commands respect.

He says a few words. There's a man's voice. Then a woman's. Then a man speaks for a long time and finally all of them talk. Words, words. I hear their rhythm and their music; I hear accents from all over Britain and vowels from every class. But I can't hear what they're saying. I hurt too much to listen. I hurt too much to think. I'm a wounded wild animal. I barely know my own name. All I know is how to use.

I start to stumble through the routines of this new place. I can't sleep at night. I don't want to eat at mealtimes. If I stand up I want to sit down. If I sit down I want to stand. I don't want to do anything. But I have to because there's a minefield of rules here. When your cup's in use it should have a saucer on top. You take your turn on the chores rota. No smoking anywhere in the house except the conservatory. Write about significant events in your life and hand it in to your counsellor. Get up at seven o'clock every morning.

Are they trying to kill me? I've been a chaotic user with no structure and this routine is like being dropped into a freezing plunge pool. I am so shocked and dazed that I hardly know what's happening.

But soon there are more rules and they are just for me. Mark is not allowed to sneak off to bed in the daytime. Mark is not allowed to crawl under the dining-room table for a nap. They give us £6 a week and if we break a rule we lose 20p. By the end of the first week I've lost the lot and I owe them some of next week's money too.

'How're you?' people ask me and my answer's always the same.

'Fucking desperate.' My head's battered. I'm battered all over.

Physical pain stops me joining in the group therapy. I sit there silently while they talk. When I'm alone with Alan, I have one question.

'Can someone like me ever get clean?'

We are in one of the therapy rooms, a wooden hut in the yard. The sun's rays reach one corner and light up the backs of the faded chairs. Alan studies my face and leans forward.

'Yes,' he says.

'I mean, is it really possible for an addict like me to change? Have a different life? A life that doesn't mean I'm injecting drugs every day?'

Alan makes a big, expansive gesture with his arms and nods his head vigorously.

'Yes, yes, yes,' he says.

'Honestly?'

'Yes. I'm a recovering addict. I've been clean ten years.'

I stare at him. Ten years. I can't imagine ten minutes, never mind ten years.

'You don't have to think about ten years. Think about today. Just take one day at a time.'

I can feel tears in my eyes. Because someone has switched a light on. The light is at the end of a dark corridor. It is weak. It glimmers like some faraway star. Hope. The possibility of change. The faint, faint chance that a day will come when I don't need to take drugs.

Alan watches me closely. He sees the light go on. He smiles at me.

But the corridor is long and dark and the light flickers and falters often. If I don't take drugs, what will I do? What other life can I have? Where is there for me to go? And, within days, Ravenscourt, with its rules, its routines, its irksome fellow inmates, its group therapy and its endless demands of a man who is still skulking on the edge of humanity, has driven me to despair. I've lost my entire week's wages this evening by curling up under the dining-room table for some shut-eye. I had to write my life story and that was one long blinding headache. Plus they're always talking about Significant Events in our lives: we're supposed to discuss them and write about them and put our sheets of paper in a brown envelope on top of the TV for our counsellor to read. I don't want to. I want to take myself off into a corner. I'm a wounded animal, but they won't let me curl up by myself. They won't leave me alone. I hate it here. I don't want to use again but I hate being clean. Clean is a state of utter desolation.

I try to tell Alan this. We're in the therapy room again and I say: 'I could join in more if my rattle wasn't so bad. If I had a bit of methadone . . .'

He raises his eyebrows.

'No, Mark.'

'The pain. It's killing me.'

'There's no recorded death from heroin withdrawal. It's terrible but you won't die from it.'

'I can't think for pain.'

'You're chemically dependent and the only thing to stop that dependence is to stop the chemical. Not by taking other things to depend on instead.'

'Whenever I've tried to stop before I just can't get through the rattle.'

Alan looks at me and thinks for a moment. Finally he asks: 'How many times have you tried to give up all drugs and alcohol?'

'Loads. Loads and loads and loads.' My life flashes past me like the London-to-Glasgow express. It is nothing more than a series of failed attempts to give up drugs.

'I mean, how many times have you actually given up completely?'

'Millions!'

'Like when?'

'Well, for instance, when I went to university to study photography. And later, when I was qualifying as a tree surgeon in Kendal, I was always giving up then. I'd rattle for months at a time.'

'What exactly did you give up?'

'Heroin.'

'Did you take anything else in those periods?'

'Nothing.'

'So you didn't drink?'

'Oh, yes, of course I drank.'

'A lot?'

'I got steaming every night. I had to. When I came off gear I needed something.'

'Did you take other things to help you come off heroin? Valium? Cocaine? Methadone?'

'Um . . . yes.'

'Which of them?'

'Erm . . . all of them.'

His voice is kind and clear as though he's talking to someone very, very young: 'Mark, that isn't giving up drugs, is it? That's just changing your drug use. You kicked heroin for a while but you took other drugs and prescription drugs and drank alcohol instead.'

'The doctor gave me the prescription!' I hear my own voice. I hear the protests of an outraged seven-year-old. I never! He give it me, I never thieved it! Okay, I may have sneaked the doctor's prescription pad into my pocket so I could supplement everything he gave me with a few prescriptions of my own but the fact is I rinsed the doc because he let me.

Alan says: 'When you wrote your life story for me I felt I was reading about an addict moving from one drug to the next. You shifted backwards and forwards from drink to recreational drugs to street drugs to prescription drugs. But that's not giving up. Taking nothing at all is giving up. That's what we do here.'

I am silent. Alan watches me. There's no sun today. The room is dark and cool. I think about my attempts to give up before. I've always believed I was desperate and sincere. Now I realise that, if you call alcohol a drug, I've only stopped using once since I was a teenager: during the few months I spent in rehab in Birmingham.

'I'm not an alcoholic,' I say at last. I feel sulky and annoyed. I could head off for Bognor station right now. No one would stop me.

'Really?' asks Alan politely. I hate him when he's polite.

'I may be a drug addict but I'm not an alcoholic. I hardly drank at all when I was on the streets. I mean, only sometimes.'

Alan nods and smiles. He's not going to argue with me. He's just going to show me that I'm wrong. I hate him for thinking he's so clever.

Over the days that follow, I learn that Ravenscourt follows the

Twelve-Step Programme that has been adopted by addicts and alco-holics all over the world. Sooner or later I'm supposed to go through all twelve of these steps. Fat chance. I can barely get my head around step one.

Step One: I admit that I am powerless over my addiction and that my life has become unmanageable.

Every day, I'm supposed to write another example of my power-lessness and my life's unmanageability. I have to put it in my brown Significant Events folder and leave it on the TV.

First, I write about visiting Rosie in rehab and losing my temper with the pastor.

Next, I write about the streets, how at the end the twins kept reaching for their knife whenever they saw me.

Then, I write about how I got chucked out of detox because I couldn't stop myself biting that kid after we argued about the TV channel.

There's a lot of other things I could tell, but I don't. I've told enough now. I can't go on with this treatment, it's too painful, it hurts too much and I need a fucking hit to help me forget all this stuff, not a middle-class counsellor who grins at me and gets me to write about it.

I'm off. I'm out of this place. I find an empty carrier bag. Sighing, I open it.

Where am I going? And how?

I don't have much to take, nothing more than a few clothes others have left behind when, like me, they've run away. I put them into the bag slowly. Then I reach under the bed for my art box. My joints creak as I bend down and pain shoots up my legs. Everything hurts when you come off heroin. Without it my body is sterile. My bones are bleached of their marrow. My cells are bereaved.

I open the art box and check that my Collection of Found Objects is complete. The paintbrushes. The spoon handle. The sewing needles. The notebook. The badges. Looking inside the box is like looking back into another world where there's no carpets or lights or ceiling any more, just my feet walking, walking on hard streets. My heart races. I'm scared. I don't want to go. It's been such a long journey to rehab. But I don't want to stay.

'What's up?' asks a voice. My room-mate, Colin. It's so late I thought he must be asleep.

'I'm in bits,' I say. 'I've been here for over two weeks and I can't stand it any longer with nothing in my body.'

He sits up in bed and yawns. 'Pain still bad?'

'It's doing my fucking head in.'

All those emotions the drugs helped me avoid are happening at once. Terror, guilt, shame, hopelessness, helplessness, loneliness, sadness, a sense of loss, jealousy, anger . . . everything I should have felt in my wasted years I feel now. After being ignored for so long, these emotions have the power of a great locomotive and they're running right over me. They're crushing me, turning me into pulp.

Colin watches me.

'What do you want?'

'To be clean. I want a new life. I want a new brain.'

'Well . . . there is a way.'

'Huh?'

'It's like this. All the stuff that's in the back of your mind, it'll have to come out. You've got to get honest. All the things that have been holding you down, all your secrets, you've got to tell, mate.'

I think for a minute.

'You mean,' I say, 'I've got to tell about what it was really like out there? On the streets?'

Colin guffaws.

'I don't mean ego stuff about how hard you were. I don't mean feeling sorry for yourself stuff. I mean that you've got to tell your secrets. Real secrets. All the small embarrassing things you've never told anyone, the sneaky things, the spiteful things, the grassing-up-your-mates keep-it-to-yourself kind of things that you swore you'd never tell a soul.'

My secrets. He must be kidding. There are a lot of things I'm not going to tell anyone. Ever.

He says: 'Talking about your weaknesses gives you back your power.'

I cross the room and open the window and smell the night. I breathe deeply, inhaling the salty air, inhaling the sea.

I hear Colin's voice, insistent, behind me.

'You've got to tell.'

I turn round and he's still looking at me.

'There's a lot of stuff that's keeping you sick. Your secrets poison your soul. It's called the Secret Side of Self. Think about it, mate, before you pack your bag.'

I lie awake all night, my body alive with pain, every nerve raw, my legs propellers that have to keep whirring, spinning, moving. I want to go but I've got nowhere to go. I don't want to do this but I've got nothing else to do. I don't want to take drugs but I can't live without them.

In the morning, I'm still here.

When I go into group therapy, I'm shit-scared. I cower in my chair and everyone can tell I'm going to talk for the first time. There's an air of anticipation. Or maybe it's curiosity.

'Ah,' says Alan, looking pleased. 'Is there a Significant Event you'd like to tell us about, Mark?'

'Yeah,' I say. I open my mouth and wait for myself to speak. For a minute nothing comes out. And then I start.

I tell them about the time I went over in the flat in Kendal. I'd banged up a half gram of gear when I was supposed to be looking after Jack and he was trapped there with me all day, the door locked, his nappy falling off, hungry, crying.

I confess that I am a terrible father and then I finish speaking. I am deeply ashamed and humiliated. The room is silent. Faces stare at me. Some are shocked, some are sympathetic. A few people look away: they're wondering what they're doing here with a man like this. One woman rocks back and forth in her chair, her eyes shut, trying to block me out.

Alan leans forward.

'If you hadn't been taking drugs, addicted to drugs, would you have treated your child that way?' he asks gently.

'No fucking way.'

'Then maybe this event isn't about being a terrible father. It's about drugs making your life unmanageable,' he suggests.

The others start to talk.

'This must be a terrible memory for you,' someone murmurs. 'Your son suffered at the time but you've suffered for years on the memory.'

I want to thank him for understanding that, however monstrous my behaviour's been, I'm still a human being.

This is group therapy and they're giving me group feedback and suddenly I experience the warmth and support of people around me. I've never felt such kindness. No one's rushing off to call the children's department of the Social Services. They're talking about similar things they've done, behaviour that has haunted them, too. One woman says that both her children have been taken into care and, crying, she explains why. A man talks about behaviour with his son that he deeply regrets. Another man identifies with Jack: he describes incidents from childhood with his alcoholic parents and when he talks he looks like a confused child, his face hurt and baffled, his eyes fighting against tears.

When the session ends I feel empty. I've been sickened and shamed by my own story. But I know one thing: whatever terrible things I've done, there are others with similar experiences. I'm not completely alone.

Later I feel drained. I just want to get away. The Committee inside my head has a lot to say today. I try to sneak up to my room. A staff member stops me and fines me. I hide under the table and am found and fined again. My body is still aching: my teeth, my eyes, my feet, every joint is heavy. Nothing's changed. Colin said I'd feel better and I don't. But I've started talking now. I'm beginning to tell.

Annie, the Irishwoman, is in charge of the bedrooms. She's been here at Ravenscourt since it was willed as a rehabilitation centre by its alcoholic owner years ago. She always ticks me off and fines me when she discovers me sleeping in my clothes. Now she tells me to change my bed linen. I take off the duvet cover and trot off down the stairs to the washing machine.

'And,' asks Annie when I get back, 'what about your sheet?'

I groan. I take the sheet off the bed and go down with it. When I get back my body is seizing up with the effort. Annie's waiting for me.

'You forgot your pillowcase,' she says.

I narrow my eyes.

'Come on,' says Annie, hands on hips. 'When you change your bed linen it's duvet cover, sheet, pillowcase.'

She is five foot of pure granite topped by a helmet of white hair. There's no point arguing with the Annies of this world. So it's back downstairs again for me.

'That's how you'll learn,' Annie tells me when I return, breathless. 'You won't forget again. And you can just stop sleeping in your clothes. Got it? At night you change into night clothes and you get into bed.'

'But I feel so exhausted.'

She looks firm. 'You change and get into bed and that's when you go to sleep. Then in the morning at seven o'clock you get up. You stay up all day. You don't go to sleep again until you've changed out of your clothes and got yourself into bed at night.'

I respect her. I understand that she is a hard woman and I see that her firmness is a sort of kindness. And I'm embarrassed that she has to teach me how to live. I'm embarrassed when a group is formed for me called Personal Hygiene. I'm clean enough now but people point out that my clothes are crumpled and I look like a tramp. I used to know when to eat and when to sleep and how to dress but bit by bit that knowledge has been stripped away from me along with my humanity. And now I have to learn it all again.

Annie gives me a cookery lesson. We get on all right. But when, afterwards, she finds that the kitchen isn't spotless, her face takes on its granite lines and she fines me without hesitation. At first I hate her for it, but many coffees and cigarettes later I'm grateful. You always know where you are with Annie. Her rock-solid insistence on the rules starts to feel reassuring.

We're allowed out in a group without supervision as long as we all stay together. We can go into town or down to the beach, all ten of us or fifteen, however many people are resident right now. We move along the streets like a huge, ragged animal. We have nothing in common except the substances we used to consume but some of these people are beginning to feel like friends. After all, we tell each other our secrets.

When we get to the beach we sit down on the sand and smoke. There aren't so many people here because they all get sucked into the massive Butlins complex along the coast. A few little kids run into the water and then out to their parents, squeaking at the joy of it. Gulls wheel overhead. Dogs are insane with happiness at the space, the water, the expanse of sand. Small waves crash. I scoop up some shells and stones in my fingers and they hold the day's heat. Each is unique and beautiful. The sun has begun its descent over to the west with a hint at the red that's to follow and for the first time since I arrived here, no, for the first time in years, I feel a sort of calm, a small fissure in my misery.

The next day a counsellor calls me out of the conservatory. She's pale and I see that her hand is shaking. There's a phone call for me.

She leads me to her office and tells me that the call comes from West End Central police station. A voice informs me that two officers will be arriving shortly to interview me.

'What about?'

'We're investigating three linked deaths in the West End and we think you may be able to help with our inquiries.'

I am winded by this. The counsellor looks shell-shocked. She is staring at me hard, wondering if the police are about to arrest me. Alan arrives, his brow furrowed. He takes me outside and we have a cigarette. I stand with my back against the wall. I feel the sun on my face. I understand that, shakily, almost without knowing it, I've started to build a new life here. It's not much more than a small, rickety structure but I know it was there because the whole thing just fell down. In my head, I hear laughter. The Committee has already judged me and found me guilty and sent me to jail.

Alan's watching me.

'I never,' I say. 'I never killed anyone.'

Suddenly I see the Japanese woman, brushing her dark hair from her sweet, sad face. I see John lying on the ramp, his lips blue.

Alan looks at me intently. 'Do you have any idea what these deaths are that they want to talk to you about?'

'I got beaten up a few weeks ago and they were asking me questions then. But it could be about anyone. People die in the West End.'

'Were you mixed up with some big criminals?'

'Probably. I don't know. I needed drugs so I did a lot of things and I knew a lot of people.'

'Did you answer their questions before? When you were beaten up?'

'No. I made up a load of rubbish because they said I might get compensation.'

He sighs.

'Mark. Do you want to stay in rehab?'

'Yes. I want to get clean.' I hear my own voice. I'm making a clear, firm statement because I want to believe myself. Even though deep down inside I still don't think it's possible. Deep down inside, when I wake up each morning, I think I'll be gone from this place tonight.

'Then tell the police the truth. All your life you've lied to others and yourself. If you really want to change, if you really want to move away from a life of powerlessness over drugs, then you can start right now by telling the police the truth.'

I throw down my cigarette butt and stamp on it.

'I've lived outside the law. If I tell them anything about myself at all then they'll fucking nick me.'

'Mark . . . you've got a choice. You can bullshit your way through this. Or you can tell the truth. It's your chance to get your slate clean. Only the truth will help you through your recovery and, if it comes to that, you can follow the programme in jail.'

When the two policemen arrive, I recognise one of them. He's the detective who was sitting by my bed when I regained consciousness in hospital. He greets me.

'You're looking better than when I last saw you,' he says. And it's true. I'm getting physiotherapy now for my withered arm, the bruises have gone and I've even managed to put on a few pounds. I don't look so bad. I just feel like shit.

Before they interview me, the policemen disappear into a room with Alan for a long conference. I don't know what Alan's saying to them but I can guess. He's saying that I really want to change my life and Ravenscourt is giving me a chance and leaving me here would be more productive than arresting me. But they're policemen. Arresting people is what they do.

When it's my turn, Annie gives us all a cup of tea and I sit in one of the therapy rooms with them. I am terrified. The policemen talk nicely to me. They say I was a victim of an interesting crime. They're now investigating three deaths in the West End and they want to show me some photos and I should prepare myself for these pictures. I don't know how to prepare myself so I grip the arms of my chair.

The people in the pictures are all known to me. They lie on identical steel trays. They look like wax effigies but they're not. They're dead. Any one of them could have been me. If I blink I can see my own face on those unmoving bodies.

I suppress my instincts to lie about these people: who they were, what they did and how I knew them. I remember Alan's voice, how he told me that I could change my life by telling the truth. I'm fairly certain that I'll change my life by landing in jail but nevertheless I talk. I tell them everything I know about drugs in the West End. I even tell them about Warren Street station.

Finally they nod and look at each other and thank me for my help. They get up to go.

'Aren't you going to arrest me?' I ask.

'No, Mark. We wish you good luck with your recovery,' they say. And then they leave. Policemen, there's no understanding them. They feed my fears and haunt my paranoia but every time I come into contact with them they show me only kindness and humanity.

Alan comes in. He's smiling. He's rubbing his hands.

'Is it going to be all right?' I ask. I want to cry. Alan puts his arms round me and I let him hold me and it feels good.

'Yes,' he says, 'it's going to be all right.'

I say: 'You're always talking about a higher power . . .'

'That's step two,' he reminds me: '"I believe that a power greater than myself can restore me to sanity."'

'It just did. I mean God, or the higher power, or whatever you want to say. Now I've been shown how I would have ended up if I'd stayed on the streets. On steel trays in the police morgue with the others. If I go back there, that's how it'll be for me. Someone must be telling me to stay here in rehab.'

After this it doesn't get any easier to stay, it only gets harder to leave. Every day is a reprieve. Tomorrow I might go back, I might find myself on the streets, I might use again. I just have to get through today.

My teeth ache but no dentist will treat me. Otherwise, the physical pain of the rattle gradually eases although it frequently returns with ferocity. But as the physical misery diminishes, my mental anguish increases. I want to run off, I want to hide in a corner, I want to scream, I want to hit someone, I want to fuck someone. It's all against the rules. Rosie and I are writing to each other now and I'd like her to visit with the kids but, after a consultation with Alan, I find that's not allowed either. He says it could interfere with my treatment. At this stage, it's important to share your feelings with the group, not to channel them into a more secluded 'special relationship'.

Just when I'm getting used to the place, just when I'm beginning to learn the routine, when I'm taking off my clothes and getting into a bed at night and occasionally sleeping, then it's time to leave. Ravenscourt is a primary recovery centre and that means you can't stay any longer than twelve weeks.

Alan has arranged for me to move on to Bournemouth, to a secondary treatment centre called the Quinton House Project. For years I kept moving and now every small change seems to ricochet around inside my body. I am frightened and unsettled. When Alan hugs me goodbye I want to cry. Twelve weeks is the longest I've ever voluntarily stayed anywhere, apart from the last rehab when the only alternative was jail. This time I stayed because the alternative was death. But Ravenscourt has become my home. Since I've been here, many addicts have been through its doors. Not everybody makes it to the end of their treatment. Those that do stand a real chance of success.

When I arrive in Bournemouth I want to turn round and go back to Bognor. From the windows I can see drug dealers at work on the strip of grass across the road. And it seems to me that many of the addicts in here have no interest in recovering: they simply regard this place as a respite from their habits.

The centre is run by Lorraine Parry, a brilliant woman who specialises in relapse prevention. She can see into your head and turn you inside out. And she is surrounded by a seething nest of counsellors and therapists. They are the thought police. You can't have a feeling about anything without them asking where it comes from, whether you experienced it in your childhood, who last made you feel that way. My counsellor, Sonia, is the scariest of all but Alan had already been in touch with her and promised me I'm in good hands.

Gradually, after intensive group and individual therapy, I come to believe that I was born an addict. I believe that addiction is a disease I've had since birth, the way some people are born with more obvious physical disabilities. My stealing and other antisocial behaviour was an indication of my illness long before I ever had a drink or a drug. And I'm learning not to blame my childhood, my parents or my background for anything because when I hear others' stories I have to admit that plenty of people have suffered more and haven't grown up like me. And now my life is in my hands. I can decide what happens next. I can decide whether to stay sick or get healthy.

One of the most astonishing discoveries I make is that I have contracted neither HIV nor Hepatitis C. I don't know how it's possible I've been spared. The knowledge makes me feel humble and grateful.

But I hate it here. I hate everyone. I hate talking over and over again about myself. I don't want to tell any more secrets. And then, whenever I think I've said everything there is to say, I find myself offering up more hideous details of more hideous actions. One day, shakily, I talk about something that still has me waking in the night sweating, which can still haunt me any time, anywhere, at unexpected moments. The Japanese girl. How I killed her. And when I've finished with her I start on John from the West Country. Talking about it can't change what I did. I still feel lonely and empty and full of shame. But I am helped a little when other members of the group identify with the experience. One girl tells how someone in her squat went over and, unsure whether he was dead but certain they didn't want a visit from the police, she and her friends rolled his blue and unmoving body up in the carpet he lay on and dumped it in a skip. Another girl woke up one morning to find her partner lying next to her, blue.

I'm vomiting up my entire life here in Bournemouth. There are days when I can't take it. After another group session where I've heard more about myself than I want to know, I arrange to meet one of the other addicts down on the beach. I ask her to fix my feelings. She smiles sweetly at me and we fuck in the sand.

Afterwards I feel terrible, as though I've relapsed. I've broken the rules. For a while I try to hide what I've done but that kind of dishonesty is becoming impossible for me now. I'm on a mission to tell, even though I know that I'll be in trouble. Having sex with another addict is as bad as having a drink or a hit and that's exactly how I used the girl, like a hit to take me away from how I was feeling.

After my confession everyone discusses whether I should be thrown out. I was predatory towards the girl, I used her for my own ends and she is a vulnerable and suffering addict who that day had been very upset by subjects that arose in group therapy.

Finally they agree I should be sent to another centre nearby. It's part of the Quinton House Project but it's a satellite, the rules are laxer and there is little supervision. I'm stronger now. I try to follow the twelve-step programme that has guided many addicts and alcoholics before me, and these twelve steps are giving me, for the first time ever, a spiritual and moral code I can try to live by.

In December it's my thirtieth birthday and there's a party and a cake with candles. My first ever. I'm so choked I don't trust myself to speak. Then I slip outside and shed a tear.

Secondary rehab lasts four months. At the end of February, I'm going to graduate. They call it graduation but to me it feels I'm being thrown out on the streets. I protest that I'm not ready. In fact, I'm terrified. Living in a community with full support, a rulebook and a clear routine is one thing. Going back out there alone is another.

My therapist, Sonia, assures me I'll be all right. I can continue to attend some group sessions at Quinton House, she will still see me and, as long as I go to fellowship meetings with other addicts and alcoholics, I'll have all the support I need. Except I don't feel I can ever have enough support. I persuade them to send me on to a third stage of rehabilitation about an hour away down the coast.

There is a moving graduation ceremony. I've travelled a long way at Quinton House and I haven't made my journey alone. I feel surrounded by people who care about me. My friends Nicole and Ryan sit on either side of me, supporting me. It's an emotional experience. And when it's over I take the train to Carlton House where my living is structured and I lead a stable life while I decide where to go and what to do.

After a few months, it's time to leave again. It's time to stop living in institutions and find my own way. If there was a fourth stage of rehab, I'd certainly try it but there isn't. I've got to get out there into that world that is awash with drugs and loneliness and I have to live in it.

The possibility of going back on the streets seems to growl at me like an angry dog, scaring me, threatening me. I must have a place of my own. I know that to rent a flat I'll need a deposit and I've no idea how I can raise the funds for this. But a lifetime of lying and manipulation has equipped me to cope. The Prince's Trust gave me the money for a camera last time I was in rehab, when I was just a kid. I know they give loans to people to help them start their own business. So I apply to the Trust for enough money to buy tree-climbing equipment. I tell them that I'm going back into tree surgery.

A bright-faced man called David Fox asks me for a brief life history. He sits in his office scribbling as I talk. Then he nods and says: 'I think we can help you.'

I stare at him in disbelief.

The Trust offers me a loan of £3000. David Fox gives me business advice and wishes me good luck.

'Let me know how you're getting on,' he says.

This man's faith frightens me. He really believes that I have the confidence, the ability, to set myself up in business.

Even more terrifying is the huge sum of money the Trust is making available to me. With money like that I could relapse tomorrow. I could go on a wild spree. I could stick a needle in my

arm and get on a crack sky rocket and travel through space knowing
I'm safe because the heroin always makes everything all right. With
£3000 I could do it over and over and over. Even though it's been
out of my body for almost a year, heroin calls me back every day.
Not only because the rattle symptoms still frequently recur but
because of the power of my euphoric recall. Every single day I want
drugs and miss drugs. The only way I stop myself taking them is to
remind myself of the consequences. I remember the ghost I was
when the detox centre took me up to A&E. I remember the maniac
I became when I shut myself in the hostel taking all that stolen
crack. I remember the police photos and superimpose my own face
on the bodies lying in the steel morgue trays.

David Fox has placed so much trust in me that I'm sure to fail
him. I don't want to steal the money but it's inevitable. I am fundamentally dishonest. The Committee tells me so.

One day at a time.

The first thing I do with the money is go flat hunting. I'm certainly going to spend a lot of it on a deposit. I tell myself that I can't
go into business until I've got an address so this is a legitimate use of
the Trust's funds.

I find a flat along the south coast and the deposit is minimal. The
£3000 is unused.

I love my flat. It's up on the fourth floor of a Victorian house and
it has sloping ceilings and interesting alcoves. On one side is a church
and in its yard is a big tree, so close to my windows that I feel I'm sitting on one of its highest branches. There is no noise here, only birds
and peace. From the other side of the flat you can see all the town's
hustle and bustle.

I've lived in many flats but this one feels like my first home. It is
my sanctuary. It is paradise. I have almost no furniture: a beaten-up
sofa and a couple of cushions to sleep on. And I still think it's perfect.
Gradually I fill it. I buy second-hand beds, bookcases, cooking uten-
sils, paint. With broad, easy brushstrokes the walls turn the colour of
the deepest sea and the brightest sunflowers. More importantly,
friends help me. I have friends now. Whatever I do, I do it with help.

Sometimes I glimpse happiness here and find some peace in my new space. Sometimes I have terrible, terrifying dreams of being back on the streets. Sometimes I wake up in the morning sweating with fear, scared that I can't do it, I mean live like other people, paying bills, sorting my laundry, buying breakfast. One day at a time. But it's hard enough learning to live, so there's no way I have the confidence to start a business. The £3000 is still waiting for me.

I rely heavily on the other members of my fellowship, addicts and alcoholics who have been through the same recovery process as me. One is a builder, Ronnie, who employs me part-time. From my wage, I pay the interest on the Trust's loan.

So this is my new life, and I mean new like life is new for a baby. I'm still learning the skills. I meditate and give myself a daily structure and I keep a diary. I go to bed at night. In the morning I get up. I try to eat regular meals, good food. I learn to take care of myself. I cook for people. They cook for me. I try to maintain friendships by being honest and true.

I work on the building site part of the week with the other lads. If we can get Ronnie to stop work and start talking, we will. We sit on buckets while he tells us about the crazy things he did when he was still drinking and I think: If Ronnie can come back from that, I can come back too. There's a lot of laughter at work. The rest of the time, I'm a beach bum. I have girlfriends. And there are days, not many of them, when I can see the glimmer of a possibility that eventually, perhaps, I might learn to live like other people. I don't think about tomorrow or whether I'll use again next week or how everything could collapse around me. I concentrate on today: getting up, meditating, living, not taking any drugs.

The Prince's Trust £3000 worries me so much that I decide to spend it. I buy some climbing gear. After all, I said I would. I don't do anything with it. Now there are ropes and karabiners taking up space in my apartment instead of in my bank account. The ropes are white and orange, the metalwork shines. After a few days I don't notice it any more, I just walk round it.

A hot summer's day and I'm busy on the building site with a brush in my hand, painting away with the other lads, when I glance outside.

The patterns of sun and shadow I see draw me towards them. I put my brush on the tin and go to look.

Out here the air is fresh, even though the site is dusty and covered in bricks and rubble. Next door there's a tree, a huge beech. Directly beneath it the ground is dark but at its edges the shadows it throws are scalloped like lace. I stare up at its silver trunk with admiration. The tree looks cool on this sweltering day. Tiny insects swarm around one branch. A bird sings somewhere so high I can't see it. The tree invites me into its world of deep shadow.

I have to get high. Without even thinking about it, I scramble up the wall and from here lever myself into the lowest branches. Concentrating on where the next foot goes, where the next hand grips, I start to climb. At first, because the branches are so thick, it's hard work. But as I get higher, I get lighter. I get more nimble. I find it easier and easier to negotiate the horizontal obstacles in my vertical climb.

When I'm high enough to look through the leaves, over the rooftops, I see the blue water evaporating on the horizon into the milk-white sky. I stop. I wrap my hand round a branch. I run my fingers over it and feel the uniquely smooth grain of beech against my palm. At the end of the branch a slight breeze makes the leaves whisper.

The tree is solid. It grows but it is unchanging. It lives by the seasons, it responds to the elements, it supports many lives, from birds to the insects they feed on. Standing here, shaded by the kind tree from the sky above, I feel a deep sense of calm. I breathe slowly. I hold the tree and close my eyes.

My life has taken so many different twists and turns but trees are what I love and what I trained for aeons ago. And it's obvious to me, I don't know why I couldn't understand it before, that trees are now my future. I don't know where my journey will take me or what awaits me but standing on a branch, holding onto a tree, shaded by its leaves, for the first time I can see the possibility of a way ahead.

Afterword

I have not taken drink or drugs since 21 July 2000, the night I last injected crack in the detox centre at Elephant and Castle. Each day is a reprieve. I still follow the twelve-step programme and it keeps me clean and keeps me growing. I still occasionally get euphoric recall. Even a rattle can steal up on me from nowhere. I sometimes wake up from dreams of using, sweating because I think I've relapsed in the night. One day at a time.

When trees came back into my life, I initially worked for other tree surgeons. Without drink or drugs to hold me back I found I worked harder and better than my bosses and I got so fed up with carrying them that I soon went back to the building site.

Then I met Vicky. She was young, gorgeous, trusting and we fell in love. We connected at a deep level even though her life, at home with her parents, had been much more sheltered than mine. Our love took us a long way and we tried to look after each other well. For me, it felt like my first relationship because until now I'd had a lot of women but only one relationship – with drugs.

I watched Vicky get up every morning and go to work. Two days a week I went to the building site. The rest of the time I hung around on the beach.

'I thought you said you were a tree surgeon,' said Vicky, looking at my charity-shop clothes, my non-functional mobile phone, my blinking TV. 'You lied to me.'

'No, honest! I've had all this training.'

'Then why don't you do it?'

'Because when I worked for people I ended up carrying them while they took all the profits.'

Vicky shrugged. 'Then how about working for yourself?'

I agonised for a while. My counsellor from Quinton House, Sonia, helped me find the confidence to make the decision at last. And that's how I came to set up my own business. Just like I'd told the Trust I would. They were so sure I'd do it. And I did. It was the Trust and Vicky and Sonia who led me there and Ronnie the builder was my guiding light.

I've been addicted to most things and for a while I got addicted to work. I turned into a businessman. Yes, me. Pricing jobs, buying trucks, employing lads, sending out invoices, getting to grips with the paperwork, the council, the regulations, advertising . . . above all, I aimed to offer training and employment to recovering addicts and ex-offenders, trying to support them the way others support me through my recovery process. I worked hard and my business gathered momentum and my reputation grew.

All this time I was learning to live, but in one dimension. Relationships are hard for addicts and probably I had further to go than many since I had no healthy reference points in my past. Finally, Vicky and I weren't able to surmount all the difficulties. We'd both grown immeasurably as a result of our relationship and it had taken us where we needed to be – sadly, not with each other. But our friendship still continues.

I feel that I've been to one of life's extremities – and come back. If I'd climbed Everest and returned alive there'd have been a welcoming party. As an anti-hero of course I don't deserve or expect that, but in a way there was a welcoming party for me. My business was strong and my reputation good when, in 2005, I was given The Prince's Trust Young Achiever of the Year Award. Later that year I went to Clarence House in the Mall. I stood outside its high old brick walls and remembered the last time I lingered here, penniless, homeless, hopeless, staring at the plane trees. And then I took a deep breath and walked through the gates, an invited guest. Inside, I met a man who has helped me more than he can ever comprehend: Prince Charles.

As a result of the interview which took place that day, I went on to receive the *Daily Mirror*'s Pride of Britain Award at a glittering ceremony in London. The Trust's Rob Cope steered me through an evening in which Prince Charles narrated my story for the cameras and Victoria Beckham presented me with my gong. Sean Evans, who saved my life, was there, and so were some of my old mates. Just to make sure I didn't get too full of myself.

Since then, I've tried to balance my life better, rebuilding the emotional side of it and learning how to live and take care of myself. I still run a business, but I allow it to shrink or expand depending on work, staffing and my other interests and commitments. I'm learning that success has got nothing to do with turnover and everything to do with the way you live. My dream now is not to focus on financial success but to be a social entrepreneur, involved in projects which help others. So now I'm out there a lot, talking to people about the things I believe in. And, at the highest level, they're listening. I'm telling them about drug addicts and young offenders, about preventative policies and how government can help bring these people back into society. I'm the first-ever ex-offender to sit on the Board of Directors of the National Probation Service and I'm working with The Prince's Trust on a nation-wide innovative mentoring project, delivered into young offenders' institutions. My life's moving on now but my business is still running and I make sure there are some clear days when I can get out and climb a few trees.

Rosie and I did try to rekindle our relationship but we soon discovered that without drugs we had no relationship. She's clean now, too, and growing through her recovery the way I am, and we're trying to build a good friendship for our sake and the boys'. And one of the best things to happen to me in these years is that my sons are now a part of my world and I see them as often as I can. I try to make amends for the dad I used to be. When I think of my relationship with my father and his with his father, it seems the odds are stacked against us. But my sons and I are beating those odds. The cycle ends here. I'm so lucky to have such bright, healthy, balanced, loving boys. They light up my life.

I am in close contact with my mother these days. We are rebuilding our relationship and it has healthy boundaries. I'm learning to let her be my mother. I can appreciate better now how she suffered during those years with Dad, although I'll never understand the sickness which kept her locked into that abusive marriage. She's found happiness now, remarried to a nice man.

I have no contact with my father or his family. I don't blame him for what happened to me: it's unhealthy for me to think that way and, besides, he must be a man wrestling with his own demons.

I've kept in touch with my brother in America and I'm in the process of making amends whenever I can to my sisters for the way I treated them. I regard my younger sister, Bethany, who suffered much more in her relationship with my father than I ever realised at the time, as one of the strongest and most beautiful women I know. She's married to a good man and has three children.

Sometimes I hear news of the old Kidderminster crowd. Vanessa is married with children and still lives on the same council estate. Daniel is serving a twelve-year jail sentence for armed robbery.

When I last heard of Jodie, she was continuing to live a blameless life in Penrith. Most of my old clubbing friends are now respectable businessmen. Some work in the music world and some, like Mark Downes, have helped me with my business and remain in frequent contact. The DIY crowd have maintained the partying and mayhem. Colin, the fellow addict who helped me so much at Ravenscourt, relapsed badly soon after finishing treatment there. Almost all of my peers at Quinton House, who voted me out after the incident with the girl on the beach, have relapsed. And there have been too many deaths. I didn't realise how vulnerable I was on the streets but I understand it now from all the silent deaths I know about: in doorways, up alleys, in lonely bedsits. The deaths have occurred not only among street people but among the friends I've made in these recovery years. I've often asked myself how it was I survived and I've come to the conclusion that there's a higher power at work in my life.

As for my Collection of Found Objects, well it's just a load of trash, of course. But I've still got the paintbrushes, the spoon, the notebook and all the bits and pieces and when I moved out of the flat and bought my own house the battered old art box came with me. So when I look round at my kitchen and my furniture and my music collection and my office, I can remember that, not so long ago, my only possession was a collection of trash that other people had thrown in bins.

I did see Dave and his dog Boots once after I left the streets. When I was meeting my girlfriend Vicky one day I dared to walk again through Piccadilly underground and there, at the bottom of the stairs, was a bundle of humanity with its feet poking out from under a blanket. Next to it were four paws.

I said: 'Oy! Wake up! Oy!'

And Dave sat up, bleary eyed. So did Boots.

'Mark! Mark, you fucking bastard!' he said, grinning all over his face. 'You wanker!'

That's a term of endearment, so I sat down next to him.

'Listen, mate,' I began, remembering how angry he was the last time he saw me, 'you don't know how terrible I've felt about that Japanese girl. What I did, it's haunted me and—'

Dave interrupted. He said: 'I married her.'

I paused.

'Who?'

'*Her!*'

'The Japanese girl?' I couldn't have heard right. She was alive? Dave had married her? But now my heart was pumping because I could feel the hint of a possibility.

Dave said: 'She never took the smack you gave her, you fucker. I had it.'

She didn't take it. She didn't whack crack and heroin into her arm and die alone in a Baker Street hotel room. I felt tears stinging at my eyes. Tears of relief.

'She's not dead? Not fucking dead!'

Dave nodded. My face was hot and wet with tears. I put an arm round him and he pushed his head against mine. I held him close. I didn't care if he had lice. I just cared that I didn't kill her.

'Came looking for me a few days later. Went back to her hotel and sort of stayed there. And then . . . erm, I married her.'

You're supposed to say Congratulations. But I still couldn't speak.

'We lived here in London, she kept me in drugs and I got her passport sorted. I'm on my own for a few days now because she's gone back to Japan ahead of me. Tomorrow I'm going too.'

'Tomorrow?'

'Yep. She's organised a taxi to take me to the airport. Picking me up at nine o'clock.'

I tried to imagine the Japanese girl in her high heels and cream raincoat with the wild animal that was Dave. He was gentle and kind and good but he lived on the streets and he was wild. She might have thought she'd tamed him but he probably sneaked back there whenever he could.

I sat next to him on the floor in the tube station, wiping my tears while passers-by threw him the odd quid. I thought that a higher power must be at work, because, if I'd been one day later, I wouldn't have seen Dave and I would have had that woman's death on my conscience forever.

Dave turned to me. He said: 'I really need a bag. How're you fixed?'

I pulled out my wallet. I opened it. But the addict in me just could not give Dave a tenner for a bag. I couldn't give him the pleasure of it if I couldn't enjoy it too. 'I'll give you six quid,' I said.

Some street lads came up. Skinny, dirty young lads who reminded me of me when I lived in the West End.

'This is my mate Mark,' roared Dave. 'He's one of us!'

The lads looked surprised but they sat down next to Boots. I would have liked to tell them about my journey but I didn't know how. I tried to tell them enough for them to understand that change is possible, that anything's possible. Sweat was running down their faces and they were sniffing and clutching their warm cans of Special Brew.

I said: 'I thought I'd never get clean. I didn't know anyone who had. But there is another way. I got into treatment and now I'm trying to sort myself out.'

'Yeah, man,' they said.

I looked at Dave. He wasn't asleep yet but his eyelids were drooping.

'I mean,' I said, 'everything's changed for me. I was living on the streets like you and now I'm clean and I'm living a different way and I'm starting this business . . .'

'Fucking brilliant,' they said. 'Good story. Yeah. You done fucking great, man.'

I looked at them and saw their eyes were closed and they were out of it. Only Boots was still awake.

'All right, mate?' I said to him.

He wagged his tail.

Last Word

Maybe you've read this book and recognised not the differences between you and me but a few similarities. Then this is my personal message to you.

If drink or drugs have stopped working and, despite your best efforts, you're now in a place without future or purpose, if you're feeling desperate, then you've been given a gift. Because I believe that we can only move forward when we've reached despair. Of course, I didn't know that when I was at rock bottom. But I know it now.

I reached a point where there were two options for me. To accept help and listen to others who had gone through it before me. Or to die. It may seem obvious, but it wasn't to me then and it took me a long time to make the right choice. But I did and now I've been given the greatest of gifts: the chance to help others the way I was helped. No drink or drugs ever made me feel so good. And in this lies the solution to my problem. I hope you make the right choice and find the solution too.

The following helped me and they, or places and fellowships like them, might be able to help you too.

Homelessness
Hungerford Drugs Project,
London W1
020 7287 8743
(run by Turning Point, a national organisation:
www.turning-point.co.uk
020 7481 7600)

Treatment
Equinox Detoxification Centre
South London
020 7820 9924
(Equinox has other centres elsewhere: www.equinoxcare.org.uk
020 7939 9800)

Ravenscourt Addiction Treatment Centre,
Bognor Regis
01243 862157

Quinton House Project,
Bournemouth
01202 392241

Carlton House,
Weymouth
01305 779084

Alcohol and drugs
Alcoholics Anonymous
0845 769 7555
www.alcoholics-anonymous.org.uk

Cocaine Anonymous
0800 612 0225
www.cauk.org.uk

Narcotics Anonymous
0845 373 3366
www.ukna.org

Directionless?
The Prince's Trust
www.princes-trust.org.uk
0800 842842

Acknowledgements

When Prince Charles talks about his 'virtuous circle', he means that if he helps someone then they go on to help others who go on to help others. I seem to be joining that circle now and that's because I was given the opportunity to change my life by Prince Charles via The Prince's Trust. I'd like to thank him here, as well as various members of his virtuous circle and The Trust's team, especially Martina Milburn, Rob Cope and David Fox.

A man called Mark Lucas read an article about me in *The Big Issue* and then had the faith to believe that my story would make a book and the patience to coax me through it. So my special thanks go to *The Big Issue* and its editor Charles Howgego, and of course Mark Lucas and the team at Lucas Alexander Whitley. The next act of faith and patience came from my publishers, Little, Brown. My thanks to Ursula Mackenzie, Antonia Hodgson, Vivien Redman and all the team.

In the course of my life, and especially since the twenty-first century began, I've received a lot of help from so many people. I just wish they were all alive to read this. Privacy laws prevent me from naming many of the living but they know who they are. This book gives me an opportunity to offer them my deepest, heartfelt thanks.